Mad Men and Politics

Nostalgia and the Remaking of Modern America

Linda Beail and Lilly J. Goren

Bloomsbury Academic
An imprint of Bloomsbury Publishing Inc

B L O O M S B U R Y
NEW YORK • LONDON • NEW DELHI • SYDNEY

Bloomsbury Academic

An imprint of Bloomsbury Publishing Inc

1385 Broadway	50 Bedford Square
New York	London
NY 10018	WC1B 3DP
USA	UK

www.bloomsbury.com

BLOOMSBURY and the Diana logo are trademarks of Bloomsbury Publishing Plc

First published 2015

Library of Congress Cataloging-in-Publication Data
A catalog record for this book is avaliable from the Library of Congress.

ISBN: HB: 978-1-5013-0634-1
PB: 978-1-5013-0635-8
ePUB: 978-1-5013-0636-5
ePDF: 978-1-5013-0637-2

Typeset by Fakenham Prepress Solutions, Fakenham, Norfolk NR21 8NN
Printed and bound in the United States of America

Contents

Mad Men and Politics

Acknowledgments

This has been, in many ways, a labor of love, since we all so enjoy Matthew Weiner's creation and we have had the pleasure of luxuriating in the curves and lines of this rendering of the 1960s. This series, rife with secrets and lies, earnestness and virtue, has made us all consider our current condition and the peaks and values of this experiment known as the United States. All of the chapters explore dimensions of the 1960s but from the perspective of a contemporary eye; all of our authors were eager to engage with these mad men and women, and we couldn't be more delighted with the outcomes.

So we must begin our thanks with our authors, many (though not all) of whom seem to have names that begin with L. We could not have produced this book without our brilliant, engaging, and diligent contributors. We must thank Loren Goldman, Laurie Naranch, Kate Edenborg, Larry Heyman, Denise Witzig, Natalie Fuehrer Taylor, and Becky Josephson for their willingness to contend with our many emails, for working on an accelerated schedule, for making time in their busy lives for revisions and edits, and to all of their respective spouses, children, significant others, and family members and friends for supporting their efforts and keeping them cared for and fed. There wouldn't be a book without Loren, Laurie, Larry, Kate, Denise, Natalie, and Becky! We must give credit where it is due: to Natalie, who originally suggested an APSA panel on *Mad Men* to urge us all towards thinking about the connection between *Mad Men* and politics. To Astrid Henry, who connected us to Denise, who came on to the project late in the game but helped make it a much stronger book. To Elissa, who brought us Larry. To Danielle Cervantes, Mary Gainey, Kali Marcino, Jenny Wilson, and Caroline Beail, who helped with all the little bits and pieces (like bibliographies, references, indexes, and episode listings) that make the book a whole. And to John Nelson, who brought us together many, many years ago.

We thank both the American Political Science Association Politics, Literature and Film section and the Midwest Political Science Association for supporting panels on *Mad Men* and Politics that allowed us to initially craft our ideas and then to refine them as we prepared them for publication. We must each thank our respective institutions, Carroll University of Waukesha, WI and Point Loma Nazarene University of San Diego, for faculty development funding that contributed to our capacity to attend those panels and discuss our collaborative work.

We also have enjoyed working with Bloomsbury Academic, especially with Matthew Kopel, who became quite excited about the prospect of this book at the Starbucks in the Palmer House and has supported our efforts to bring this project to fruition. We also have enjoyed working with Michelle Chen, who has been quick and gracious in all of her interactions with us.

Finally, we each need to acknowledge those who contributed to maintaining our individual sanity and our lives during this process.

Lilly would first like to thank her co-editor and partner in crime on this project and on a few others as well, Linda. What a joy to work with someone who makes all of my writing so much better, who makes my ideas clearer, and who can impart a paragraph's worth of emphasis with one raised eyebrow. Even with technical difficulties, differing time zones, looming deadlines, and thousands of other demands, Linda knows how to stay calm, maintain equilibrium, and keep all the plates spinning in the same direction. You are my hero. Lilly also needs to express her gratitude to Ed, her other hero, who has minded the store more than usual during this home stretch and has helped keep everything in perspective, while making us all laugh. Eli and Sophia bring me hugs, and smiles, and joy, and delight, even when I am staring at the reflected glow of my computer screen. With boundless love for Sally and Ralph, my adoring and supportive parents who in the midst of the tumultuous 1960s decided to strike out on their own frontier and bring me and my brother Benjamin into this turbulent world, with some hope that we could contribute to making the ideal of America a more perfect union.

Linda is exceedingly grateful for the opportunity to work with Lilly, and for the many hours of fun and vigorous conversation about popular culture, politics, identity, and history. In addition to being incredibly smart, Lilly is fantastic at assembling a talented and creative group of people to collaborate with and at making each of them write and think better. I'm grateful to be among them. She is also quite talented at finding amazing places to eat and wonderful people to share the table with, so if she invites you to dinner in the course of some academic gathering—go! Thanks, Lilly, for your generosity of spirit, your steadfast friendship, and your incisive but encouraging voice. I'm already looking forward to the next collaboration. Linda is also more appreciative than she can say to her family, who endure the chaos before a deadline with good humor and patience. To Eric and Joshua, my own intrepid guys, though certainly not "mad men"—this one is for you. You two make me laugh and feel loved every single day. Caroline, you continue to light up my world and I love watching you grow into the person (and writer) you were meant to be. You three have my heart. Part of this project involved looking back at how far we have come (or not) as Americans since the decade of my birth; I feel lucky to have had you with me on the journey so far, and hopeful as we look toward the challenges and possibilities our future holds.

Contributors

Linda Beail is professor of political science and director of the Margaret Stevenson Center for Women's Studies at Point Loma Nazarene University, where she teaches courses on gender and race politics, campaigns and elections, and political theory. Her book *Framing Sarah Palin: Pit Bulls, Puritans and Politics* (Routledge, 2013, co-authored with Rhonda Longworth Kinney) examines gendered and partisan narratives about the first female Republican vice-presidential candidate in the 2008 election, with particular attention to popular culture, social media, and religion. She is the co-editor of *Results May Vary* (Wipf & Stock, 2013) and author of several articles and book chapters, including work on feminism, politics, and popular culture in *Women and the White House: Gender, Popular Culture, and Presidential Politics* (University Press of Kentucky, 2012) and *You've Come a Long Way, Baby: Women, Politics, and Popular Culture* (University Press of Kentucky, 2009). Dr. Beail has served as an NGO delegate to the United Nations Commission on the Status of Women. She has appeared on local television and radio, as well as authoring newspaper editorials commenting on gender and religion in presidential elections. She recently returned from Amman, Jordan, where she participated in a seminar on women, tradition, and revolution in the Arab world. Dr. Beail earned her BA *summa cum laude* from Wheaton College and her PhD from the University of Iowa.

Kate Roberts Edenborg worked professionally in communications for almost 15 years. She started out in journalism as a reporter and editor and then moved to a career in healthcare communication. She did her PhD work at the School of Journalism and Mass Communication at the University of Minnesota, Twin Cities. Edenborg is now an assistant professor at the University of Wisconsin–Stout for a professional communication and emerging media program, where she coordinates the applied journalism concentration and teaches courses on media history, mass communication, and journalism. Edenborg's research includes examining gender representations in children's literature and popular culture as well as exploring the strategies of communicating complex information. Her recent publications include contributions to *Seeking a Voice: Images of Race and Gender in the 19th Century Press* (Purdue University Press, 2009), *The Civil War and the Press* (Transaction Publishers, 2000), and *Girl Culture: An Encyclopedia, Volumes 1 and 2* (Greenwood Press, 2007).

Loren Goldman teaches political theory at Ohio University. Much of his scholarly work concerns teleology, progress, and hope in political thought, with particular emphases on Pragmatism, Critical Theory, and German Idealism. His articles have appeared in *Political Theory*, *Transactions of the Charles S. Peirce Society*, the *Journal of the Philosophy of History*, and *William James Studies*, of which he is book review editor; he has also contributed essays to several edited volumes and encyclopedias. In addition to a translation of Ernst Bloch's *Avicenna and the Aristotelian Left* (Columbia University Press, forthcoming), he is completing a book on hope in modern political philosophy. He has degrees from Yale, Oxford, and the University of Chicago, and held postdoctoral positions at Rutgers and the University of California, Berkeley prior to arriving in Athens.

Lilly J. Goren is professor of political science and global studies at Carroll University in Waukesha, Wisconsin. She teaches American government, the presidency, politics and culture, gender studies, and political theory. Her research often integrates popular culture, literature, and film as means to understanding politics, especially in the United States. Her published books include *Women and the White House: Gender, Popular Culture, and Presidential Politics* (University Press of Kentucky, 2012, co-edited with Justin Vaughn)—winner of both the 2014 Susan Koppelman Book Award and the 2014 Peter C. Rollins Book Award, *You've Come a Long Way, Baby: Women, Politics, and Popular Culture* (University Press of Kentucky, 2009), and *Not in My District: The Politics of Military Base Closures* (Peter Lang, 2003), as well as articles in *Political Research Quarterly*, *White House Studies*, and Berkeley Electronic Press's *The Forum*, and she has served as guest editor, with Justin Vaughn, for a special issue of *White House Studies* on the presidency and popular culture in 2010. Goren has served as chair of the American Political Science Association's Politics, Literature, and Film section and she has also served as an executive board member for the APSA's Presidents and Executive Politics Section. She is currently revising a manuscript on the role of anger in modern democracies. She is a regular political commentator for both local and national media outlets. Professor Goren earned her AB in political science and English from Kenyon College and has an MA and PhD in political science from Boston College.

Lawrence Heyman is an adjunct professor of properties design, fabrication, and set decoration in the Oklahoma City University School of Theatre and also at the University of Oklahoma School of Drama. He holds an MFA in properties design and production from the University of Illinois at Urbana–Champaign and a BFA in scene design from the University of Wisconsin–Whitewater. He has worked researching, designing, procuring, and fabricating props for theaters such as The La Jolla Playhouse, The Goodman Theatre, The Huntington Theatre, and the Utah Shakespearean Festival. He has also worked as a freelance set decorator, set dresser, and motion picture greens man on feature films including *The Crucible*, *To Jillian on her 37th Birthday*, *Rushmore*, *Hope Floats*, *Varsity Blues*, and *Pearl Harbor* and in the art departments of events for Mercedes Benz USA and Toyota. He understands that to produce convincing props and set decoration requires an understanding of history, technology, design, and crafts.

Rebecca Colton Josephson earned her MA in literature at the University of New Hampshire, and is currently an MDiv candidate at Andover Newton Theological School. She teaches at the Derryfield School in Manchester, NH. She has also published work examining democratic implications of and feminist approaches to the popular police procedural, "The Closer." Rebecca is also a singer and enthusiastic walker.

Laurie Naranch is Associate Professor of Political Science and director of the Women's Studies Minor at Siena College, NY. She has published in the areas of democratic theory, gender theory, and popular culture. Her current research is on debt and citizenship. She is also continuing work on the Greek–French thinker Cornelius Castoriadis and democracy. She recently published entries in the updated *Encyclopedia of Political Thought* (2014) from Wiley Blackwell on "women's rights" and "gender and identity." She has also published in *differences* and *Peace Review* and in the collection *You've Come a Long Way, Baby: Women, Politics, and Popular Culture* edited by Lilly Goren (University Press of Kentucky, 2010). Naranch also contributes blog entries on the political thinker Hannah Arendt, democracy, and labor through the Hannah Arendt Center at Bard College.

Natalie Fuehrer Taylor teaches political philosophy at Skidmore College. She is the author of *The Rights of Woman as Chimera: The Political Philosophy of Mary Wollstonecraft* (Routledge Press, 2007). She is also the co-author (with Daryl Tress) of "Betty Friedan and Gloria Steinem: The Popular Transformation of American Feminism in the Late Twentieth Century" in *The History of American Political Thought* edited by Bryan-Paul Frost and Jeffrey Sikkenga (Lexington Press, 2003), and the author of "The Personal is Political: Women's Magazines for the 'I'm-not-a-Feminist-But' Generation" in *You've Come a Long Way Baby. Women, Politics, and Popular Culture* edited by Lilly J. Goren (University Press of Kentucky, 2009).

Denise Witzig is Associate Professor and Director of the Women's and Gender Studies program at Saint Mary's College of California, where she teaches a variety of courses on feminist theories and popular culture, including classes on *Mad Men*, the sixties, and the sexual revolution. Her article "My Mannequin, Myself: Embodiment in Fashion's Mirror" appeared in *Fashion Talks: Undressing the Power of Style* (SUNY Press, 2012). Witzig has presented her research on fashion theory, popular narrative in fiction, film and television, advertising, and consumerism at numerous conferences in cultural studies, women's studies, and film. She has also written on representations of the woman writer in twentieth-century short fiction. Her work on sexual authority and the epistolary in Edith Wharton has appeared in the critical anthologies *A Forward Glance: New Essays on Edith Wharton, Edith Wharton: New Critical Essays* and in the *National Women's Studies Association*

Journal. Her recent research and presentations have focused on feminism, masculinity, and cultural memory in *Mad Men*, part of a book-length project focusing on the series. Witzig continues to be enthralled by the nostalgia and glamour of the popular history presented on *Mad Men*—she is just the viewer she is writing about.

Part One

The American Century

1

Mad Men and Politics: Nostalgia and the Remaking of America

Linda Beail and Lilly J. Goren

Nostalgia literally means the pain from an old wound. It's a twinge in your heart far more powerful than memory alone. This device isn't a spaceship. It's a time machine. It goes backwards, forwards. It takes us to a place we ache to go again.

Don Draper, pitching an ad for the carousel slide projector to Kodak, in The Wheel *(1.13)*

Since its premiere in 2007, *Mad Men* has been designated as one of the great television dramas of all time, winning four best drama Emmy awards, among many other accolades. It has been hailed as ushering in a new "golden age" of television and credited with creating one of the great new breed of "anti-heroes" of contemporary broadcasting in Don Draper, played by Jon Hamm.[1] Its aesthetic of mid-century modern cool has inspired fashion lines, interior design, and other stage and television shows mining the 1960s for drama and comedy. The show has been recapped, tweeted, and written about by fans and cultural critics alike, who weekly dissect its visual allusions and dialog like forensic detectives, looking for clues to its hidden meanings with as much care as any literary scholar, while swooning over the fashion.

Yet *Mad Men* is an important political text for reasons that include, but reach beyond, its significant impact on popular culture. The show has much to tell us about American identity, not only in the 1960s—a period of major change and importance in American social and political life—but in our own twenty-first-century milieu. In depicting a post-war America defining itself as a political and economic superpower, while struggling with its inequalities of race, gender, and class, *Mad Men* offers viewers a way to explore contemporary facets of American identity through the lens of the recent past. Our nostalgia for the 1960s fuels the show's appeal. This is a time just far enough away to have acquired a romanticized gloss of history. Yearning for a past that never was, we can watch *Mad Men* to immerse ourselves in that "uncomplicated" and glamorous era. Gender roles were separate and clear, African Americans were nearly invisible in the corporate world, and ice clinked seductively in a crystal glass as the secretary poured whiskey for her boss. Yet simultaneously, the show undoes the fiction of the 1960s as cool perfection before the tumult of the decade hits; its characters are lost and unhappy, adulterous, and alcoholic with no idea how to relate to their children or find contentment; they lose jobs, companies, and even take their own lives. Creator Matt Weiner describes the show as "science fiction"—but in the past.

> Just as science fiction often uses a future world to say things about the present you can't say directly (it's both figuratively and literally ahead of its time), his show uses the overtly sexist and racist atmosphere of a 1960 New York advertising office to talk about issues that persist today but that we are too "polite" to talk about openly.[2]

Never a documentary, *Mad Men* instead tells stories set in the 1960s that appeal to those who never actually lived through or remember that era, stories that illuminate our continuing political dilemmas of freedom, identity, inclusion, consumption, and authenticity.

Weiner noted that the script, when he wrote it, reflected some of his own *ennui* at the time. He explained that he had a lovely family, a good job, but he felt "really unhappy, dissatisfied, and wondered what was wrong with me … I had a complete lack of gratitude for what I had."[3] He has also explained that the idealized Madison Avenue advertising executives of the 1960s were his heroes, given their excessive lifestyle and general disregard for authority.[4] Weiner went on to write for a number of other shows—most particularly *The Sopranos*—before finally getting the go-ahead from AMC to produce *Mad Men*. Weiner's particular creation in *Mad Men*, Don Draper/Dick Whitman, has become a touchstone within the canon of television "anti-heroes." This canon, demarcated by the late James Gandolfini's Tony Soprano, through Don

Draper, includes Bryan Cranston's Walter White on *Breaking Bad* (also on AMC), Michael Chiklis on *The Shield*, Kiefer Sutherland's Jack Bauer on *24*, and characters on *Deadwood*, *Six Feet Under*, and *The Wire*. It can be traced all the way back to the earlier 1990s and the dueling police procedurals *Homicide: Life on the Streets* (1993–7) and *NYPD Blue* (1993–2005).

One of the central themes of *Mad Men* is the contradiction between appearance and reality. Don Draper, we quickly discover, is not who he seems; in the pilot episode, he is seen in his Manhattan office and with a lover in Greenwich Village, but in a surprising twist in the last moments of the episode we discover he has a wife and children in suburban Ossining. Later we learn he isn't even Don Draper; his real name is Dick Whitman. Draper is the identity he stole from an officer killed in the Korean War. While everyone around him wants to be suave, successful Don Draper, this is merely a role Don himself plays. As viewers gradually learn his actual life history, we see what a self-created man he is, seizing opportunities to leave his unhappy, rural upbringing behind and cheerfully, desperately conning Roger Sterling into hiring him at the advertising agency. Yet the counterfeit becomes the reality. When Pete Campbell, a jealous account executive, discovers Don's true identity, he threatens to reveal it and destroy Don. Importantly, Don maintains his cool bravado, and boss Bert Cooper dismisses Pete's melodramatic allegations in an instant: "Who cares who he really is?" As long as Don is creative and charismatic, wooing clients with perceptive pitches, Cooper is happy enough to count the profits. Don's excellence in creating the illusion of Don Draper has created the reality of Don Draper—he is who he says he is, because the money and motives of those around him accept and desire that reality.

This preoccupation in American politics with style versus substance, appearance versus reality—the concern that political ads "sell" us a candidate with a false smile or lies, for example—is a theme that is explored throughout the entire series of *Mad Men*, and in the essays in this volume. What is real in politics? Who and what can we trust? Is it all shiny surfaces and lies? Beyond simply the interplay of reality and appearance, surface and what lies beneath, the show examines the very American notion of self-creation. As a nation, we have created the myths of our young history. Our iconic heroes—from

Huck Finn to Jay Gatsby—light out for the territory and reinvent who they are. It's a supremely American mythos, one that Don Draper fits into in interesting ways.

Don Draper is a self-invented creation, one who "refounds" himself. We see him live a life of quiet desperation, terrified of vulnerability in his personal and professional relationships. This fear of vulnerability may also be a feature of American political identity—to quote Ronald Reagan, the belief that we can only achieve peace through (overwhelming and intimidating) strength. There is no room for weakness or vulnerability. We see the personal costs of this belief for Don, and through his experience can examine the political costs to our national identity of this mythos. Other characters in *Mad Men*, such as Peggy Olson, represent a challenge to the old ideas. Peggy, as "the new girl" in episode one and the first female copywriter who climbs far up the ranks at Sterling Cooper, embodies other possible elements of this social and political evolution: the immigrant experience, blue-collar social mobility, feminist change, progress.

As Machiavelli reminds us, republics require founding myths. The 1950s and 1960s are a key period in modern American history. Post-World War II economic prosperity, the rise of the middle class (thanks to the GI Bill, Veterans Administration loans for home mortgages, and federal funding of interstate highways that made suburbanization possible), and the emergence of the Cold War create the modern American identity. The nation is "refounded" in this period as a super power, both militarily and economically—this new America is one that strides across the globe, not one that stays home, inside her borders. Our notions of social mobility and "the American dream" are shaped by this era in ways that resonate into the present: culturally we still refer back to 1950s television sitcoms as a sort of baseline for "traditional" family life (though 1950s family patterns were actually more "blip" than baseline, as the Baby Boom and low divorce rates represented were not the norm for most in the preceding half of the twentieth century). Even as the 1950s created a more prosperous, anti-Communist and imperial America, this refounding was challenged by the social and political events of the 1960s. The sixties are characterized as the end of American innocence: the sexual revolution, race riots, Vietnam, and the assassinations of John F. Kennedy, Martin Luther

King Jr., and Robert F. Kennedy are evidence of the turmoil bubbling up from underneath the placid and powerful post-war American landscape. This decade—in which the entire arc of *Mad Men* unfolds—is important because of the way these changes contribute to the refounding myths of the United States, myths that are more inclusive and democratic, yet more violent and disruptive as well. This political refounding is still being contested in contemporary politics. The issues raised still confound us: free love, the Pill and sexual equality, or traditional morality and femininity? A post-racial society that is color-blind, or blind to continued racism? A country of increased social mobility, or increasing income inequality? White male privilege was undermined by the civil rights and women's movements, but these were not traditional or complete revolutions with clear-cut victors. The social mores and political power threatened by these changes remain contested. We are still fighting over contraception, equal pay, the causes of poverty, and the systemic racism of re-segregated schools and the prison–industrial complex.

The nostalgia evoked by the show raises questions about the politics of popular and fictional uses of the past. We need to pay attention to the strategies used in representing this era, and to the responses that the narrative makes possible. With its matter of fact portrayal of 1960s sexism, racism, and anti-Semitism, the show shocks contemporary viewers with the chasm between what was normalized then and what we expect now. However, there is a political critique to be made that it allows us to feel superior to "the bad old days" (when bosses not only routinely expected to sleep with their secretaries and refused to hire Jews, but mothers also let children play with plastic dry-cleaning bags over their heads, women smoked and drank through pregnancies, and families casually left all their trash on the roadside after a family picnic). The temptation is to pat ourselves on the back for how far we've progressed—without recognizing the potential indictment of our own continued, convoluted experiences with sexism, racism, domination, and privilege. Additionally, there is a political irony to the way that *Mad Men* works on one level to indict the white male class privilege of the 1960s, revealing its ugly flaws, while letting its viewers vicariously revel in the pre-revolution aesthetic style, glamour, and even clarity of roles. Is there something politically appealing, not only in the Herman Miller chairs or

Sally's go-go boots, but in the ways that women and people of color knew where they belonged—and stayed in their place? Can we have equality but keep Joan's swaying hips, or the three-Martini lunch? Are we more attracted to the allure of this "dangerous" past than disgusted by its injustices? As Katie Roiphe opined wistfully in the *New York Times*:

> The phenomenal success of the show relies at least in part on the thrill of casual vice ... Watching all the feverish and melancholic adultery, the pregnant women drinking, the 7-year-olds learning to mix the perfect Tom Collins, we can't help but experience a puritanical frisson about how much better, saner, more sensible our own lives are. But is there also the tiniest bit of wistfulness, the slight but unmistakable hint of longing toward all that stylish chaos, all that selfish, retrograde abandon? ... Can these messy lives tell us something? Is there some adventure out there that we are not having, some vividness, some wild pleasure that we are not experiencing in our responsible, productive days?[5]

Nostalgia, indeed. The show has created a longing for "stylish chaos" and "wild pleasure" in this past, a past that our "better, saner" selves know they do not really want to go back and live in. But oh how we wish we could visit—or maybe just be photographed there. How the past is portrayed in contemporary texts is acutely political in the kinds of imaginative responses it makes possible. As Kent Ono points out in his analysis of how representations of race work in *Mad Men*, "the show depicts race as a product of the past. The past thus functions as a container for racism, making racism's *present* disappear," making current grappling with persistent, complex, and evolving instances of racism much less possible.[6] It's not simply that the show does not deal with race deeply or correctly in its depictions of the 1960s; it's that by depicting race and racism in certain ways in the 1960s, it creates both a distance and a whitened, privileged perspective that makes it harder to see the power dynamics and structural racism of our own twenty-first-century "post-racial" present.

The marketing that has been catalyzed by the show demonstrates this political paradox as well. While one might read the text of the show as critical of consumption and the illusory nature of advertising, manufacturing artificial desire, the show has also contributed to wider marketing and consumption. Banana Republic has created a clothing line modeled on the show, and Mattel sold Barbie dolls representing the main characters. Mid-century modern design in clothing and furnishings grew more popular, and *How to Succeed in Business Without Really Trying* (which years ago originally starred Robert Morse, who plays Bert Cooper) had a successful revival on Broadway. A book of poetry by Frank O'Hara, read on the show, suddenly spiked in Amazon sales; Roger Sterling's fictional "memoir" created within the show became an actual book also available on Amazon. Viewers were even invited to commodify themselves on the AMC website, where they could take quizzes to determine "Which Mad Man Are You?" (or, better yet, "Which Of Don's Women Are You?").

Of course it is relevant that the show is set in an advertising agency. On the one hand, it is a more realistic or relatable setting than that of some of the other high-profile dramas of this "golden age" of television—ordinary corporate America, not a meth lab or a mafia boss's turf (as in *Breaking Bad* or *The Sopranos*). It allows viewers a bit less distance between their own lives and that of the fictional world they are entering. On the other hand, advertising itself is about the myths of creation, of manufacturing desire, and of glossy packaging as opposed to internal content. Over and over, various characters in the show try to assert that advertising itself is politically neutral, that it only exists to serve the interests of clients and consumers, to make money. But events belie that claim, as choices are made about whether or not to continue marketing cigarettes, hire African Americans, trade on female employees' sexuality, or work for clients who don't want their product turned into a "Negro" product. There *is* no such thing as apolitical. Advertising creates and naturalizes desires. We watch as the SCDP team begins to market products based on affect and the feelings they evoke in consumers—the love associated with the chocolate of a Hershey bar, or the nostalgia of traveling back home again to a place we are loved via Kodak's slide carousel—not by showing literal pictures or attributes of a product. Don Draper and his colleagues are inventing our contemporary world, a world of hyper-consumer culture. The show interrogates our own reality, allowing us to ask, how did we get here?[7] How does the use of advertising as the background narrative help us examine the conflation of capitalism and democracy as they were becoming more inseparable in the minds of most Americans? Is advertising all a huge deception, or a service to consumers, giving us useful information? Does it shape the world, or simply respond to it? Or, like popular culture itself, does it reflect, refract, and shape all at once?

Mad Men looks back to invoke the trope of the traveling salesman as well. It reminds us that travel is an important dimension in American ideology: we are always headed toward the frontier.[8] By the 1960s, this means not only the "final frontier" of space exploration (and again, Matthew Weiner tells us that this whole show is a kind of science fiction). We also get the idea of the eroding Eastern establishment being replaced by the lure of California. Early on, it is the place to which Don escapes to see Anna Draper, the "only person who really knows [him]" and where he can be "himself." Disneyland is where Don realizes he wants to marry Megan, and when their marriage is strained, he pleads with her to come with him to California, "where we were happy." By the end of season six, not only has Harry Crane headed to Hollywood to work the television ad business of the agency, but Ted Chaough and Pete Campbell have opened the West Coast branch of Sterling Cooper & Partners, and Megan has moved to Los Angeles for her burgeoning acting career. Yet twenty-first-century viewers know that the golden attraction of California in the 1960s and 1970s doesn't last; not only are the Manson murders and Altamont looming, but so are an energy crisis, smog, wildfires, and scandals ranging from the O. J. Simpson trial to allegations of child molestation by Michael Jackson. From the very real struggles of immigrant farm workers to the vapid veneer of celebrity tabloids and TMZ, the sunlit glow of California faded, not offering a lasting answer to questions of identity and self-reinvention.

The show also politicizes femininity. Great attention has been paid to the character development of women in *Mad Men*, and to how the evolution of women's roles and opportunities changed in the 1960s. The gender politics of the series offer nuanced examination, not only of men and women's changing power dynamics, but also of the very construction of femininity. Through the advertising agency, we see how products are used to construct very particular notions of femininity, challenging the ideology of a natural or essential womanhood. The multiple central female characters offer a variety of women's perspectives and experiences; their juxtaposition offers viewers a chance to enter into debates about power, domesticity, sexuality, and femininity that are not merely historical, but also have contemporary resonance.

All of these themes come together in *Mad Men* as the series poses considerations for the contemporary viewer, whether we are paying close attention, or simply enjoying the sleek drama on Sunday nights. How and what do we think about the way that gender or race or sex are engaged within the narrative? What do we make of the way that ad campaigns are developed as we see the building blocks for today's consumer culture and the fusion of marketing and ideas? How do we understand the relationship between reality and social construction, authenticity and illusion (or are those distinctions themselves even meaningful in our postmodern landscape)? *Mad Men* is, on some level, more subtle than we may acknowledge, because there are so many dimensions of the current cultural landscape that are reflected within the series itself.

The shifting television landscape: Characters and narratives

There has been a shift in the television landscape that has produced not only changes in the productions/products themselves, but also in the way they are made, consumed, and integrated into popular culture. The business model associated with television production is in flux and likely will continue to be in flux, but that has also produced narrative adventures and the analysis thereof in ways and with impacts much more extensive than in the past. Thus, this television revolution has been at least twofold; it involves not only change regarding the shows and their content, but also the type of people working in television and the quality of artists contributing to the creation, writing, and production of these shows.

In the early 1990s, Baltimore journalist David Simon sent Barry Levinson, the Academy Award-winning filmmaker, a copy of his book *Homicide: A Year on The Killing Streets* with a proposal to make it into a feature film. Simon's work chronicled the life of homicide detectives in Baltimore, and provided the basis not only for the network television show *Homicide: Life on the Street*, but also for the subsequent HBO television show *The Wire*. Levinson, who saw the opportunity to tell these longer, multi-dimensional stories within the televisual format, was the executive producer for *Homicide* throughout its tenure on television. *Homicide* presented a gritty and more realistic vision of issues around law and order, urban policing, urban crime, and violence than much of what was on television up to that point and also teased out the humanity and moral complexity of homicide detectives. This was clearly demonstrated by Andre Braugher's character Frank Pembleton, who often struck an extremely religious and morally upright position, but who was surrounded by colleagues who had different perspectives, and who were not always as certain of everything. Pembleton's usual partner on *Homicide*, Kyle Secor's Tim Bayless, while not necessarily a foil for Pembleton, provided a distinctly different approach to life and certitude, presenting a kind of contrast.[9] But *Homicide* also did a few other fairly revolutionary things in terms of the police procedural, including the depiction of imperfect police who don't always catch "the bad guy" and who face their own conflicted actions and inclinations. These police officers experienced the psychological, emotional, and moral conflicts that actual police officers regularly face and, in so doing, showed a side of our society as seen from within local political institutions. The audience that watched *Homicide*, while not as extensive as the audiences for *Law & Order* or *NYPD Blue*, was extremely loyal to the show as noted at the time: "Other shows have higher ratings, but few have more dedicated fans."[10] What was encapsulated in *Homicide*, more so than other contemporary television shows, were three-dimensional characters and interactions, morally complex situations, and critiques of political institutions. Those aspects of the show were attractive not only to the actors and actresses on the show, but also to those who would write episodes and direct them. Barry Levinson and other film directors and film actors saw opportunities to engage in a project on television that was considered "serious" and important and laid the groundwork, in many ways, for the era of "prestige television."

In parallel to—or slightly preceding—the creation and production of *Homicide* and *NYPD Blue* was the British creation and production of *Prime Suspect*. The original *Prime Suspect* four-part program was first aired in the UK in 1991, in the US in 1992. In many ways, *Homicide* and *Prime Suspect* examined similar terrain, with the capacity of the main character (Andre Braugher's Frank Pembleton and Helen Mirren's Jane Tennison) to induce the likely suspect to confess in the interrogation room. *Prime Suspect*, especially in the initial program, also integrated the overt sexism and discrimination that Jane Tennison experienced at the hands of many of her colleagues, supervisors, and subordinates. While there was some corruption within the police force that she came across in the course of her murder investigation, there was also the presentation of the morally compromised situation in which many prostitutes found themselves, and their expectation that the police would not pursue the murderer or threat to them because they were involved in the sex-trade. This theme continued in a number of the *Prime Suspect* episodes throughout its multi-year production.[11]

This would continue to be the path that "prestige television" staked out— that participating in television was not considered a "step down" for actors, actresses, writers, and directors when they were participating in a series that was critically acclaimed, award winning, and laying claim to a place within the cultural landscape. Brett Martin explains in his book *Difficult Men: Behind the Scenes of a Creative Revolution* that there is also a difference in the very operation of television during this period of ascendency. Not only are celebrities potentially more inclined to pursue options on television instead of in films, but the individuals in charge, the showrunners (as they are called), are the writers, the "authors" of the shows, instead of the directors (though directors do create a lot of the atmospherics that are so important). This is distinct from films, where the writers are important and produce the script, but the individual given most credit for the finished film itself is the director. Martin analyzes this situation, explaining that:

> all the showrunners shared … the seemingly limitless ambition of men given the chance to make art in a once vilified commercial medium. And since the Hollywood film industry had long been in a competitive deep-sea dive toward the lowest common denominator, chumming the multiplexes with overblown action "events" and Oscar-hopeful trash, Alan Ball, the showrunner of *Six Feet Under*, was entirely justified in his response to hearing [David] Chase's stubborn assertion that he should have spent *The Sopranos* years making films.
>
> "Really?" said Ball. "Go ask him, 'Which films?'"[12]

Alan Sepinwall argues in his book *The Revolution was Televised* that this "golden age" of television is in part due to writers and showrunners having finally figured out the benefits of television (as opposed to films)—namely, that there is much more time to tell a story, and for characters to develop in complexity, and to evolve and shift with time, circumstances, and contexts.[13] Indeed, this is what has been transpiring. Even on shows that are less critically acclaimed, narrative and characters have been developed following the initial episodes:

> dramas like *NYPD Blue* and *Homicide* … tapped into what I had seen for years as the limitless potential of TV storytelling … [Television] could tell very long stories. It could allow characters to grow over extended periods of time. And by coming into my home rather than making me go to it, it could forge a more intimate bond with me.[14]

Sepinwall's point is particularly relevant to the discussion of the "politics" of *Mad Men*, as he is noting the engagement that the television audience has with narratives and characters. It is a deeper and more attenuated relationship, intimate and ongoing, lasting often a few years/seasons. The stories themselves can often juggle more characters and narrative dimensions than most films because of the longer lifespan of a television series. *Mad Men*, in particular, is doing something unique within popular culture—even within the context of prestige television dramas—because of the moral complexity of the characters themselves, but also by situating the drama quite consciously and overtly within an historically complex context, where the narrative engages with the contested understanding of that historical period, the 1960s.

There is an additional aspect of this fluid television landscape that centers on how the television audience reacts to and interacts with or about the shows themselves. This subsequent dimension to the revolution remains very much in flux as social media and the various platforms and ways in which individuals watch television continue to shift and change. The recent advent of Netflix's and Amazon's production of original content is just one more example of the shifting "playing field" in which television is created, distributed, and consumed. This shift, along with the rise of fan sites, where avid watchers of shows comment on their every aspect, narrative, and character evolution, has contributed to a changing landscape in the way in which television is both constructed and consumed. It is more interactive than ever before, with input from those who watch it often followed by comments from those who are making the shows themselves. The rise of Twitter—and the experience of live-tweeting episodes of shows—has further contributed to this interactive engagement with television. "The social media can provide networks with real-time feedback on what they are doing."[15] Studies are demonstrating this interactive engagement, and television networks are trying to capitalize on it in an effort to get the audience to watch the television show during its initial airing and to drive more viewers to watch.[16] More than simply a marketing or ratings ploy, though, these digital means of responding to the text of a show like *Mad Men* create the opportunity for community around a text. This community of fans and critics contains political dimensions and practices. As Lisbet van Zoonen notes, citizenship has a lot in common with being a "fan" of some cultural phenomenon: fandom, like citizenship, keeps a person involved in seeking information, talking with others in order to make sense of what happened, or persuading them of one's own interpretation and preferences, and investing emotionally in the (political/cultural) object, securing continued commitment.[17] Matthew Weiner is well aware of the fan investment and interaction with *Mad Men*. The aura of secrecy and ambiguity he has created around the show's plot points has encouraged even more analysis and conversation among its audience, and provided more opportunities than a typical television show for viewers to interpret and make meaning(s) of the text. As Weiner has noted in interviews,

> No matter how definitive I am with the show, it always seems to be ambiguous for the audience. For me, that's just the nature of the show and the nature of the audience. Convincing the audience that Lane had actually died and was not coming back … I mean, that's why we showed his body! I'm always, honestly, not being coy—just surprised at what people do get and don't get. I don't even question it anymore. I am seriously, deeply flattered that there's a conversation. And I love that the conversation—I hope that the audience isn't disappointed that their theories are better than what we did.[18]

Far from lulling audiences into a complacent, de-politicized role, popular culture texts like *Mad Men* encourage the development of political skills and practices—negotiating the meanings of the text, arguing with other citizens/ viewers about those interpretations, recognizing the multiplicity of views and voices, and responding back to cultural and political messages being disseminated. This volume examines a variety of those messages and practices.

Morally complex universes

For a long time, there was not much in terms of variety of access points to television shows and the content was generally designed to appeal to the broadest possible audience, thus often eschewing controversial presentations or ideas.[19] This seemed to be truer of evening dramas than of half-hour comedy shows, in part because comedies could often engage with controversial topics while poking fun at reactions to those topics. The one-hour evening drama fits into somewhat clear categories: police procedural, soap opera (often including medical dramas), action drama, legal drama. These shows often dealt with controversial and topical issues (as *Law & Order* always advertised, its plots were "ripped from today's headlines"), but they were not necessarily morally complex in structure or in plot development, and in many ways the characters remained fairly static. One often knew who the "good guys" and the "bad guys" were and, more often than not, the "good guys" won/solved the case/caught the bad guy/came out on top. The rise of the "anti-hero," while not upending this plot trajectory, presents viewers with characters and outcomes that are more complex than was previously the case. These characters and shows engage viewers by asking the viewer to consider affection for a character who doesn't do the right thing, or who is known to be corrupt and immoral. The characters are also drawn in more dynamic dimensions—they are not static, always heroic, or villainous. They change based on the situation and the other individuals involved, demonstrating growth (and decay). In this way, the shows themselves have been "more realistic," with fully human, multi-dimensional protagonists who are confronted with situations that ask them to consider the moral basis of their actions. Audiences continue to watch, empathize, and debate, but most of all want more of the same.

The audience also continues to want to engage with the shows themselves as well as the creators and the writers, and the porous nature of the Internet, as previously mentioned, has provided far more opportunity for interaction.

Fansites, online blogs, growing numbers of websites that include recaps and commentaries, and the use of Twitter during the actual airing of shows have all contributed to a changing dynamic around television shows and how we watch them. These changes have made for much more extensive engagement between and among the shows themselves (writers, creators, actors, designers, directors), the audience, and television critics (professional and amateur). This has furthered the popular cultural reach of many television programs, dubbed "water cooler shows" because individuals in work settings (who may not have very much in common otherwise) discuss the latest plot developments and character arcs around the water coolers. This is one of the ways in which popular culture works its way into the broader "political" discussion, since characters and shows become touchstones, common dialog, and points of reference. And, as the more complex television shows are the shows that spark conversation and dialog, the discussions are not about how funny a show was the night before or how tragic, but actual conversations about the complicated situations in which complex characters find themselves and what they choose to do in those situations. This brings in considerations of fairness, justice, legality, the treatment of others, and a myriad of issues and topics that are constantly being debated within political institutions themselves. The morally complex universes and characters presented on television often reflect more nuanced analysis of political questions than elected representatives provide for voters during campaigns.

In fact, these morally complex narratives, while still being produced within a commercial system that requires viewers (or consumers) to sit through advertisements during the course of a television show, stand in some contrast to the previous eras of television shows that were made and distributed through the three national networks. The productions that have marked this new age of prestige television have been delivered through less-than-traditional avenues and this has been a significant factor in terms of the narratives and characters. In certain capacities, these shows have demonstrated deviations from the arguments made by the Frankfurt School scholars, who articulated the way that art would become mass produced as a part of industrialized economies. This mechanization of art—broadly construed—included the advent of film, which Walter Benjamin, Theodore Adorno, and others considered a means for controlling culture and thus controlling the masses of citizens. Much of the Frankfurt School argued that film and other forms of mass-produced "art" would, by definition, politicize art within a society, but that same art would inevitably traffic in soothing (or numbing) narratives and ideology, thus placating the citizens. This would provide an avenue for controlling the "ideas" of a society—reinforcing cultural tropes, founding myths, and the like. Adorno explains that:

> The total effect of the culture industry is one of anti-enlightenment, in which … enlightenment, that is the progressive technical domination of nature, becomes mass deception and is turned into a means for fettering consciousness. It impedes the development of autonomous, independent individuals who judge and decide consciously for themselves. These, however, would be the precondition for a democratic society, which needs adults who have come of age in order to sustain itself and develop. If the masses have been unjustly reviled from above as masses, the culture industry is not among the least responsible for making them into masses and then despising them, while obstructing the emancipation for which human beings are as ripe as the productive forces of the epoch permit.[20]

The Frankfurt School was particularly concerned with the capacity of "the masses" to realize their deception by the newly mechanized culture. Citizens of the twenty-first century are so inundated by this that it is often difficult to parse it and consider the influence that culture has on us as citizens, as consumers, as "the masses." We are well beyond the scope of the concern articulated by Benjamin, Adorno, Horkheimer, and others. And, while there often seems to be a unified culture in which many of us participate, the fracturing of media has contributed to a more fluid or porous culture—perhaps still unified, but certainly not as fortified or immutably structured as in the past.[21]

Thus, this wave of complex television narratives, anchored by writers and directors from multiple visual experiences, is being produced at a point where the entire televisual landscape has shifted rather dramatically. Still hewing to a format and production modality that is contextualized by the mechanization of art, many of these television shows (and narratives) are urging the viewers (the consumers) to consider themes more in keeping with literature. *Mad Men* is particularly situated in this context, since the meta-analysis of

Mad Men deconstructs not only the narrative and the characters but the context in which they are presented, the postwar advertising world. "Reading" *Mad Men* provides the opportunity to not only examine the story development and understand the interactions of characters, but, because the story and timeline are set in a particularly vibrant and not-all-that-distant past, the viewer finds him or herself overlaying particular cultural understandings on to the analysis.

There is also a connection between the abstract nature of mass-produced cultural artifacts as the molders of popular culture and thus contributors to the broad political landscape, and the ways in which themes and ideas conveyed through these mechanisms also interact with individuals in a dynamic, rather than a static, way. The "examples" of fictional multifaceted situations provide an overt connection between fictional presentations and cultural artifacts and the "real world" of politics. So much of electoral politics is also about controlling "the narrative" and sending messages to voters in one form or another. These two aspects of politics integrate electoral politics and popular culture without much acknowledgment. The morally complex characters we find on television reflect the moral complexities of our lives and generally contribute to our expectation that those in elected office are also morally complex (if not downright corrupt). Scholar Jeffrey P. Jones has noted the integration of what is generally considered "politics" with popular culture and how the two are fundamentally connected in the way we understand the world in which we live and vote:

> politics is increasingly a textual practice, both in how it is constructed and presented for publics and how it is consumed or "read" by audiences. But as texts, this engagement does not happen in a vacuum. It happens in the swirl of other images, narratives, and ritual practices with which we invest our time and make commitments through all forms of popular culture. And it happens in the context of our primary social relationships—among our families, friends, or colleagues and in our homes, workplaces, or gathering spots. Politics occurs for many people in what one author calls our "media surround": the forms, types, places, and contexts in which media are inserted into our lives. It is this complexity to our relationship with politics via media—its simultaneously private and public nature—that provides a location for reexamining the notion of television's role in civic (dis)engagement.[22]

Television is not the static entity it once was. It continues to evolve, as does the content of the shows, events, and information that are conveyed. Television is becoming more interactive—between the activities that viewers pursue and the engagement by the actors and actresses, writers, showrunners, and the networks themselves in responding to the viewers. Television as a cultural entity is also more porous than it has ever been in the past—amid YouTube posts, web series, smaller and newer networks, subscription cable, and platforms like Hulu, Netflix, and Amazon Prime creating their own content, it is easier and cheaper to write and create a television pilot and show than at any time since the advent of television. The industry is in a state of flux itself, with declining viewers for the "big three" networks and changing viewing patterns established by the advent of the DVR, On Demand, and subscription options like Netflix and Hulu Plus. Time shifting and, in particular, "binge watching" multiple episodes or whole seasons of a show at once have further blurred the lines between episodic television and feature films in terms of the viewing experience, allowing audiences to immerse themselves fully in the worlds of these shows and characters for extended, uninterrupted periods of time, if they like. All of this has contributed to a kind of renaissance in television dramas. *Mad Men* has become an example of what this changing platform can and has produced: a period drama that explores human interactions and the repercussions of recent political/historical events through the prism of myriad imperfect characters at a Madison Avenue advertising agency during the explosion of consumer culture in postwar America.

An overview of *Mad Men*

Mad Men presents the audience with a narrative story that, in large measure, revolves around the character of Don Draper/Dick Whitman. From the stylized opening segment, with the dark image drawing of a man sitting on a couch smoking and then tumbling down through tall buildings, to our introduction to Jon Hamm's rendering of Don Draper, we, as the audience, are drawn towards Don's story. At the same time, the show clearly draws its strength from an ensemble of intriguing characters as they interact in midtown

Manhattan, Brooklyn, Ossining, California, and elsewhere. The outline of the show points the viewer towards Draper as the character in whom we should be most invested. It is definitely a show about Don Draper, just as *The Sopranos* was a show about Tony Soprano. But it is also about Peggy Olson, the new secretary who arrives for her first day of work at the Sterling Cooper advertising agency early in the initial episode. These two characters provide much of the framework through which the audience experiences the post-war politics and culture of this 1960s drama. The narrative unfolds, over the course of the entire series, with much emphasis on Don Draper, whose family life is portrayed alongside his professional life. At the same time, Olson's personal and professional life grows increasingly central to the narrative. With Peggy's move from the secretarial pool to a position as a copywriter, and finally as a "creative" in her own right, Olson's storyline and her own trajectory pull at the audience, as we watch her negotiate both her professional and her personal lives in the context of changing gender roles within American society in the 1960s. Over the course of the series, the perspective of Don's daughter Sally—who enters adolescence and, like the show's viewers, is vigilantly watching and trying to make sense of her parents' world—becomes increasingly important to the narrative structure as well. So not only do we experience *Mad Men* from these multiple perspectives that allow viewers to notice gender positions and power dynamics, but generational perspectives and changes as well.

In books exploring the rise of this new "golden age" of television dramas that include *Mad Men*, *The Sopranos*, *Breaking Bad*, and *The Wire*, Alan Sepinwall, Brett Martin, and other authors examine not only the shows themselves but also their creators, and the "Hollywood" machinations around the development and finally production of many of these excellent dramas. Brett Martin notes that Weiner, when he started working on the script for *Mad Men* (at night, since his day job was as a writer on the sitcom *Becker*), was fascinated with "the decades of his parents', and his grandparents' youth—those years' shiny, attractive surfaces and the darker realities beneath."[23] As it weaves together the professional world of advertising along with the personal foibles and travails of the various characters, the story splits its focus between the shiny and attractive surfaces—of Don Draper, Joan Holloway Harris, Betty Draper, Peggy Olson, Roger Sterling, Pete Campbell—and the realities of their lives, lives that are not as shiny or as attractive. *Mad Men* pulls together lots of images and historical contexts with which Americans are familiar, and works those images and historical events into the daily lives of a small coterie of individuals, who respond to the events themselves and, in particular, to the cultural and political shifts that are transpiring all around them. These stories are buttressed by traditional American narrative tropes, with the emphasis on the wealth of the East Coast elite in contrast to the poor and distraught Midwestern youth of Dick Whitman, the tug of the West Coast and the ideals of the tamed frontier, and the comforts of modern American suburbia. *Mad Men* has, as a story, taken on significant pieces of Americana and has been exploring them through the perspectives of the characters who dominate the show. This is not an historical exposition, but it consciously integrates historical touchstones like the Civil Rights Movement, the assassinations of John F. Kennedy, Martin Luther King Jr., and Robert Kennedy, as well as the burgeoning Women's Liberation Movement and the space race, while more subtly engaging the cultural currents that infused the 1960s. As skirts got shorter and ties got wider, characters experimented with LSD and sex. Weiner has acknowledged that he deliberately started the show in 1960 because he wanted to make sure that the birth control pill was available and viable for the female characters.

The richness and depth of *Mad Men* has inspired numerous essays and blog posts analyzing its messages about culture, history, human nature, and psychological identity. *Mad Men and Philosophy* was one of the first texts to delve into an academic analysis of this show, noting that the book was

> written by *Mad Men* fans for *Mad Men* fans who can't help but think about the characters, events, and issues long after they turn off the television. Whether you want to think more about the role of women in the series, or the morality of advertising, or the way to lead a meaningful life, you will find guidance in [this book].[24]

Gary Edgerton, editor of *Mad Men: Dream Come True TV*, explains that he was "fairly certain that the programme was going to be significant enough culturally and aesthetically to warrant" an edited volume analyzing the show from a variety of perspectives.[25] Edgerton goes on to note that "[e]very few years a new television programme comes along to capture and express the zeitgeist. *Mad Men* is ... that show."[26] Edgerton's book incorporates commentary and analysis of diverse aspects of *Mad Men*, from the use of music, sound, and silence throughout the series to the gender dynamics explored within the show, to explications of the particular narratives within the series. Edgerton explains that *Mad Men*

> traffics in presentism by unapologetically framing its characters' small personal dramas through the eyes of the present .... The series uses the language of myth—the conventions of the domestic and workplace melodrama—to represent the sorts of places where friends and relatives in the not-so-distant past lived and worked ... The characters of *Mad Men* ... are merely an earlier, confused and conflicted version of us, trying to make the best of a future that is unfolding before them at breakneck speed ... Where better to begin to make sense of yet another transformative moment like our own than in a narrative such as *Mad Men* where the characters are similarly caught in a kind of limbo wedged between the recent past and a shadowy uncertain future.[27]

Edgerton's point is an important one in terms of understanding the proliferation of all kinds of commentary about television in general (by television critics and by the host of bloggers, commentators, academics, and others) and *Mad Men* in particular. *Mad Men* has been a kind of three-way telescope in the way in which it presents an idea of how the 1960s felt and operated as determined by writers, directors, set and costume designers, and actors all making the television show in the early twenty-first century. The show is then consumed, analyzed, and dissected by an audience (both in the United States and internationally), members of whom perhaps have other perspectives about not only the history, cultural, and political dynamics of the 1960s, but also how those dynamics might inform our current cultural and political dilemmas. This is where *Mad Men and Politics* enters the discussion.

Mad Men's conscious 1960s setting allows it to chart many of the socio-political changes that transpired within the United States during the period. The aforementioned birth control pill radically changed the opportunities and potential life choices for many, many women (and men). It heralded not only second-wave feminism, but cultural upheaval and changes with regard to sexuality—what became known as the sexual revolution. Sexual relationships and the gender dynamic within them are extensively explored in *Mad Men* from both male and female perspectives. This is but one example of the many political issues that *Mad Men* takes on and integrates into the broader narrative of the show and the characters. Why should a show about the 1960s be of so much interest not just to television viewers, but to the many people who are also responding to it by writing about it, critiquing it, analyzing the characters, and the plot trajectories? Why does Edgerton consider this a "zeitgeist" show? Because it touches a political and cultural nerve, examining. issues—gender, race, and ethnicity, nationalism, consumer culture, power, American identity—that are not merely historical but are still being debated, discussed, and disagreed about by many today.

What the themes of the show are, who the target audience is, and from whose point of view the story is written are interesting questions that help determine the political meanings and messages we read from it. Whose perspective governs the show's narrative? Initially, most critics and viewers seemed to think it centered on its main character, the (anti-)hero Don Draper. Over the seasons, there has been increasing insistence that Peggy Olson's character is perhaps equally central to the arc of the show, and the evolution of Peggy and Don's relationship governs the storytelling. Moving toward the end of the series, there has been more discussion and dawning realization that perhaps the best way to understand the show's perspective is from that of the Draper children, especially Sally: "the most important 'eye'—and 'I'—in *Mad Men* belongs to the watchful if uncomprehending children, rather than to the badly behaved and often caricatured adults."[28] Matthew Weiner attributes the idea for the show to his own curiosity about his parents' lives, viewed from his perspective as a child born in the 1960s. As Sally becomes an increasingly important character in the show's storyline, and as viewers come to see her father Don Draper through *her* eyes, it seems plausible that this is a story not told by (or primarily watched by, if one looks at the demographics of its audience and fan base) the "Dons" and "Bettys" who lived the events it drama-tizes. Rather, it is their "watching, hopeful, and so often disillusioned children" who are now re-membering them in order to make sense of both the past and the present.[29] One critic explains: "Who, after all, can resist the fantasy of seeing what your parents were like before you were born, or when you were still little—too little to understand what the deal was with them, something we can only do now, in hindsight?"[30] We would argue that this appeal is not merely literal—one generation nostalgically and critically looking back at its parents' generation—but political. *Mad Men* offers us a seductive and subversive window into our collective American past, and not just to make sense of our parents' identities, but our own.

There are "companion" books that provide information on understanding the show itself, including texts for each season of the show, or that explore the clothing styles, or design elements incorporated into the series.[31] This book integrates a lot of the foundation that has been laid by many of these texts and critiques, building on them to explore aspects of the show that fall under the umbrella of *politics*—not partisan electoral politics, but the broadest understanding of politics—which includes cultural interpretations, gender interaction, sexuality, familial structure, social mores, citizenship and identity, social constructions and movements, the relationship between the individual and work, the individual and the state, the sense of self, issues of nationalism and patriotism, and more. These essays explore a host of topics that help the audience (and reader) understand not only the show and its characters, but also the way in which issues and narratives developed within the series help us to understand ourselves, our place within a culture and society, our relationships with others, and the impact of these events on our lives, our country, and the nature of American political identity.

The chapters in the first part of this book, The American Century, examine the political themes that run throughout the narrative of the series. These themes include the mythos of American identity and the limitations of that identity, the conceptualization of power as pluralist or elitist and understanding the relationship of political power to economic structures, and the idealized promise of happiness where individuals often seek but rarely find either satisfaction or joy. Lilly Goren's essay "If You Don't Like What They Are Saying, Change the Conversation: The Grifter, Don Draper, and the Iconic American Hero" explores the notion of the mythical American hero—as defined within literature and other cultural artifacts—and how Don Draper embodies and challenges that understanding. Specifically, she draws parallels between Draper and Jay Gatsby, that archetypical American hero. Draper's chosen career path, where he can "con" Americans through his insightful pitches to their consumerism, as well as through a re-invention of his original identity, is a modern version of Gatsby—but there are also important deviations from the Gatsby narrative. Don, over the seasons of the show, establishes his credentials as a wealthy and powerful individual, who, for a time, comes to take his place among those who form established American society. This chapter examines the dichotomous presentation of Don Draper and Dick Whitman, the contrast between the backbone of establishment society and the grifter, especially within the framework of a common understanding of the American hero.

Loren Goldman plays with assumptions of democratic pluralism and power in "The Power Elite and Semi-Sovereign Selfhood in post-War America." By engaging the dialectics of appearance and reality in mass society, this chapter reads *Mad Men* as a variation on the common American trope of the self-fulfilling prophecy and argues that it stages an important debate in then-contemporary political science about the nature and limits of pluralism in mass democracy. Since before its founding, the idea of America has been linked to the notion of realizing an idealized collective self that breaks with the feudal past and forges a new identity out of the wilderness by dint of labor and gumption. *Mad Men* presents both the promise and fragility of the self under conditions of late capitalism: while most evident in the figure of Don Draper/Dick Whitman, each major character attempts to make a radical break with the past, only to find that greater social power structures limit sovereign agency. Writ larger, the tensions *Mad Men* represents in each character reflect a greater debate in Cold War political inquiry concerning the standard pluralist understanding of American politics, as the hopeful visions of democracy offered by thinkers like Robert Dahl and John Dewey were challenged by Reinhold Niebuhr, E. E. Schattschneider, and C. Wright Mills. The characters' struggles to escape their pasts parallel the tensions between structure and agency confronting contemporary pluralist narratives of American political life and suggest the ironic character of the self's sovereignty.

In her essay "Cash or Credit: Sex and the Pursuit of Happiness" Laurie Naranch analyzes how *Mad Men* illuminates the importance of exchange—specifically focusing on sex as the currency in the transaction—and how the ordinary experience of individuals may find that exchange politically and personally isolating: a dark reading of the American Dream. If we think of sex as a privileged site through which *Mad Men* works out anxieties about self-invention, sexism, security, and commerce in the 1960s as well as in our present age, we come to see the way in which sex—as intimate activity, desire, and identity—structures the world of *Mad Men*, with its implications for the classical liberal dream of the pursuit of happiness.

The second portion of the book, Business and Identity, explores the business of capitalism in postwar America and how business, economics, and American identity fuse within *Mad Men*. These chapters examine nationalism, patriotism, and the Cold War; the post-war economic boom, twentieth-century free market capitalism, and the changing approaches to consumer culture; and the framing of sex as a calculation within the *Mad Men* narrative. In "Appearances, Social Norms, and Life in Modern America: Nationalism and Patriotism in Mad Men," Lawrence Heyman begins by examining how a changing sense of nationalism and patriotism are woven into the fabric of our understanding of modern American life as it is presented in the show. The embedded evaluation of nationalism, patriotism, and what "America" is during this period reflects the contested nature of American patriotism as the nation emerges from the post-World War II period into the Cold War and the 1960s. By focusing on this specific decade, *Mad Men* weaves in examinations of nationalism as seen through growing consumer culture, especially in the boardroom discussions around products and advertising campaigns. Matthew Weiner purposefully set the work environment for *Mad Men* in a Madison Avenue advertising agency because advertising has become the tapestry that signifies and validates the modern American identity. Advertising is the canvas through which change is reflected and communicated. Significant emotional events were carefully woven into the fabric of the ads produced by Madison Avenue during the time in which the show is set—and the conversations among the characters on *Mad Men* are, in fact, discussions of these shifting understandings of national identity and patriotism during the Cold War, social unrest, and American involvement in Vietnam.

In "Going Groovy or Nostalgic: *Mad Men* and Advertising, Business, and Social Movements," Kate Edenborg specifically explores the changing nature of the advertising industry in conjunction with the cultural and political upheaval of the 1960s. The companies served by Sterling Cooper were themselves evolving with the time—there were growing markets in military hardware, aeronautics, cars, and motorcycles, and these were not so much replacing but contesting more "female"-oriented markets (food items, bras, cold creams, etc.). The structure of companies themselves were also shifting, from mostly "family businesses" (i.e., owned and operated by fathers and their children, spanning the generations) to a more "modern" corporate structure (with managers, CEO, etc.). This move toward administrative control is reflected in the Sterling Cooper ad agency itself with the mounting tension between management (Lane Pryce and his counting of paperclips) and "creative." Edenborg demonstrates that the well-known and caricatured cultural and political shifts of the 1960s are not divorced from or in opposition to the business world; rather, business and advertising mirror and adopt many of the same attitudes, modes, and changes.

The third section of the book, Those Seen and Not Seen, Heard and Not Heard, directs attention to our understanding of particular identities, of gender, of race, of "other." The three essays in this section specifically focus on, respectively, masculinity, femininity and feminism, and race and other demarcations of difference within American society. Denise Witzig, in her chapter "Masculinity and its Discontents: Myth, Memory and the Future of Mad Men," explores masculinity in the context of postwar America, where men were often evaluated on the basis of their wartime heroism as well as economic status. This exploration—which focuses on many of the male characters on *Mad Men*, but especially protagonist Don Draper—integrates a Freudian analytical lens with contemporary feminism as it evaluates the connection between masculinity, sexuality, and modernity. Melancholia is a reaction not only to the (still salient) crisis in masculinity that the show explores, but to history, repression, and loss of the modern self as well.

In her essay "'You Can't Be a Man. So Don't Even Try': Femininity and Feminism in *Mad Men*," Natalie Fuehrer Taylor examines the three main female characters of the series—Betty Draper Francis, Joan Harris Holloway, and Peggy Olson—as they define and redefine themselves within the decade that inaugurated second-wave feminism. The women of *Mad Men* are complex characters who respond to the social, political, and cultural changes swirling around them from a multitude of perspectives, experiences, limitations, and positions of privilege. The women's movement brought greater equality and opportunity to the workplace, as seen over the course of the series in the advances that Peggy and Joan make professionally. The barriers they faced, and the sexist assumptions these women lived with both at home and in the workplace, may not be tolerated by or familiar to contemporary viewers. But the show also presents these three women facing the dilemmas of negotiating love and respect, home and work, sexuality and power—quandaries all too familiar to twenty-first-century men and women. *Mad Men*'s exploration of feminism and femininity raises questions about our own contemporary issues of gender identity and politics.

Mad Men and its creator Matthew Weiner have been criticized for ignoring or downplaying racial issues in their portrayal of the 1960s. As the Civil Rights Movement and racial integration made major progress through the decade, many viewers and critics wonder why the show has not taken more advantage of the opportunity to depict these social changes and tell the stories of African Americans as fully developed characters. In "Invisible Men: The Politics and Presence of Racial and Ethnic 'Others' in *Mad Men*," Linda Beail argues that while these criticisms are plausible, perhaps the show is consciously choosing to immerse viewers in the experience of "white privilege" typical of the time period. This is a theme still relevant to understanding race relations in the United States today with public reactions to the Trayvon Martin and Michael Brown shootings polarized along racial lines and blacks and whites appearing to live in different worlds. *Mad Men* problematically but realistically presents the marginal position of people of color in the 1960s, and illustrates the political challenges of becoming visible and gaining power. The show's treatment of race also offers an interesting comparison to narratives of social change with regard to the status of women and the assimilation of Jews in the U.S. posing questions of intersectionality and the politics of representational strategies.

Finally, the book concludes with Rebecca Josephson's assessment of the changing American self of the 20th century, with the 1960s as the fulcrum on which that self was pivoting, redirecting, shifting, and changing. In her concluding chapter, "Tomorrowland: Contemporary Visions, Past Indiscretions," Josephson engages the idea of the American self, both politically and culturally. Her reflection on this concept, contextualized within the world of *Mad Men*, knits together the many strands that have been examined in the preceding chapters as she explores the more philosophical dimensions of what contemporary Americans think of themselves, while nostalgically viewing their former selves within this televisual presentation.

Together, these chapters aim to help viewers and fans think about the political work being done within *Mad Men*. We hope that it deepens the pleasure of watching and talking about the show, even as it engages readers in the political practices of meaning-making, and in theorizing, evaluating, and debating the notions of power, democracy, identity, and truth offered by this fascinating and complex text.

Notes

1 Though *Mad Men* creator Matthew Weiner does not agree with the classification of Draper as an "anti-hero."

2 Bernie Heidkamp, "New 'Mad Men' TV Show to Reveal Racism and Sexism of Today," Alternet.org, August 24, 2007, http://www.alternet.org/story/60278/new_%22mad_men%22_tv_show_uses_the_past_to_reveal_racism_and_sexism_of_today (accessed March 7, 2014).

3 A 2008 *Washington Post* interview with Matthew Weiner, quoted in Alan Sepinwall, *The Revolution Was Televised: The Cops, Cooks, Slingers and Slayers Who Changed TV Drama Forever* (New York: Touchstone, 2013), p. 307.

4 Ibid., 306.

5 Katie Roiphe, "The Allure of Messy Lives," *New York Times*, July 30, 2010, http://www.nytimes.com/2010/08/01/fashion/01Cultural.html (accessed March 31, 2014).

6 Kent Ono, "*Mad Men*'s Postracial Figuration of a Postracial Past," in Lauren M. E. Goodlad, Lilya Kaganovsky, and Robert A. Rushing (eds), *Mad Men, Mad World: Sex, Politics, Style, and the 1960s* (Durham, NC: Duke University Press, 2013), p. 315.

7 In a conscious reference to "Once in a Lifetime" by Talking Heads, which highlights the reality of not only desire for the American *dream* (big automobile, beautiful house, beautiful wife) but also the conflicted nature of wanting things

to stay the same as they ever were but having them constantly shifting and changing, much like the dichotomy of *Mad Men*.

8   *Mad Men* makes much of this trope with ad campaigns for airlines, tourism, and Samsonite luggage. The fourth season episode *The Suitcase* (4.7) is a kind of distillation of many of the broader narrative arcs on *Mad Men*, forefronting the tense friendship and mentorship between Don and Peggy while pressing the emotional implications of Don's dual identities and his beleaguered quest for love and acceptance.

9   Police procedurals allow for this kind of contrast, often presenting contrasting but complementary qualities among the partner duos on the force. HBO's recent production *True Detective* is yet another version of this presentation.

10   Tom Jicha, "'Homicide' Tries a Shift on the Internet," *Sun Sentinel*, April 3, 1997, http://articles.sun-sentinel.com/1997-04-03/lifestyle/9704010269_1_homicide-fans-second-shift-ratings (accessed June 20, 2013). The show also won a number of Emmys, Critics' Choice Awards, and Peabody Awards during the course of its run.

11   The show, over the years, also brought a variety of British actors to the attention of American audiences, especially Helen Mirren.

12   Brett Martin, *Difficult Men: Behind the Scenes of a Creative Revolution* (New York: Penguin Press, 2013), p. 9.

13   Critics such as John Fiske have long pointed out the polysemy of popular culture texts, and feminist analyses of soap operas note the subversive feminist potential of these shows—they are open-ended, have room for complexity that can go unresolved, and audiences can make meaning that isn't overdetermined from the authors/directors/producers. See, for example, the work of Tania Modleski, Ien Ang, and Christine Geraghty for further exploration of this point.

14   Sepinwall, *Revolution was Televised*, p. 2.

15   David Bauder, "Television & Social Media: Viewers Use Twitter as a Part of the TV Experience," *Huffington Post Entertainment*, December 3, 2012.

16   Live-tweeting *Mad Men* has not become the social media phenomena that live-tweeting has around *Scandal* or *Orphan Black*, but *Mad Men* has produced substantial, nearly-instant analysis and has led to the creation of websites that are devoted to analyzing all aspects of the show itself. These range from the implications of the costume choices on the plot and our understanding of the characters (TomandLorenzo.com) to broad-based analysis (BasketofKisses.com). Television critics at all major online and traditional media outlets have also been compelled to post reviews of each episode, usually within the following 12–24 hours, often followed by full-season reviews and subsequent commentary.

17 Lisbet van Zoonen, *Entertaining the Citizen: When Politics and Popular Culture Converge* (Lanham, MD: Rowman & Littlefield, 2005), p. 145.

18 Denise Martin, "Matthew Weiner Talks About *Mad Men*'s Next and Final Season," *Vulture*, March 11, 2014, http://www.vulture.com/2014/03/matthew-weiner-sets-up-mad-mens-season-7.html (accessed March 31, 2014); Alan Sepinwall, "Mad Men Creator Matthew Weiner on Don's Confession, Bob Benson's Origin and More from Season Six," Hitfix: What Alan's Watching, June 24, 2013, http://www.hitfix.com/whats-alan-watching/mad-men-creator-matthew-weiner-on-dons-confession-bob-bensons-origin-and-more-from-season-6 (accessed March 31, 2014).

19 This was certainly not always the case, and the 1970s saw quite a few controversies erupt in shows written by or created by Norman Lear, who also brought Americans *Archie Bunker/All in the Family, Sanford and Son, Good Times, The Jeffersons, One Day at a Time,* and *Maude,* among others. Larry Gelbart, who created the television show *M*A*S*H* in the 1970s also contributed to this period of television renaissance, though the shows were generally half-hour situational comedies as opposed to hour-long dramas.

20 Theodor W. Adorno, *The Cultural Industry: Selected Essays on Mass Culture* (London: Routledge, 1991). Quoted from Adorno, "Cultural Industry Reconsidered," in Raiford Guins and Omayra Zaragoza Cruz (eds), *Popular Culture: A Reader* (London: Sage Publications, 2005), p. 108.

21 There are quite a few texts that explore many dimensions of popular culture. A few of the contributors to this volume have also written chapters in *You've Come a Long Way, Baby: Women, Politics and Popular Culture* (Lexington: University Press of Kentucky, 2009) and *Women and the White House: Gender, Popular Culture and Presidential Politics* (Lexington: University Press of Kentucky, 2012). Both books use the lenses of gender and politics (in different forms) to explore popular culture.

22 Jeffrey P. Jones, *Entertaining Politics: Satiric Television and Political Engagement,* second edition (Lanham, MD: Rowman & Littlefield, 2010), p. 24.

23 Martin, *Difficult Men,* p. 242.

24 Rod Carveth and James B. South (eds), *Mad Men and Philosophy: Nothing is as it Seems,* Blackwell Philosophy and Pop Culture Series, ed. William Irwin (Hoboken, NJ: John Wiley & Sons, 2010), p. 2.

25 Gary Edgerton, *Mad Men: Dream Come True TV* (London: I. B. Tauris, 2011), p. viii.

26 Ibid., p. xxvi.

27   Ibid., pp. xxvi–xxvii.

28   Daniel Mendelsohn, "The *Mad Men* Account," *New York Review of Books*, February 24, 2011, http://www.nybooks.com/articles/archives/2011/feb/24/mad-men-account (accessed March 7, 2014).

29   Ibid.

30   Ibid.

31   See, for example, Nelle Engoron, *Mad Men Unmasked: Decoding Season 4* (Amazon Media, 2012); Will Dean, *The Ultimate Guide to Mad Men: The Guardian Companion to the Slickest Show on Television* (London: Guardian Books, 2010); Stephanie Newman, *Mad Men on the Couch: Analyzing the Minds of the Men and Women of the Hit TV Show* (New York: St Martin's Press, 2012).

2

If You Don't Like What They Are Saying, Change the Conversation: The Grifter, Don Draper, and the Iconic American Hero

Lilly J. Goren

The world is a great dodger, and the Americans the greatest. Because they dodge their own very selves

D. H. Lawrence, *Studies in Classic American Literature*

Don Draper has inhabited the living rooms of many Americans for seven seasons on AMC's *Mad Men*.[1] He has presented us with dual identities: that of Don Draper, the name of his commanding officer in Korea who was killed and from whom Dick Whitman stole his identity and also his discharge from the military; and Dick Whitman, the name he was given at birth, by his prostitute mother, as she was dying.[2] In many ways, Don Draper, the character, seems to be inspired by F. Scott Fitzgerald's Jay Gatsby. However, he ultimately is more akin to Ralph Ellison's Invisible Man. There are some quite obvious similarities between Draper and Gatsby, not only of fact (changed names, obscured pasts, etc.) but also a certain willingness to bend in morally compromised directions. Draper/Whitman, Gatsby, and quite a few other characters who dot the American landscape have a certain fluidity to their identities that connects them to the romantic idea of the United States, both historically and conceptually. This flexibility with identity, with who they really are, makes it much more difficult for them to fully connect to others, and to forge the bonds of friendship or intimacy that join people together. This has often been the dirty little secret of the American ideal of individualism and freedom—the subsumed value of community and connection, friendship, and engagement.

Who is Don Draper?

Dick Whitman grew up in a desperately poor home in rural America with a half-brother named Adam. He was drafted into the military and is the only enlisted soldier with his commanding officer in a remote location when they are hit. Ultimately, through subsequent mishaps on Dick's part, their foxhole blows up, killing Draper and injuring Whitman. Whitman, in the midst of this mess, switches dog tags with Draper, having learned that Draper was about to be sent home. No one questions the newly reborn Draper or his identity; he is sent to hospital to recover and he becomes Donald F. Draper. Although Whitman committed at least two illegal acts, identity theft and desertion, he takes on a new life, a new identity, and very consciously leaves behind the remnants of his family (including his half-brother Adam). These events come to be known to the viewers over the course of the first two seasons of *Mad Men*. Draper's secret identity leads to the undoing of his first marriage, and periodically complicates, even threatens, his work life.

In the season six episode *The Tale of Two Cities* Don hallucinates his death after perhaps too much hookah at the Hollywood Hills party he, Roger Sterling, and Harry Crane attend as Harry tries to track down movie moguls. Don's image of his death comes after a hippie version of his wife Megan appears and is then followed by Private Dinkens, whom Don met in the opening episode of season six. Dinkens was on active duty in Vietnam. In Don's hallucination Dinkens is now dead and tells Don that he, too, is dead, noting to him how bad he looks. Don's next vision is standing poolside, looking down at himself floating, facedown, in the water while partygoers surround the pool. Don actually "comes to," soaking wet, on the side with Roger, also soaking wet, kneeling beside him. The implication is that Roger has pulled Don out of the water and saved him from drowning, and that the hallucination was Don's deathlike experience/reverie.

The image of Don facedown in the pool has prompted many a comparison to *Sunset Boulevard*, especially given the West Coast location where these events transpire. But this image comports with the image of Jay Gatsby's death that Nick Carraway conveys in *The Great Gatsby* just as much, as Gatsby is killed in his pool, and is found by Nick and his staff dead, adrift on a float, shot by George Wilson. Draper, like so many an American literary hero, is a creation akin to Jay Gatsby—heroic, flawed, imperfect, a liar, and from common and, to a degree, corrupt or impure beginnings. Gatsby was hardly the first incarnation of this image. Our literary and actual landscape is littered with conmen and grifters—their stories permeate both our mythical understanding of the United States and the reality of our day-to-day life. We, as a people, have long believed what people have told us, perhaps naively. The question becomes, how much of a grifter is Don?

Edgar Allen Poe goes to great lengths to explain how a grifter—or diddler, as he calls them—works in his brief text "Raising the Wind: (Diddling Considered as One of the Exact Sciences)."[3] A grifter (or diddler, or confidence trickster) is a person who tries to obtain money or goods through fraud or deception, especially while playing on the confidence or integrity of the individual being conned. Grifters often move from place to place so as to avoid detection. Herman Melville's 1857 novel *The Confidence-Man: His Masquerade* is another fictional presentation of this theme. Fitzgerald published *The Great Gatsby*, his rather romantic take on the grifter, in 1925. Ralph Ellison's 1947 masterpiece, *Invisible Man*, while not exactly a tale of a grifter, certainly explores some of these same themes within the story of an ultimately "nameless" African-American man. Even as recently as Tom Wolfe's 1987 bestseller *The Bonfire of the Vanities* we have the tracings of this same trope, if contextualized a bit differently. This story is particularly familiar within American literature and, by extension, cultural artifacts that can be considered broadly within our understanding of "American letters." According to Kevin Courrier in his book *Randy Newman's American Dreams*, this concept is not uniquely American, but has "[taken] a stronger hold on the American imagination."[4] Melville scholar Stephen Matterson noted that "[t]here is actually a peculiarly American delight in confidence tricksters ... In part such affection has to do with America's emphasis on and admiration for individual enterprise and ingenuity, which are considered notably 'Yankee' qualities."[5]

Don Draper certainly embodies this individual enterprise and ingenuity, as he works his way from car salesman to furrier to, finally, advertising executive (and back again). Over the course of seven seasons of this series we have learned, mostly through flashback, how Don was able to work his way onto Madison Avenue—through cunning and shading the truth, if not outright lying.[6] Draper had been doing some advertising work at the furrier where he was working but certainly had little to show by way of a "book." To break into the field and obtain a job at Sterling Cooper, Draper employed something of a confidence scam on Roger Sterling. As seen throughout the series, Draper does have a keen sense of what will make a good advertisement, and he is one of the best "salesmen" at the agency in terms of pitching a campaign to the clients.

While we are quite familiar with this trope, Draper's story—and Peggy Olson's parallel but slightly more morally upright story—pulls us in, and one is left to consider why our fascination persists, even though we already know many of the problems that our protagonist will face. This individual, while not necessarily heroic in the classic sense, is very much the center of activities and experiences in various narratives that have given shape to popular understandings of the United States and the myth that is a kind of constant trope within our culture.[7] This trope can be seen in all aspects of American culture—from high "art" where (mostly) men of letters have written "the great American novel" with this narrative in mind, and where American poets and playwrights have integrated this idea into their work—to middlebrow cultural presentations; they are reflected in many a Western (novel and film), as well as in films that are often ranked as the "best" movies, such as the first and second *Godfather* films, and *Citizen Kane*. The American ideal, the land where one can achieve anything, is based on the theory that this is a classless (and, according to Alexis de Tocqueville, formless) society so that an individual is not encumbered by rank or position in the ways of so many of our European friends. While this is a vast blanket of a trope, it is a constant within American culture. Daniel Frick highlights it in introducing his portrait of Richard Nixon and the United States, puzzling about the conflict inherent in this myth: "Does, as the myth of the self-made man would have it, America provide unlimited opportunity for self-expression and fulfillment? Or does the nation's glorification of individualism maim, and even ultimately defeat, the self and destroy our larger social community?"[8] And as a context for American fiction—not just written, but all fiction—this tale has been with us and continues to frame stories portrayed on television, in film, and in writing. *Mad Men* continues this tradition and, I would argue, the television show draws its broader picture (and may intrigue us so) based on this same trope. Though unacknowledged, this literary trope is often implied within our political discourse. We see it consistently—it is emphasized by the stories that politicians tell about themselves (person next door, mom in tennis shoes, simple roots, etc.), claiming a connection to "every" man (and woman) and thus not emphasizing elite differences (wealth, family, academic achievement, position). This idea of reinvention, of the "everyman" success story, has embedded within it the fissures of American democracy: the desire to become part of the elite (either economic or political, or both) and the intention to maintain the democratic or common aspects of one's self. This is particularly the case among contemporary office seekers and holders, who, more often than not, come from the moneyed elite but who convey to citizens that they are, in fact, just "like you and me."

While it is simple to point out the commonality between Don Draper and Jay Gatsby, I would also argue that Peggy Olson, initially Don's secretary and later a copy writer and "creative" herself, is as integral to our understanding of the ideas that structure *Mad Men* as Nick Carraway was to our understanding of Fitzgerald's ideas within *The Great Gatsby*. Don may be the tragic figure at the center of *Mad Men*, but Peggy is the character who engages with and, in many ways, adapts to the shifting cultural and political environments that surround her. Peggy also has her own secret that she has deftly learned to conceal, in part because Draper taught her how to do so.

Though they certainly share the capacity to charm people, Draper and Gatsby both maintain a general reserve. Don is, in some ways, much like the central figure of Fitzgerald's novel, but in other ways he is distinct. His general reticence is at odds with Gatsby's chattiness. Yet the trajectory and the tropes are quite parallel, from the changing of names (and, with them, identities) to leaving behind of family and lives that seemed to hinder the growth of the hero. Alexis de Tocqueville, in *Democracy in America*, explains that this is the norm among democratic peoples:

> new families constantly issue from nothing, others constantly fall into it, and all those who stay on change face; the fabric of time is torn at every moment and the trace of generations is effaced. You easily forget those who have preceded

you, and you have no idea of those who will follow you. Only those nearest have interest.[9]

Gatsby moves from his poor origins in the rural Midwest (North Dakota), and the name Jimmy Gatz, to the wealth and culture of New York and Long Island. Draper, too, leaves the Midwest (rural Pennsylvania, Indiana, and Illinois) and, by way of the Korean War, goes from being Dick Whitman, son of a prostitute and a drunk, to being the toast of Madison Avenue as Donald Draper. Gatsby's "parents were shiftless and unsuccessful farm people—his imagination had never really accepted them as his parents at all."[10] We learn from Don himself about his mother—after she died, "they took him to the man who was his father" and he was raised by that man, Archie, and his wife, Abigail. When Don was ten, Archie, a drunk and a liar, died from being kicked in the face by a horse, right in front of his son. Abigail and her subsequent husband, Mack, brought him up in a whorehouse. Not unlike Gatsby, Don explains that he was "raised by those two sorry people" (*Long Weekend*, 1.10). Both Draper and Gatsby distance themselves—physically and mentally—from their birth families and generally hide their origins. This is in keeping with Tocqueville's analysis of the difference between citizens of aristocratic regimes and those who inhabit democracies, especially a kind of pioneer or frontier democracy as in the United States: "not only does democracy make each man forget his ancestors, but it hides his descendants from him and separates him from his contemporaries."[11] Draper is seen by the viewers and by his colleagues as separate: in the early seasons of the series, many of the younger men at Sterling Cooper are anxious about meeting with Draper, and, while they are impressed with his abilities, he holds most of them at arm's length. Gatsby and Draper, through force of will, forget their ancestors, and keep many of their contemporaries at a distance. In both examples, Gatsby/Carraway and Draper/Olson, each "hero" takes an interest in another outsider, individuals who are, in some particular ways, not part of the primary social group with whom they associate.

On the surface, the similarities between Gatsby's story and Draper's story—and the tragedy that has punctuated Draper's story during the seven seasons on AMC—are quite stark. The Gatsby/Draper parallel pursuits of fitting in to what they believed to be the American ideal, of accumulating money as part of a bigger or grander quest, and the need to hide the unseemly parts of themselves that might not comport with whom they wanted to seem or be, are seminal elements in both *The Great Gatsby* and *Mad Men*. These qualities outline the trope within American culture of the "self-made man" who figures out how to find the right opportunities and make the most of his particular gifts—Gatsby is said to be "quick and extravagantly ambitious."[12] When the agency is being purchased by Putnam, Powell, & Lowe at the end of the second season (2.13), in "*Meditations in an Emergency*," Don is described as the "prized possession" of Sterling Cooper, although his potential exit from the agency almost scuttles the whole deal. Ultimately, both men become wildly wealthy; in Gatsby's case, that wealth provides him an opportunity to try to create roots or a position for himself within upper-class American society. For Draper, it often provides potential freedom and the capacity to leave his job/family if necessary. One of the images that is conveyed a number of times during the first season of *Mad Men* (and subsequently) is how much cash Don has hidden away in his locked desk drawer.

This is one of the points of distinction between Gatsby and Draper. Gatsby's drive to establish himself and accumulate wealth was to become part of the society from which he had, in his youth, been ostracized. This was part of his scheme to win Daisy back from Tom Buchanan. If Gatsby could rival Buchanan's wealth and position, then he could rival him for Daisy's affections in a way that he could not when he first met her. We don't observe a similar plan by Draper, though we do observe what he has achieved over the years since he returned from war with his new identity. Draper, like Gatsby, finds his ideal woman: Betty Hofstadt, a Bryn Mawr graduate who pursued a brief modeling career before becoming Mrs. Donald Draper. Betty epitomizes the American ideal of beauty: figure-eight shape, blond hair, ruby lips, and porcelain skin.[13] Gatsby was not as accomplished as Draper in terms of his capacity with women, as he missed his opportunity to marry Daisy. But the ideal of Betty, similar to the ideal of Daisy, is not the same as the reality; thus Don and Betty separate and ultimately divorce over the course of seasons two and three. In each situation, the illusory prize—the beautiful woman who proves less satisfying in achievement than in pursuit—implies the structure of the classical literary narrative: the romantic quest for purity and beauty as embodied by unsullied women. In Gatsby's case, Daisy cannot deny that

she loved Tom, and thus she is not as pure as she had been in Gatsby's imagination. In Draper's case, *Mad Men*'s seven seasons have indicated that Don/
Dick is desperate for both intimacy and love, a kind of classical friendship
that he continuously pursues, and fails to achieve, with the women with
whom he has sex. Both men are greatly disappointed by the women they
pursue. At the same time, Don and Peggy have been building a relationship
in fits and starts, which includes mutual respect and shared emotional, but
not physical, intimacy. For Don, this takes on the form, in many ways, of the
idea of "political friendship"—the relationship between two individuals that
is distinct from private or social friendship. While Don and Peggy have a
relationship that is not between equals, as Don is Peggy's boss for most of the
series, the interactions between the two during seasons six and seven wrestle
with that inequality and, to a degree, arrive at a place of rough equality in the
way they see and treat each other, and a more equal friendship.

Because of the episodic and extended life of television series, we see more of
Don Draper, over a longer period of time and in more detail, than we ever see
of Gatsby in Fitzgerald's novel.[14] But both characters come out of this particular
American aesthetic tradition: the interlinking of rugged individualism and
material success combined with the grifter, the confidence man, a secret identity.
But Gatsby and Draper seem to be in quest of somewhat different pursuits, with
the intervening years between their stories directing them towards distinct
ideals. Gatsby's plan all along was to belong—to somehow take on the deep
past and lineage of the aristocracy that he longed for across the sound in East
Egg. Draper's plan is both more muddled and more fully embedded within
Tocqueville's analysis of the restive Americans who in the "midst of their well-
being" often find themselves undone, distracted, and ultimately unsatisfied.

Draper: Understanding this particular version of the grifter

We first meet Donald Draper, advertising executive and "creative," in the first
episode of *Mad Men, Smoke Gets in Your Eyes*. He is in a bar, writing on a
napkin, with a cigarette in one hand and a drink next to him, and we learn that
he is trying to come up with a way to sell Lucky Strike cigarettes now that they

have been deemed a health risk. Don is flummoxed because he seems to have reached an impasse and is already anticipating that "he is over and that there will be a bunch of young executives picking at his bones tomorrow" (*Smoke Gets in Your Eyes*, 1.1). He can't figure out the way in which to sell one brand of cigarettes over any other now that he is stripped of any health pitches that can be made about smoking. He explains all of this to the second person viewers meet, another "creative" type, Midge, who illustrates greeting cards. Draper arrives at her apartment quite late in the evening and she welcomes him with a drink, some music, witty remarks, and the unbuttoning of her blouse as she reclines on the bed. We follow Don through the evening and into the next day where he returns to his office, still without a clear idea for the pitch. None of this seems odd or out of the ordinary, from what we know. In retrospect, of course, these actions reveal the multiple layers of Don Draper as we come to know him. Much seems normal (including his interlude with Midge at her apartment) until the last two minutes of this very first episode, when Don returns to his suburban home in Ossining and we meet his wife, Betty, and his children, Sally and Bobby, all of whom are asleep. As a viewer, one is then compelled to revisit all of our conclusions about the Donald Draper we have met during the previous 55 minutes. It seems that the Don we met is not necessarily "the real Donald Draper."

In his pitch during the course of this first episode, Don explains to the Lucky Strike executives that what they are selling is not a cigarette: they are selling happiness, and happiness is whatever the advertisers say it is. The eventual resolution is that Don persuades them that they can completely redefine the image of the cigarette, and the activity of smoking, because health claims are no longer legitimate. The ad campaign moving forward will be "wholly new" and postmodern in how it functions, creating the value of the cigarette by re-envisioning the act of smoking itself. We learn, through *Mad Men*'s seven seasons, that this re-envisioning, this capacity to create anew, is how Don operates. This is why advertising, especially in the post-war period, as American consumer culture grew and expanded, is the ideal career for Don Draper. America is reinventing itself as a global superpower, and an international economy; domestically, the 1960s embodied American reinvention with myriad political, social, and cultural revolutions. Don has lived his adult life re-envisioning himself—there is little work that would suit him quite as well as advertising, and especially his role as the head of the creative department. This section of the advertising firm comes up with the copy and the art for advertising products.

From one perspective, Don is a grifter by profession. This is the easiest avenue for him to pursue, far easier than getting a law degree and passing the bar exam or pursuing some other kind of profession requiring particular credentials or academic qualifications. Advertising is a creative process. The copy, the taglines, the drawings themselves are all forms of art, but the art is being applied for a particular purpose: to sell an item. As the series unfolds, there is an ongoing commentary about the value of the items themselves; whether the things being advertised (cigarettes, laxatives, cars, airlines, lipstick, etc.) are of any particular value or necessity, or whether they are, in fact, completely unnecessary and advertising must create the demand for consumers to buy them. Thus, while Don's profession has a creative, artistic component, as he rudely tells Peggy in season four it is money that drives the process, and not the drive to fulfill a creative desire. Rather, creativity and reflection are harnessed and directed towards the sale of products.

As the seasons unfold, Don's personal journey and his professional pursuits are knit together because he has become, since his "original sin" of changing identities in Korea, a grifter, a confidence man. His professional cons—the advertising ideas that he creates and sells, not unlike the ideas that candidates sell when running for office—are "legitimate," at least to a point. While there are certain commentaries made throughout the earlier seasons about the nefarious or disreputable nature of advertising (most specifically by Pete Campbell's father, who finds·the whole thing unseemly), the main protagonists are able to live quite nicely and "appropriately" from their income and their work at the ad agencies.

At the same time, there are a number of instances where the agency itself operates in a corrupt and disreputable manner, most specifically in the effort to land the account for Jaguar cars. This is what makes Don's professional choices so complex in the context of who he is and how he has trained himself. In season five, the executives at Sterling Cooper Draper Pryce fall off the knife's edge upon which advertising, at that point, was balanced—between being legitimate and being a form of prostitution (something with which Draper is quite familiar, given his background and upbringing). A proposition is made to the agency that it will win the Jaguar account if Joan Holloway Harris spends the evening with the president of the Jaguar Dealership Association, Herb Rennet. Don is the sole partner to speak vocally against this proposition. Don respects Joan as a long-time colleague and, at least by the standards of the 1960s, appears genuinely to value her as a friend. In the episode that precedes the Jaguar proposition, Don escorts a hysterical Joan from the office, just after she has been served with divorce papers from her estranged husband. In *Christmas Waltz* (5.10), Joan and Don enjoy some retail therapy at the Jaguar dealership and then spend the afternoon at a midtown bar, talking about life, and comparing stories about lovers. As demonstrated by his caring friendship for Joan in *Christmas Waltz*, Don does possess a certain amount of integrity, especially about his work; this perversion of the agency (the account management side of the business that Don generally stays as far away from as possible) both undermines it and, in Don's eyes, undercuts the validity of his and his team's work, their creativity, and their genius. It also puts Joan into the position of a prostitute, and casts a shadow over the respect and (non-sexual) intimacy that Don and Joan have developed over the years.

Joan ultimately goes through with the proposition and the Jaguar account is landed—until Don dismisses Rennet and the account in season six. During the course of *The Other Woman* (5.11), we learn that Don tried to stop Joan from going through with the evening with Rennet, but he came to her after the fact. Disgusted that his colleagues would operate in such an immoral manner, Don protests throughout the episode that their work needs to "stand on its own." While certainly operating in a protective (and paternalistic) way towards Joan, Draper also displayed a particular code of honor by which he operates, at least in regard to his work.

Changing the conversation: Who is Donald Draper?

Don is almost always willing to, as he says, "change the conversation," and he himself is a reflection of that inclination; he didn't like who he was or what people said about him, so he changed who he was. He literally changed the conversation. But he balances on a different edge from the rest of his colleagues at Sterling Cooper Draper Pryce: he focuses on the integrity of his work in the creative department, and when he is put on leave at the end of season six, he finds a way to continue to create by working with Freddy Rumson as his Cyrano-like stand-in. It is the rest of his life that is lacking in integrity—this missing element stems from his secret identity, his duplicitous departure from his military service, and his constant infidelity to both of his wives. In this way, he is in keeping with Melville's Confidence Man, who keeps shifting his identity. The Confidence Man is nameless and, as the reader sees him, constantly changing his "masquerade" so that it is never clear "who" he is.

Season four of *Mad Men* opens with the question "Who is Don Draper?" asked by a reporter in the context of an interview (*Public Relations*, 4.1). But this question hangs over the entire series and certainly drives not only the series itself, but the commensurate commentary on *Mad Men*. One of the overarching themes of the series is whether or not Don is a consummate grifter. Is there some integrity to Donald Draper/Dick Whitman, a "true" or "real" self? There are aspects of Don's life that have made him face this question, most particularly in regard to his relationship with his daughter, Sally. He has found himself needing to be more authentic with her than with anyone else with whom he interacts (with the exception of Anna Draper, the California widow of the actual Don Draper, with whom he can be himself and drop his masquerade).

While Don often displays excessive self-confidence in most aspects of his life (in his approach to women, his job, his capacities on the job, his inter-action with his friends and colleagues, and to a lesser extent in relation to his children), he does not always have the bravado to "bluster" through all situations. Like Gatsby, Don can seem full of confidence, "[t]hat's the thing about Don: he's all surface and image … but on those very rare occasions when he allows someone (and us) to see the fear under the mask, it can be emotionally devastating."[15] Tocqueville discusses this fear, explaining that it is part of the pursuit of equality and of material well-being within democratic states, and that it makes it often impossible for citizens to be satisfied: "In America I saw the freest and most enlightened men placed in the happiest condition that exists in the world; it seemed to me that a sort of cloud habitually covered their features; they appeared to me grave and almost sad even in their pleasures."[16] We occasionally are given a look behind his mask of bravado, as when Don is melting down on Rachel Menken's couch, sweating after Pete Campbell threatens him, or having a full-blown panic attack when he thinks that the US government might find out that he switched identities and was thus a liar and a military deserter. The final episode of season six presents Don with an enforced sabbatical from Sterling Cooper because of his *dual* performances at a pitch meeting for Hershey chocolate. Don makes the perfect pitch to the executives based on a romantically idealized childhood, but then drops his façade and makes essentially another pitch, in which he describes how Hershey bars were the one thing in his whorehouse childhood that was good, that made him feel normal, which served as his communion. What transpires is an extended presentation of this dissolving bravado at the same time that Don is wrestling with who he is in the world, and without alcohol, another mask behind which he functions.

In many of these situations, Don initially considers running away for one reason or another, reconsiders, and then knits himself back together enough to figure out how to get out of his situation. Don often wants to flee, to "shape shift" again, and become someone else. It is easy for him and he knows how to do it. But as he grows more "established" it becomes more emotionally difficult for him to leave, though that has certainly not stopped him from risking his position, his marriages, the love of his children—at least Sally—or even his wealth.

Gatsby was interested in establishing himself as part of society from the beginning. Draper lives much more on the edge, the edge of leaving, and he occasionally does "step out," sometimes pursuing sexual partners distinct from his wife, sometimes effecting a full-fledged disappearance, as he does late in season two, episode 11 (*The Jet Set*). He and Pete Campbell go to California for a trade show and Don just disappears for two weeks, hooking up with a group of rather unencumbered and nomadic European aristocrats. We watch Don perform his disappearing act (for hours or days) more frequently in the earlier seasons of the show, when no one but Anna Draper knows about his dual identities. As Don reveals his secret to more individuals (mostly women with whom he is involved), he goes on this kind of "walkabout" less frequently—though he disappears into more alcohol-induced hazes, which make him equally absent from his daily life. In later seasons, as Don holds a position of more responsibility and import at the agency, he has more difficulty escaping his past (or present)—in some ways, Don's inability to realistically "escape" mirrors post-war America, a country that could no longer close up its borders and pay little attention to the rest of the world.

Seasons six and seven witness even more of Don's unraveling, after he seems briefly knitted back together through his marriage and relationship with Megan and the apparent financial solidity at Sterling Cooper Draper Pryce. Season six highlights the general unraveling of Don Draper as he becomes more acutely alcoholic and pursues a dangerous affair with Sylvia Rosen, who lives one floor below the Drapers. Don admires and is quite friendly with Dr. Arnie Rosen, her husband. However, Don seems continuously to miss a beat in his advertising campaigns at work. The decline of Don Draper, which really began in season four of *Mad Men*, becomes more acute, and by season six and the beginning of season seven he really does seem to have become a most extreme version of Tocqueville's democratic individual, who is "constantly [led] back toward himself alone and threatens finally to confine him wholly in the solitude of his own heart."[17] Many of the images of Don from season six portray him as distant from Megan, distant from his lover, Sylvia, distant from many of his colleagues, and disengaged from the work he usually relishes. Don was never quite comfortable at his suburban home in Ossining; he was so *un*comfortable that he left home for hours when he was supposed to be picking up the birthday cake for his daughter's party in *The Marriage of Figaro* (1.3). Ultimately, he is no more comfortable in his Manhattan high rise with Megan than he was in Ossining with Betty, and when Megan moves to California and sets up residence there to pursue her acting career, their marriage slowly dissolves over the physical distance, while a lack of connection and intimacy comes to characterize their estrangement. Don has once again walled himself off from someone who loves him.

How do we understand and contextualize Don's discomfort? In this regard, he fits into the position of the traditional American literary hero. We first learn at the beginning of *The Marriage of Figaro* (1.3) that Don Draper is actually named Dick Whitman. Don is recognized, on the train into Manhattan, by another member of his service platoon. At this point, there is no real context for us, the viewers, to understand what the story was with regard to his name. We do know that Don Draper was in the military; we saw his purple heart in the first episode, *Smoke Gets in Your Eyes*. And one would have expected that Don/Dick had been in the military because, at that point, all able-bodied men were drafted. This interlude on the train in 1.3 puts Don in a bad mood—he comes into the office and snaps at everyone. Although some of the mood may be attributable to the Volkswagen ad in *Playboy* that seems to have caught everyone's eye, clearly Don is more irritable than usual.

This early part of Don's day is followed closely by a visit from Rachel Menken, of Menken's Department Store. We meet Rachel in *Smoke Gets in Your Eyes* (1.1), when she comes to Sterling Cooper for a possible bid on the advertising account for her family's department store, which shares a wall with Tiffany & Co. on Fifth Avenue. Initially, Don is quite rude to Rachel, suggesting that she—perhaps because she is female, perhaps because she is Jewish—doesn't know what she is doing and has come to the wrong advertising firm looking for the wrong kind of marketing for Menken's. Don leaves the meeting in a huff and Menken departs, rather disgusted with the way she has been treated. Roger Sterling speaks with Don after the meeting and suggests that it might be wise to try to make a play for the account since it would be a hefty one; at the same time, Sterling concurs with Don's opinion of Rachel's "uppity-ness." Don tries to smooth over the situation with Rachel Menken by inviting her for a drink.

When they meet, Don attempts to charm her, and he and Rachel have a very interesting, albeit brief, conversation. Don starts out by asking Rachel why she isn't married, and she notes the gendered offense of the question. She responds by explaining—long before second-wave feminism—that she shouldn't have to choose between "putting on an apron and working," that she actually enjoys working in an exciting position, and that she has never been in love. Don explains that "love doesn't exist. What you call 'love' was invented by guys like me to sell nylons" (1.1). Here, in the first episode, he is bursting one big myth: that *love*—that emotion that takes your breath away, the "big lightning bolt to the heart"—was invented to sell things. With a very arrogant delivery, Don continues, explaining that "you're born alone and you die alone, and the world just drops a bunch of rules on you to make you forget those facts, but I never forget" (1.1). Don is explaining that he is living outside of the myths; he knows that the images on the cave wall are just that, images, and he is on to the game. In his haughty reply to Menken, Don admits essentially to designing his own life, his own rules, and knowing the illusions by which others are living. But this may not have led him to reflect on the meaning that he is creating. And Menken picks up on Don's essential discomfort with who he is, noting that she has just realized how difficult it must be to be a man; she continues by saying that she doesn't know what he believes in, but she does know what it feels like to be out of place, to be disconnected, to see the whole world laid out in front of you the way other people live it—"there is something about you that tells me that you know it too" (1.1). Draper is taken aback, and he is discomfited by Menken's evaluation of him, but instead of engaging with her about this dislocation, he changes the subject. This brief interlude, with a character we have been led to understand is an outsider because of her gender and her religion, is all the more interesting in retrospect, as we learn over the course of seven seasons just how much of an outsider Don Draper really is.

From the start we are given a window into Don's separation, his standing apart from the world in which he lives. Don's secret identity, which unfolds over numerous episodes, certainly contributes to this separation; his separation also contributes to his iconic position as yet another version of this classic American hero. Draper, in enunciating his understanding of the rules that are "dropped on you," again has much in common with Ralph Ellison's Invisible Man, who notes that "the mind that has conceived a plan of living that must never lose sight of the chaos against which that pattern was conceived. That goes for societies as well as for individuals."[18] The Donald Draper that we initially meet in *Mad Men* seems to have it all, and yet, as the plot unfolds over the course of a decade, we learn that not only is Don's life an illusion, but that he often loses sight of the chaos against which he occasionally attempts to establish order. He has internalized the idea of the "American dream" and pursued wealth, marriage, and family—yet none of it is satisfying, and he is constantly in danger of losing any and all of these trophies. He may need to heed Bert Cooper's final instruction to him, in a reverie after Cooper's death, that the best things in life are free (*Waterloo*, 7.7).

Rachel Menken is given a particularly interesting position within the series, since she and the audience together get to know Don Draper better throughout the first season.[19] When she doesn't appear in the final episode of the season, *The Wheel* (1.13), Don is upbraided by Bert Cooper, who has received a call from Abraham Menken, explaining that Rachel would be unavailable for the next three months as she is on a European sea voyage. Don had turned to Rachel in the previous episode, *Nixon vs. Kennedy* (1.12), and asked her to run away with him to Los Angeles when Pete Campbell discovered Don's secret identity as Dick Whitman and tried to blackmail Don with this information. In this instance, Rachel had fled from Don, as opposed to Don opting to flee either from his life in New York, or from Rachel. She has, once again, seen Don for who he may well be; even if she doesn't know the particulars of his invention, she knows the contours of the kind of grifter that Don/Dick embodies.

When Pete comes to him with the blackmail information, in an effort to compel Don to make Pete head of Accounts Services, Don rebuffs Pete—again with more conviction than it is clear he really has—and heads over to Menken's to try to convince Rachel to run away with him. She thinks he means for the weekend, and when it becomes clear to her that the proposition is for something more permanent, she is aghast. She notes that he can't just run off—what about his children? What about her father's store? Don, who has already recreated himself at least once, notes that "people do it all the time" (*Nixon vs. Kennedy*, 1.12). As the seasons progress, we become more and more aware of Don's tendencies to want to flee, even if he always seems to return eventually. Dr. Faye Miller, whom Don dates during part of season four, notes to him that he "only likes the beginnings of things," by which she means relationships. Her analysis is that once Don gets to know someone else and she gets to know him, he tires of the experience and his natural inclination to hide himself, to exit, kicks in and he "moves on." One of Don's most unexpected responses was not to "move on" at the end of season six but to stay in New York, having been put on leave by Sterling Cooper Draper Pryce. He had exposed himself to his colleagues—by dropping his mask—and by default he had exposed himself to the advertising world, where gossip was rife. At this point in the narrative Don had also given up his dependence on alcohol, at least to a degree. He takes his children to see the house where he grew up, exposing them to a part of his reality (*In Care Of*, 6.13). Don chooses to eschew the land of reinvention (California), and instead he tenuously seeks his own rebirth, but this time within the confines of some dimensions of the truth as Don Draper/Dick Whitman. Perhaps this is his Lincolnian "rebirth of freedom," freedom from the confines of his constructed self.

The art of the con

Don is always ready to leave at a moment's notice and he has the means to do so. In this way, Don Draper (or, rather, Dick Whitman) appears to operate as a grifter, a conman. But Don (like Gatsby), while involved in a complicated and rather extensive deceit, is not, oddly enough, interested in "the con," aside from having people believe that he is someone other than the person he was named at birth. The American literary landscape is littered with conmen and grifters and one of Fitzgerald's great accomplishments in Gatsby is the portrayal of the self-created man, a character distinct from a grifter, a character who knew exactly who he was in his created persona. As Nick Carraway explains, "[t]he truth was that Jay Gatsby of West Egg, Long Island, sprang from his Platonic conception of himself. He was a son of God—a phrase which, if it means anything, means just that."[20] Draper did not, as premeditatedly, assume his new self, but he went to Korea (or joined the army) to get away from where he was, and when the opportunity to re-create himself arrived, he took it, even as it meant cutting himself off from his family, who would believe that Dick Whitman died in Korea. The real Donald Draper died in Korea, while Dick Whitman dies and is reborn as Don Draper.

Don, ultimately, bears the hallmarks of a conman, but he isn't necessarily operating like one, at least as regards conning people out of their money by nefarious means. He does con Betty with regard to who he is and his many infidelities, though this deceit does not seem deeply malicious. Don's fundamental difficulty in understanding intimacy and friendship and his constant need to keep people at a distance so they cannot know him, is the heart of his con. Ultimately, Betty discovers the same box of secrets that Pete Campbell had found and leaves Don for good because he is not who he says. After they separate and divorce, Betty often casts Don as immature, while still wistfully considering his truer self, especially in the context of love and entanglement. Betty's reflection about Don's actual self comes after the two of them, each married to someone else, engage in an evening of sex when they are visiting Bobby at summer camp in *The Better Half* (6.9). Betty has come to understand Don in much the same way that Faye Miller characterized him: she says she can only hold his attention so long, then it decays, but she enjoys the nostalgia of their briefly shared intimacy because it indicates to her that she is quite desirable. Don contemplates intimacy as they lay next to each other, wondering "why sex is the definition of being close to someone … it doesn't mean that much to me." He notes that lying with Betty in his arms would make him feel just as close to her as having sex with her, highlighting Don's muddled sense of how he understands intimacy with others, especially women. Betty responds by telling Don that she feels sorry for Megan—who has recently admitted how lonely she feels—because Megan "doesn't know that loving you is the worse way to get to you." Don's instincts often give him insight into the connection between a feeling or sense and how people will respond to that sense, but these same instincts make him even more afraid to open himself to others. But he works in a profession that is, more or less, based on conning people to believe that they need or want something that will then improve their lives, even if he can't persuade himself how best to do this personally.

At the same time, Don's inclination is, at times, to pursue the "con," to pursue the option that is untruthful in order to prompt designated outcomes. In the season three finale, *Shut the Door. Have a Seat* (3.13), Don asks Lane Pryce to fire himself, Roger, and Bert. Don and a select number of staff members work through the weekend to dissect Sterling Cooper and flee before the British company that owns them, and is in the process of selling them, learns of any of these machinations. While this move is a group effort, Don instigates it, and the whole undertaking is, in fact, a con of Putnam, Powell, & Lowe. In season four, Sterling Cooper Draper Pryce is in contention for a new Honda account in *The Chrysanthemum and the Sword* (4.5). Roger Sterling is opposed to working with the Japanese, and more or less scuttles their chances of getting the account. But in an effort to prevent Cutler Gleason Chaough from landing it, Don, with assistance from others at Sterling Cooper Draper Pryce, instigates a deceptive con to compel Cutler Gleason Chaough to spend more than is allowed according to the terms laid out by the Japanese. Don rents space and camera equipment to make it appear as though Sterling Cooper Draper Pryce is making a television ad, which would cost more than the limited budget allowed. Cutler Gleason Chaough responds in kind, developing and producing a television ad and thus undermining the company's own chances of getting the Honda business because it didn't abide by the regulations set out by the Honda executives.

This move is quickly followed by Don's decision, upon learning that his agency has lost the Lucky Strike account, to run a full-page ad in the *New York Times* delineating why Sterling Cooper Draper Pryce would no longer be doing any work with tobacco companies. Upon losing this account, it became quite public that the company was unstable and, possibly, going to go under as a firm, a conversation that Don and others keep having with clients and potential clients. In the midst of this maelstrom, Don moves to make good on his adage "If you don't like what they are saying about you, change the conversation," moving the focus away from Lucky Strike's decision and the company's potential demise. This circles back to the first episode of *Mad Men*, "Smoke Gets in Your Eyes," and the campaign that Don creates, out of whole cloth, for Lucky Strike—selling the virtues of smoking as something that makes people happy, regardless of health issues. As he had noted in that episode, without any health benefits accorded to smoking, advertisers are left with a clean slate to *create* the appeal of cigarettes.

This time the content of the ad explains that Don Draper, not the entire agency, has decided he can no longer work for tobacco companies given the health risks involved in smoking. While he admits to being a smoker, the content of the ad is disingenuous given that Sterling Cooper Draper Pryce had pursued any number of tobacco companies (up until the minute he writes the ad). He makes a moral argument that Sterling Cooper Draper Pryce will "no longer take tobacco accounts" because tobacco kills people, and staff had been "addicted" to the work from tobacco companies. Draper argues that his is "an ad for the agency," but he is accused of having a tantrum in the *New York Times* (*Blowing Smoke*, 4.12). He successfully changes the conversation, but he sets the agency on a rather unsteady course and this provokes the firing of any number of company employees. While Megan, Don's secretary and future wife, thinks that it is "great that Don stands for something" (*Blowing Smoke*, 4.12), his move is certainly extravagant and rather radical; it appears to everyone else as dangerous and potentially damning for the company. Don came up with the idea after he had run into his old girlfriend Midge and had talked with her about her heroin addiction. Don himself, during this section of season four, had significantly reduced his dependence on alcohol, having become more aware of his own inclinations toward addiction. The letter/advertisement he writes, which he alone pays for, makes the argument that Sterling Cooper Draper Pryce had an "addiction" and was no longer going to be held captive to it by selling this harmful substance to the public. Don's effort was to present the other advertising agencies who did work for the tobacco industry as corrupt—since they were selling such a dangerous product—and to turn others against those competitors.

Peggy responds to Don's asking her opinion of the ad with "I thought you didn't go in for those shenanigans"—she and Pete had been reprimanded by Don when they tried to create artificial demand for Sugarberry Hams so that the company would put the product into more stores (*Public Relations*, 4.1). Peggy, certainly more than anyone else, understood that Don was trying to finesse the conversation and the situation. Regardless of her opinion of the ad, she acknowledges to Don that she understands that this is all a bit of a con job.

Don's story over the course of these seven seasons integrates his personal duplicity with his career choice: selling products to eager consumers. At the same time, we see his occasional unmasking in the form of the exposing of his actual past, or in the line in the "sand" that he draws in terms of "selling." And while he tries to keep his work from becoming a kind of con as well, he periodically slips and uses the same ploys at work—to keep accounts and to outwit competitors—as he does to keep his past and his identity secret. A grifter or con who loses his confidence usually loses the capacity to sell "the con," and Don seemed precipitously close to this edge during season six. This also distinguishes him from the man we meet throughout *The Great Gatsby*, since we are never given any reason to question Gatsby's confidence. Don has only ever depended on himself to make his way in the world and to bolster his self-confidence and, ultimately, to create himself. Don does not have the self-confidence that he should, given his success and position, although he demonstrates degrees of confidence, especially when dealing with people he thinks are inadequate, to whom he usually shows contempt. In contrast, he often shows confidence in those in whom he has faith, especially Peggy Olson.

Don and Dick

Season six of *Mad Men* took many of the pieces that compose Don Draper. During the course of the season Draper struggles to keep Dick Whitman under wraps and is slowly undone. Many of his better inclinations are subsumed by his dual vices of infidelity and alcoholism, neither of which is satisfying, but both of which serve the purpose of allowing him some freedom. These vices serve to increase the distance he puts between himself and his wife, Megan, and things spiral out of control when Sally, Don's daughter, walks in on him and Sylvia, his downstairs neighbor, having sex (*Favors*, 6.11). As an audience, we become accepting of Don's ethical limitations, especially in regard to his infidelities, in part because he often operated more ethically in the workplace than he behaved towards either Betty or Megan (or Faye Miller, or Bobbie Barrett, or Sylvia Rosen, etc.). Season four's plots had caused the audience to become disgusted with Don's excesses with regard to sex and alcohol, but as that season evolved, Don redeemed himself and pulled back from the brink. In season five he continues his redemption, to a degree, with his marriage to Megan, but the Don Draper of season six tests the audience's attachment to the series' main protagonist, especially in the way he responds to Sally after she finds him in a compromising position. In discussing how they conceive of Don (and some of the other characters), two of the regular writers on *Mad Men*, Andre and Maria Jacquemetton, note that "despite their sometimes questionable choices, [characters like Don] … generally uphold a certain standard of morality and/or dignity."[21] According to Slate.com's television critic Patrick Radden Keefe, "[t]he morality bit seems clear to me: Don is a bad guy in many ways, but he's a decent bad guy, a bad guy with a code, which is a deeply appealing archetype of American popular culture."[22] But this code doesn't quite resonate in season six, and leaves us, the audience (along with Don's colleagues at Sterling Cooper, who come together to put him on "leave" from the agency), with little tolerance for him. The audience's frustration, which has emerged in critiques of the show, suggests that season six is the weakest season of *Mad Men* (to date), and that Don Draper has become boring and vacuous, a shadow of his character in previous seasons.

> [*Mad Men* Creator Matthew] Weiner seems to have pushed Don to [an] … extreme this year, reinflating his testosterone but strip-mining him of any remaining charm, competence, or swag. What we're left with isn't quite the 'monster' that Peggy accuses him of being, but it's just as ugly: a scared little boy who managed to con the world with an opaque exterior. But what's he hiding now, other than an insatiable appetite? In 1968, Don Draper is an empty Jaguar with tinted windows: great to look at it, but a disaster under the hood.[23]

Draper has lost his charm; he has alienated his colleagues, friends, and family. He has, as Tocqueville suggested, turned in on himself. His elaborate personal con apparently starts to unravel at the very end of the final episode of season six, *In Care Of* (6.13), when he takes Sally, Bobby, and Gene to see the house (presented as completely dilapidated and in a sketchy part of town) where he grew up. He is showing his children that he started out in a very different environment from that in which he currently lives and in which they are growing up. Is this Don taking responsibility for himself? That remains to be seen. He spends a good deal of season six enjoying a kind of freedom that he himself has created—freedom to sleep with his neighbor, freedom to not abide by the usual demands of work (like showing up sober and on time for meetings), and freedom to do as he pleased—without regard for how his actions might impact others (personally or professionally). This is an unromantic portrait of a conman, yet the extent to which he has become used to life as Don Draper is evident, until everything starts to fall apart as he reveals the truth about his past in the pitch meeting with Hershey.

Don has already decided it is time to flee when the opportunity arises to open a California office for Sterling Cooper. Instead of the "middle-of-the-night" flight that he has considered (and even pursued) in the past, Don instead decides to put the pieces in place so that he can flee his current life in New York in an "establishment" way—he can continue to be Donald Draper, but he can do so on the West Coast with the promise of a new life, if not a new identity. This could be a hybrid of Dick Whitman and Don Draper—the man who is always ready to reinvent himself as someone new at any moment when his past might be revealed, combined with the wealthy, powerful, established executive. However, there is a consistent difficulty for Don: his name might have changed, and he might well understand that he did, in fact, reinvent himself at one point, but unlike Gatsby, who is presented as completely divorced from the qualities or characteristics of his past, Draper/Whitman never really moves beyond his past, his childhood, and the peril that they seem to pose, either in terms of his being unmasked or the way that his current self is a result of that past and those experiences.

In a sense, Don has become distorted by this internal conflict, and his reliance on alcohol and unencumbered sex distract from some of this distortion, if only for a moment. Grantland.com's television critic Andy Greenwald notes this conflict: "A self-made man whose astronaut looks once allowed him to travel effortlessly into anyone's orbit, Don now seems perpetually floating in the wrong direction, haunted not by the roads not taken but by the ones he already took."[24] This image, this Don Draper who can't quite erase the Dick Whitman that still forms him, marks the first half of the final season of *Mad Men*. In many ways, this has been the story that has propelled *Mad Men*'s narrative throughout—Don Draper has never been able to be rid of his origins, not in the way that Nick Carraway characterizes Gatsby's image of himself. As he noted, Gatsby saw himself as Athena-like, having arrived fully formed as the "son of G-d" and "to this conception he was faithful to the end."[25] Gatsby, once he took on that new persona, fully inhabited it. Draper remains a conflicted individual, trying to determine if his freedom is more valuable than his responsibility, in search of an intimacy that he cannot establish because of his hidden self. He is much more in keeping with the idea of a masquerade, of shape-shifting. Ralph Ellison speaks of this in the conclusion of *Invisible Man*, where his creation decides to re-create himself in a new skin, to come out of his hibernation: "I'm shaking off the old skin and I'll leave it here in the hole. I'm coming out, no less invisible without it, but coming out nevertheless."[26] Don has been hibernating in a bottle. He isn't invisible in the same way as the Invisible Man, but his actual self has been invisible to those with whom he works, and to his children. The Invisible Man knows he can't hide forever; the Don Draper of the sixth and seven seasons seems to be coming to the realization that he can't escape his identities. Though he certainly doesn't know exactly what he needs to do, he does seem to understand that he cannot continually try to outrun his past, in part because that leaves him unmoored, bereft, and alone.

Thus we see Don Draper not in the romantic vision of Fitzgerald's Gatsby, but more in keeping with this American tradition of grifters. He demonstrates an essential goodness on occasion, but he also shows his selfish and corrupt capacities. The question to consider is whether, like the Invisible Man, he speaks for many of us, even if we don't have secret identities. Don's quest for authenticity, for real affection, for a reciprocal love, makes him potentially less corrupt than most con artists and grifters. His problem is often that he loses himself in the facades. Don's efforts with Sally and, haltingly, with Peggy in seasons six and seven highlight his quest for real connections. He occasionally wants to allow people to know him, but his masquerade has gone on so long that it is often hard for him not to rely on alcohol, or sexual pleasure, or his disengaged Draper mystique to open up an avenue toward intimacy.

Notes

1   Throughout this chapter, I will refer to the character as Don Draper, unless it is specifically his earlier incarnation as Dick Whitman that is being discussed.

2   We also come to know that she cursed Dick's father and said that if he got her pregnant she would cut off his dick; she passes this on to her son as she passes away.

3   Edgar Allen Poe, *Saturday Courier* (Philadelphia), October 14, 1843, Vol. XIII, No. 655, p. 1.

4   Kevin Courrier, *Randy Newman's American Dreams* (Toronto: ECW Press, 2005), p. 13.

5   Matterson quoted by Courrier in ibid.

6   We learn that Draper actually got Roger Sterling to hire him by taking him out
     and getting him drunk—after selling him a fur stole for Joan Holloway—and
     then turning up at the offices at Sterling Cooper the next day, explaining that
     Roger had offered him a position at the agency. Sterling was too drunk to recall
     if he had done such a thing and simply went along with Draper's story.

7   This hero is also distinct from the "anti-hero" that is also popular within
     American literature and culture. The anti-hero, in the more modern form of
     Michael Corleone, Tony Soprano, Walter White, and Vic Mackey, all knowingly
     work outside the law, breaking laws, fully aware of the moral or amoral universe
     in which they live. Gatsby, Draper, and the Invisible Man operate slightly
     differently, as this chapter will explore.

8   Daniel Frick. *Reinventing Richard Nixon: A Cultural History of an American
     Obsession* (Lawrence, KS: University Press of Kansas, 2008), pp. 6–7.

9   Alexis de Tocqueville, *Democracy in America*, Volume II, Chapter 2, translated
     and edited by Harvey C. Mansfield and Delba Winthrop. (Chicago: The
     University of Chicago Press, 2000), p. 483.

10   F. Scott Fitzgerald. *The Great Gatsby.* (New York: Charles Scribner's Sons, 1953),
     p. 99.

11   Tocqueville, *Democracy in America*, p. 484.

12   Fitzgerald, *The Great Gatsby*, p. 101.

13   In many ways, Betty and Don's suburban life epitomizes the post-war ideal that
     also reifies Cold War gender politics. Betty is kept at home, in her beautiful
     clothes, with her children. Her identity, as Natalie Fuehrer Taylor details in
     Chapter 8, is closely tied, especially in the earlier seasons, to her understanding
     of femininity and motherhood, with the contrast of Don's outward identity as
     consistent with hegemonic masculinity so well explained by Denise Witzig in
     Chapter 7. Don's masculine virility is also in keeping with the political identity
     of the United States at the beginning of the 1960s, the sense among Americans
     that whatever they did was right, even if it wasn't. Lawrence Heyman's chapter,
     "Appearances, Social Norms and Life in Modern America: Nationalism and
     Patriotism in Mad Men," delineates this aspect of *Mad Men.*

14   Gatsby is made elusive by Fitzgerald, and he is generally presented to us
     through Nick Carraway, who is not always honest and who is also presenting
     Gatsby in recollections.

15   TomandLorenzo.com, review of *Mad Men*'s season five episode *The Other
     Woman*, May 28, 2012, http://www.tomandlorenzo.com/2012/05/mad-men-the-
     other-woman.html (accessed June 4, 2012).

16   Tocqueville, *Democracy in America,* p. 511.

17   Ibid., p. 484.

18   Ralph Ellison, *Invisible Man* (New York: Vintage Books, 1972), p. 567.

19   Midge, whom we meet in the first episode, is dispatched by episode eight. She resurfaces in season four, briefly, in *Blowing Smoke* (4.12). Having contrived to bump into Don, she subsequently tries to "con" him—though he does make this into a legitimate business arrangement. She admits that she is a heroin addict and needs money; although her body is offered as part of the deal (by her partner), Don doesn't take up the offer, and ultimately buys one of her paintings.

20   Fitzgerald, *The Great Gatsby*, p. 99.

21   Patrick Radden Keefe, "*Mad Men* Season 5," Tuesday, June 5, 2012, http://www.slate.com/articles/arts/tv_club/features/2012/mad_men_season_5/week_11/mad_men_review_betty_and_sally_still_need_each_other_.html (accessed June 20, 2012).

22   Ibid.

23   Andy Greenwald, "Men in Crisis: *Mad Men*'s Curious, Frustrating, and Ultimately Disappointing Sixth Season," Grantland.com, June 19, 2013, http://www.grantland.com/story/_/id/9402724/mad-men-disappointing-sixth-season (accessed July 15, 2013).

24   Ibid.

25   Fitzgerald, *The Great Gatsby*, p. 99.

26   Ellison, *Invisible Man*, p. 568.

3

The Power Elite and Semi-Sovereign Selfhood in Post-War America

Loren Goldman

The powers of ordinary men are circumscribed by the everyday worlds in which they live, yet even in these rounds of job, family and neighborhood, they often seem driven by forces they can neither understand nor govern.

C. Wright Mills, *The Power Elite*, p. 3

Introduction

It is for good reason that much scholarly work on *Mad Men*—including some essays in the present volume—concerns the fraught relationship between appearance and reality. Soup to nuts, the show revels in irony and nostalgia, cataloging the ways that, as one volume dedicated to it is subtitled, "nothing is as it seems."[1] The tension between appearance and reality indeed suffuses *Mad Men*'s universe. Even if one overlooks the obvious symbolism of its setting in advertising, and its Protean protagonist Don Draper/Dick Whitman (who is he *really?*), the dramatic appeal of *Mad Men*'s central figures stems from the audience's understanding of the conflicts between the private selves presented to us and the selves they feel compelled to present to others in everyday life. Peggy's suppressed feminism, Pete's alpha-male front, and Betty's hidden depression reveal a world in which dissemblance is normal: such people lie professionally, cheat casually (usually with impunity), and keep dark secrets from their closest confidantes. In its smaller details, *Mad Men* also plays on the uncertainties of being and seeming: to take·but one example, when insult comedian Jimmy Barrett first meets Don, he exclaims, "I loved you in *Gentleman's Agreement!*" (*The Benefactor*, 2.3), a 1947 film in which Gregory Peck plays a journalist passing as Jewish for a scoop, thereby (unwittingly) mirroring Dick's own passing as Don.[2] Even *Mad Men's* theme music deceives upon first listening, with the descending strings suggesting a classical composition before the drums enter, unveiling a slickly produced hip-hop beat.[3] This is a show in which nothing is as it seems—at least not initially.

Mad Men also suggests, however, that beneath the veil of appearances there are realities that cannot be avoided. Its characters operate within social structures they feel impotent to transform, and even though the ground appears to be shaking under their feet, the hierarchies of power that form the horizons of their agency remain firm. This essay aims to tease out the implicit structure of the social power *Mad Men* portrays as lurking beneath the surface, the structure of which most of its inhabitants are only faintly aware. Political theory's resources for reflecting on this problem of appearance and reality are vast, and *Mad Men's* densely woven characterological fabric offers numerous exemplary points of entry.[4] Rather than enter the fray, as usual, from the perspective of its main *dramatis personae*, I begin instead from one of the show's more apparently marginal characters, albeit one who in *Mad Men's* reality wields extraordinary power: Bert Cooper, Sterling Cooper's founding partner.[5] Cooper stands out among the falling men and women of *Mad Men* in that he never seems bewildered by the rapidly changing world around him. For him, things are ultimately very simple: great men shape the world through force of creativity, full stop. Consequently, however bemusing and befuddling appearances may be, at root an elite group of extraordinary individuals runs the world, and that is how things should be. Cooper's self-certainty as a captain of industry ironically reflects a compelling line of analysis propounded in the period during which *Mad Men* takes place and which is typified by sociologist C. Wright Mills' elite theory, my guide for the rest of this essay.

Mad Men, grand theory, and social inquiry

In 1959, C. Wright Mills discerned three tendencies in contemporary sociology hindering its basic mission of analyzing problems "of direct relevance to urgent public issues and insistent human troubles."[6] One was a tendency "toward a theory of history," the insistence on fitting empirical findings into a foreordained narrative, a failure Mills associated with Auguste Comte, Karl Marx, Herbert Spencer, and Max Weber.[7] A second methodological tendency he rued was "toward a systematic theory of the nature of man and society," in which "sociology comes to deal in conceptions intended to be of use in classifying all social relations and providing insight into their supposedly invariant features".[8] Mills complains that such supposed insights are ultimately "concerned with a rather static and abstract view of the social structure on a quite high level of generality."[9] Finally, Mills worried about a tendency "toward empirical studies of contemporary social facts and problems" that assemble data and cultivate methods for their own sake rather than engage concrete issues, and in which one finds miscellany "transformed into a style of thought."[10] Against "Grand Theory" (Tendencies I and II) and "Abstracted Empiricism" (Tendency III),[11] Mills preached the gospel of a Pragmatism-inspired "Sociological Imagination" that situates its object of study within "historical social structures," or concrete relations of power prevalent in a given place and in a certain time.[12]

I suggest we proceed by heeding Mills' call with regard to *Mad Men*, teasing out the concrete historical social structures the show portrays rather than using Grand Theory (be it in Marxist, Weberian, Freudian, or other guise), or focusing, in the manner of an Abstracted Empiricist, on its exceptionally wrought production design. In following Mills' lead, we're also following *Mad Men*'s lead, for the show practically begs not to be viewed through a Grand Theoretical lens. Although the production is intimately related to then-contemporary American culture, the long sweep of history never really enters into frame, and anti-capitalist challenges to the system in which Don, Peggy, and the rest find themselves are confined to marginal figures portrayed unflatteringly—Midge's beatnik friends, Peggy's self-righteous boyfriend Abe, and Megan's dogmatically Marxist father,[13] for example—and explicitly rejected by Bert Cooper and his bourgeois brethren as just so much communism.[14] In season two, when one of the new, young copywriters hands Don the Port Huron Statement, moreover, the ad men immediately reflect on how to commodify youth rebellion (*The Golden Violin*, 2.7):[15] perhaps because advertising so often trucks in noisy sloganeering, they are deaf to a genuine call to arms.[16] In any event, what is true for the external world of socio-economic relations goes just as well for the internal world of the self, as *Mad Men* treats its psychologists even more roughly: Dr. Arnold Wayne is an unhelpful therapist betraying Betty's confidence from the start, Roger mocks the very idea of therapy in his own sessions (*The Doorway*, 6.1), and, in its very first episode, when Sterling Cooper's research director Greta Guttmann (who studied "with Adler in Vienna") proposes to incorporate the Death Drive into the Lucky Strike campaign, her late-Freudian insight is met angrily by Lee Garner, Jr., their most important client: "What the hell are you talking about? Are you insane? I'm not selling rifles here; I'm in the tobacco business! We're selling America! The Indians gave it to us, for shit's sake!" (*Smoke Gets In Your Eyes*, 1.1). (Greta disappears from *Mad Men* halfway through its first season.) While Grand Theoretical readings of *Mad Men* are plausible, I will accept these warnings forthrightly, and approach the show instead with an eye to how it represents the historical social structures of post-war America without the narrowing gazes of teleological thought or fixed notions of human nature.

For this task, C. Wright Mills can remain our guide, as the ultimate structure of social power portrayed in *Mad Men*—the real forces behind the curtain—mirrors the framework he provides in *The Power Elite* (1956).[17] With all the caveats that accompany a short summary of a sophisticated, controversial, and celebrated classic of social analysis, Mills' vision can be roughly characterized. While acknowledging that his contemporary moment was one of radical social transformation,[18] Mills did not, like William Whyte and David Riesman, focus on how the corporatization of post-war American life undermined the sovereign self's already shaky foundations. Instead, he emphasized the centripetal transformations of American society that both underlie and belie the apparent fragmentation of power at the level of ordinary experience. In Mills' view, the post-war United States was dominated by an overlapping network of elites,[19] the most important of whom sit atop the economy, the military, and the government. Contrary to the rosy picture of social mobility and interest group representation sketched by the pluralist theorists of his day,[20] Mills argued that the most significant tendency in contemporary American society was the increasing concentration of national power in fewer hands:

> Within each of the big three, the typical institutional unit has become enlarged, has become administrative, and, in the power of its decisions, has become centralized. Behind these developments there is a fabulous technology, for as institutions, they have incorporated this technology and guide it, even as it shapes and paces their developments ...
>
>   As each of these domains becomes enlarged and centralized, the consequences of its activities become greater, and its traffic with the others increases. The decisions of a handful of corporations bear upon military and political as well as upon economic developments around the world. The decisions of the military establishment rest upon and grievously affect political life as well as the very level of economic activity. The decisions made within the political domain determine economic activities and military programs. There is no longer, on the one hand, an economy, and, on the other hand, a political order containing a military establishment unimportant to politics and to money making. There is a political economy linked, in a thousand ways, with military institutions and decisions. On each side of the world-split running through central Europe and around the Asiatic rimlands, there is an ever-increasing interlocking of economic, military and political structures. If there is government intervention in the corporate economy, so is there corporate intervention in the governmental process. In the structural sense, this triangle of power is the source of the interlocking directorate that is most important for the historical structure of the present.[21]

The upper echelons of these domains comprise America's "higher circles," whose members "occupy the command posts" of society.[22] These elites are not a natural class, and rarely coordinate action to exert their force; their members nonetheless have "awesome means of power available to them."[23] If elites in some sense always govern any society, the structural consolidation of economic, political, and military power in post-war America means that "those now in command of them have come into command of instruments of rule quite unsurpassed in the history of mankind."[24]

In the midst of making these claims, Mills asks that his framework not be taken as a philosophy of history, for he denies that the power elite *determines* world events.[25] For one, its members are limited by the world's complexity, not to mention the usually prohibitive costs of conspiratorial manipulation of mass society.[26] Indeed, Mills' conception of social elites chafes against conspiratorial interpretations, as the powerful in his account comprise individuals who do not recognize themselves as a distinct class with particular interests,[27] and he cautions against assuming that the fact of social exclusion indicates intentional design aimed at the latter.[28] For Mills, moreover, the power elite does not comprise a distinct economic class, but a diffuse network of persons united by their leadership of society's various command posts; wealth is a factor in their power, yet—unlike Marxist accounts—it does not define their interests or self-conception.[29] Practically, then, the elites do not have the group sense of common interests that invites conspiratorial claims. In a more philosophical sense, the elites may not have much agency over themselves, at least when they are acting *as elites*; they play roles functionally required by the social structure itself, speaking in line with what James Scott calls a culture's "public transcript,"[30] thereby making it impossible to determine *generally* whether any one individual is, as Mills puts it, "role-determined" or "role-determining."[31] Put simply, people in business are just expected to act as businessmen, and play to form. Bracketing such concerns, Mills' aims are instead diagnostic, to identify those on the command posts, making the decisions that affect vast swathes of ordinary people.[32] Influenced as Mills was by American pragmatism, his diagnosis is accompanied by a call for the intelligent democratic reconstruction of social power, now that its contours have been outlined. In his words:

> To be sure, the will of such men is always limited, but never before have the limits been so broad, for never before have the means of power been so enormous. It is this that makes our situation so precarious, and makes even more important the understanding of the powers and limitations of the American elite. The problem of the nature and power of this elite is now the only realistic and serious way to raise again the problem of responsible government.[33]

*

Like most everybody's everyday life, the bulk of what happens in *Mad Men* occurs on a level far removed from the concerns of the power elite, and my aim here is not to suggest that Mills offers more for understanding the quotidian interactions of its characters than other contemporary commentators like the aforementioned Whyte, Betty Friedan, Theodor Adorno, or Erving Goffman.[34] At its higher frequencies, however—and amongst its higher echelons—the show offers a vision of a society whose command posts remain manned by the power elite identified by Mills, where the decisions of a thinning number of business, political, and economic leaders set the quotidian horizons of its characters' lives. What's more, *Mad Men* conveniently provides its own Millsian commentator in the person of Bert Cooper, Sterling Cooper et al.'s founding partner and resident sage,[35] who alone among the characters never seems to doubt himself and who, also alone among the show's characters, regularly opines on sociological analysis.

Bert Cooper, power elitist

A telling scene comes in season two, episode seven, following the successful pitch to Martinson's Coffee. This season as a whole concerns the radical social transformations occurring in early 1960s America, with several younger copywriters, including Smitty and Kurt, hired by Sterling Cooper to connect with youth culture (in contrast to the ridicule that greeted VW's now-iconic Lemon ad in *Mad Men*'s first season, diegetically several years prior).[36] The Martinson's pitch is a collaborative effort; Don is shown here as a manager, while Peggy, Smitty, and Kurt are the creative brains of this particular operation.[37] After receiving word that the firm has landed the account, Bert asks Don to join him and Roger in his office.[38] Bert offers congratulations, and when Don protests that he didn't do the job alone, Bert marvels at what he takes to be naiveté or modesty (although viewers know Don's statement is simply factual): "Fascinating!" Small talk out of the way, Bert and Roger explain that Don's success at Sterling Cooper means they expect him to take on more professional burdens for the agency, in this instance joining, at Joe Martinson's invitation, the board of a planned but non-existent Museum

of Early American Folk Arts. The purpose of the museum itself is inconse-
quential for these organization men, and viewers are effectively instructed to
doubt the supposed cultural sophistication of *Mad Men*'s characters—Bert
admits in the same episode to Harry Crane that he bought his Rothko as
an investment.[39] Don assumes initially that Bert and Roger want him there
in order to create a brand campaign, but Bert explains their real purpose:
"philanthropy is the gateway to power," to which Don skeptically replies, "If
you say so."[40] Sensing that Don doesn't quite appreciate what they're asking
of him, Bert tells Don he is "going to be wearing [his] tuxedo a lot more,"
adding "it's time for the horse to catch the carrot." So as to give Don some
real straight talk, Bert asks Roger to leave, and continues, "Would you agree
that I know a little bit about you? … [Don: "A little."][41] *There are few people
who get to decide what happens in our world. You are about to join them. Pull
back the curtain and take your seat*" (emphasis added). The next scene shows
Don, having taken his seat, buying his Cadillac, the post-war power elite's
mobile throne.

   While this moment is the most explicit and full-throated endorsement of a
power elite in the show, Bert regularly gives voice to a Millsian view of post-war
America: appearances notwithstanding, he knows how "the sausage is made"
(*New Amsterdam*, 1.4), and the process involves great men collaborating,
conflicting, conspiring, or some combination of all three. When the Nixon–
Kennedy election results arrive, Bert asserts that Mayor Daley rigged votes; his
outrage is not at the fact that a politician has pulled some strings—he himself
spent the entire evening watching returns "literally in a smoke-filled room at
the Waldorf, with every Republican· luminary save MacArthur and Jesus"—
but that the "widespread fraud" was so brazen (*Nixon vs. Kennedy*, 1.12).
What's more, Bert doesn't see the race so much as one between Nixon and JFK
than as a fight between different sets of elites, as he explains that Daley gave
"*Joe* Kennedy every corpse in Cook County; otherwise Nixon wins." When
Don protests that the whole electoral race "doesn't seem fair," Bert responds
with bemusement similar to his reaction to Don's forthright denial of sole
responsibility for winning the Martinson's Coffee account: "Fair …" he echoes,
and ends the conversation, seemingly in wonder at the naiveté of his star
player. For Bert, the existence of the power elite is a fact that must be accepted,

and since the power elite set the rules, one should simply aim to join their ranks. Nixon lost, and now Sterling Cooper will have to (happily) play ball with the Kennedy administration, for even if elites lose, the elite always wins. The whiff of snobbery in Bert's comments about the bare-knuckled nature of Chicagoland politics reflects a pragmatic appreciation for stability, a concern evident early in the show when he chooses not to fire the conniving Pete Campbell, since Pete belongs to one of the original patrician families of New York City—the highest echelons of the "local society" leaders Mills classed as the earliest members of the American power elite (*New Amsterdam*, 1.4).[42] For Bert, within the stable structure of elite control, individuals have the latitude to show their mettle, as long as they don't upset the structure itself: faced with the truth that Don Draper is Dick Whitman, he offers that "this country was built and run by men with worse stories than whatever you've [Pete] imagined here … The Japanese have a saying, a man is whatever room he is in, and right now, Donald Draper is in this room. I assure you, there's more profit in forgetting this …" (*Nixon vs. Kennedy*, 1.12).

Particularly interesting is Bert's affection for Ayn Rand, whose work he recommends enthusiastically (*The Hobo Code*, 1.8; *Indian Summer*, 1.11), as it reveals a social imaginary at odds with the systemic nature of power in modern society. Undoubtedly, Bert has worked hard for his success (though we know little of his own backstory), and we can infer that in the mirror he sees John Galt—*Atlas Shrugged*'s mysterious protagonist—having, through force of will and ingenuity, forged himself from nothing into a corporate titan. This self-understanding is at odds with both the social hierarchy the show represents as well as what Bert himself *does*. For all of Bert's enthusiasm for rugged individualism and self-transformation, it is evident that the hope of bootstrapping is hollow, circumscribed as we are in our agency by the various privileges and exclusions encoded into the social structure. The Randian fantasy of creative prometheanism, of a self that is sovereign over both itself and the world it inhabits, is belied, furthermore, by the fact that we never see Bert doing anything productive. His paeans to leadership (*Waterloo*, 7.7) and his rare flashes of authority notwithstanding (consider his quashing of the argument between Harry and Pete about MLK's assassination in *The Flood*, 6.5, and his refusal to countenance Don's desire to pursue new business with

IBM in *The Monolith*, 7.4), Bert's value to Sterling Cooper is dubious—his underlings consider him an old loon (*The Gold Violin*, 2.7; *The Beautiful Girls*, 4.9), and Bert spends his camera time receiving massages, doing crosswords, and reading *The Chrysanthemum and the Sword*, Ruth Benedict's seminal (and controversial) study of Japanese culture. Indeed, despite his self-image as a restlessly productive individual, the character of Bert Cooper reveals the power elite—in Millsian fashion—as a privileged group profiting off the spoils of those who toil under them, yet who conceive of themselves as the legitimate beneficiaries of a system made in the image of a bygone time, before regulation and mass democracy stifled the capacities of individuals to beget great things in the world. Don's anger at Bert upon hearing of the agency's impending sale to McCann Erickson betrays an awareness of this contradiction: he wakes Bert from a catnap and suggests the partners buy the firm, only to have Bert tell him, "Young men love risks because they can't imagine the consequences," to which Don ripostes, "And you old men love building golden tombs and sealing the rest of us in with you" (*Shut the Door. Have a Seat*, 3.13). Yet also like Mills, Bert denies that elites conspiratorially manipulate the masses: in the only scene where his worldview is explicitly challenged (by Peggy's journalist boyfriend Abe Drexler and her fellow copywriter Stan Rizzo), he vociferously rejects the accusation that the Vietnam War is being waged (solely) for the sake of the military industrial complex's bottom line (*A Little Kiss*, 5.1). Bert may think that elites manage society, but he does not believe that they do so with any particular end in mind apart from stability.[43] What is crucial for him is that "the adults" are in charge (*The Other Woman*, 5.11). Bert's excursus on leadership in *Mad Men*'s final season gives an indication of what this means for him. Bert tells Roger that leaders have vision and are loyal to their team; Roger is loyal but he isn't a leader, while Jim Cutler has vision but isn't on Bert's team.[44] Don is a genuine leader, but one who may not be reliable—Bert compares the idea of asking him to return from leave like Napoleon returning from Elba. Those who deserve their perches on the command posts are rare birds indeed.

Mills' primary domains in *Mad Men*

Bert may be the show's most explicit commentator on the power elite, but *Mad Men* reflects the centrality of elites in the contemporary social structures in myriad ways. Here I will sketch how *Mad Men* represents power elitism in Mills' three main domains of the economic, political, and military orders—domains that the show suggests are (increasingly) intertwined. *Mad Men* represents the choices of its characters—including those of Bert Cooper—as framed by "forces they can neither understand nor govern," as Mills comments in *The Sociological Imagination*.

a. The economic order

The decisions of economic elites are the most direct constraints in the lives of *Mad Men*'s characters. This is true despite the fact that many of its primary characters are themselves consummate businesspeople, for to be so in advertising means to be at the whim of clients' often arbitrary and misguided desires. Advertising is an industry predicated on image, and image often has little relationship to reality—this very arbitrariness underlies the tenuous place of men like Don (and even Bert) among the elites—and the absurdity of advertising's aim is clear from Don's counterintuitive assurance that the Federal Trade Commission's declaration that cigarettes are carcinogenic presents "the greatest advertising opportunity since the invention of cereal. We have six identical companies making six identical products. We can say anything we want" (*Smoke Gets in Your Eyes*, 1.1). This allows Sterling Cooper to suggest "everybody else's tobacco is poisonous. Lucky Strikes are toasted," and in this case the metonymic association of Luckies with one step in their production process is a smashing success. The slippage of signifier and signified, however, this ability to say anything, also means that the client can reject anything; as *Mad Men*'s very first scene reveals, nobody knows why anyone chooses one cigarette brand over another.[45]

A long tradition of twentieth-century thought, most closely associated with Frankfurt School Critical Theory, critiques the advertising industry as bent on undermining individual agency through the manipulation of desire.[46] In

the *Mad Men* universe, we see this sort of manipulation regularly as Sterling
Cooper seeks to catch up with its rivals in the "creative revolution" of the
1960s. When Smitty reads Don the Port Huron Statement, the two immediately begin strategizing how to use the concept of "wanting to *be*" in pitching
products (*The Gold Violin*, 2.7), reflecting the commodification of dissent that
developed over the course of that decade.[47] That advertising affects consumers
is clear, yet *Mad Men* also represents the ad men themselves as subject to
arbitrary elite *business* power they cannot control. We see this in the pitches,
high-stakes presentations that succeed or fail on clients' whims: most of the
ones we witness underline how Don and his team can do little wrong, but
every now and again the clients' arbitrary desires reveal the tenuousness of the
entire enterprise. Maidenform's representatives balk at the "sexy" campaign
they had requested (*Maidenform*, 2.6), Conrad Hilton is disappointed with
a pitch because it didn't include his eccentric desire for a lunar hotel (*Wee
Small Hours*, 3.9), Mountain Dew is unhappy with Sterling Cooper's "witches'
brew" idea because it diverges from the industry norm established by Pepsi
(*The Summer Man*, 4.8), and Heinz rejects Peggy's "bean ballet" spot because
kidney beans resemble "bloody organs" (*A Little Kiss*, 5.1).[48] The fragility of
the ad man's position as an intermediary between the business elite and the
masses is emphasized, furthermore, in Sterling Cooper's vain attempts to land
American Airlines. Mohawk Air is dropped in order to show their commitment
to the potential new client, but the desired pitch never even takes place. The
agency's play for Jaguar underlines this positional insecurity even more.
Promising national exposure and a steady stream of considerable income, a
car company is an advertising firm's ultimate client.[49] The cost of pitching to
Jaguar is steep, however: the head of its dealers' association—a major voice in
deciding who gets the account—demands a night with Joan for his support.
In return for a partnership stake, Joan assents, and the other principals agree,
with the notable exception of Don. The night before the pitch, Pete enters his
office and explains that Joan's willingness means that they have "removed all
other impediments" to landing Jaguar, yet "no matter what else goes on, it's
the creative that's going to win this" (*Christmas Waltz*, 5.10). The drama that
precedes this scene shows that Pete is lying, of course, for the pitch will be
won by Joan's prostitution, and his comment that he'd seen the campaign and

it was "something I couldn't have imagined yet exactly what I expected" takes on special resonance as a parallel description of the unseemliness beneath the ostensible liberation of competition. The metaphor of advertising as a form of prostitution is particularly apt in the case of Jaguar, moreover, as Sterling Cooper's collective desire for success transforms them literally into peddlers of flesh.[50] Thus despite the hob-nobbing with elites and despite their proximity to society's upper echelons, *Mad Men* reminds us that advertising firms are ultimately the speculative middlemen of mass consumption, at the beck and call of a business order they only sometimes understand and over which they exert control at the pleasure of its real motors. At the extreme, clients can make or break firms: Lucky Strike's departure from Sterling Cooper leads Roger to declare "We're dead" (*Hands and Knees*, 4.10),[51] just as landing Jaguar puts the agency once again in the industry's higher echelons. As the show progresses, the talk around the office revolves more and more around the possibility of landing the major account that will propel Sterling Cooper et al. to the top of the heap. Dow (*The Other Woman*, 5.11) and Chevy (*The Flood*, 6.5) both hold the promise of finally and unquestionably taking that seat behind the curtain, so much so that the agency is entirely restructured in order to compete with larger ad firms for Chevy. Even then, however, Sterling Cooper and Partners' positional security is fragile, as Chevy, the jewel in their crown, ultimately decides to move its advertising in-house (*The Strategy*, 7.6).

The relative impotence of *Mad Men*'s characters *vis-à-vis* the business elite is further underscored by the seeming uncertainty of Sterling Cooper's very existence. At first, it is acquired by Putnam, Powell, and Lowe, whose Lane Pryce sets about slashing staff, to the dissatisfaction of its employees and executives alike. Putnam, Powell, and Lowe is subsequently bought by McCann Erickson, reinforcing the fact that even the relative elites at Sterling Cooper are impotent to control their own fates—Bert, for example, is expected to be "put on an ice floe," in the words of Conrad Hilton (*Close the Door. Have a Seat*, 3.13), a *real*, secure member of the business elite, and indeed Bert loses his office for the rest of the show. Although the reinvention of the firm as Sterling Cooper Draper Pryce (among further iterations) returns nominal power to its principals (power that gets again diffused as they merge with Cutler, Gleason and Chaough in season six), as ad men, they nonetheless remain in thrall of the captains of industry to whom they pitch.[52] Even when the ad men *create* products (as in the executive savings account of *5G*, 1.5) rather than just sell them, they ultimately remain errand boys for the men whose decisions shape the world: at the close of season three, when Don indignantly asks Hilton if he comes and goes as he pleases, unlike the ad men themselves, Hilton is unrepentant about his privilege as an indispensable member of the power elite: "Yes I do" (*Close the Door. Have a Seat*, 3.13). Don, by contrast, cannot. As ad men, they go, as Roger Sterling puts it in the same episode, "from one John's bed to the next." It is meant as both an insult and a compliment when Roger tells Bert in season seven that "Don Draper can work anywhere" (*Waterloo*, 7.7).

At the extreme, success in business literally requires the loss of self, a possibility dramatized in the final season by Don's willingness to leave Sterling Cooper & Partners in order to land Philip Morris (*The Runaways*, 7.5); everything he had worked for would have been destroyed. Don's words are all about a cancerous product on the verge of execution, and he's a "cigarette man." His pliability, his willingness to sacrifice everything he stands for, his integrity and his character, his name even, is what might allow him to save himself. Like the prostitutes who socialized him, Don's success in business requires the renunciation of sovereign power over his social self. When Commander Cigarettes (whose name is replete with significance) is "dead," Don's life is spared, and Jim finds consolation in the resurrection of Sterling Cooper as a recognized tobacco-friendly agency (*Waterloo*, 7.7).[53]

b. The political order

Mills' second central domain of the political order in the power elite is also present in *Mad Men*, albeit often more muted than the business order.[54] In terms of electoral politics, mass movements, and the ambient terror of the Cold War alike, we are presented with a vision of the world in which a small network of elites sets events into motion that shape history; indeed, even the characters who are *close* to those networks of power are impotent to control them. Recall Bert's take on the 1960 Nixon–Kennedy presidential contest, which provides the background to season one: elite fraud enabled the

Massachusetts Senator to reach the White House. It is plausible that Bert's anger is misguided, for had the boys at Sterling Cooper had a better read on the pulse of the American public, they might have been able to assist the campaign with better results—a possibility Bert suggests when he notes that JFK's efforts turned a corner after Frank Sinatra began stumping for him (*The Wheel*, 1.13). The general bewilderment suffusing Sterling Cooper at Nixon's defeat is reflected in Bert's overdetermined and contradictory accounts of what went wrong (the election was won either by fraud *or* metonymic manipulation), but in either case, the default assumption is that a power elite ultimately determined the election's outcome.[55]

This emphasis on political elites is further dramatized by Betty's marriage to Henry Francis, an advisor to both New York Governor Nelson Rockefeller and New York City Mayor John Lindsay, and (ultimately) a Republican State Senator. The romantic relationship between Betty and Henry begins when Betty asks him to help stop the construction of the Pleasantville Road Reservoir. Although Betty and her friends in the Junior League of Tarrytown have done all the organizational footwork, their concerns are ignored by the local power elite (Tarrytown's mayor calls the reservoir "old business," a done deal) until Henry arrives; as Rockefeller's director of public relations and research, he holds considerably more sway than the town council, whose members agree to delay the reservoir pending a study of its need and impact (*Souvenir*, 3.8). In this instance, the power elite aligned with Betty and helped her cause, but Henry's presence also reminds us of the relative impotence of average people: were it not for him, the reservoir would have gone up as planned. This relative impotence is further underscored by the fact that Henry's willingness to help Betty is based on romantic interest rather than the justness of her cause, and that Henry arrives at the Tarrytown meeting at the absolute last minute; in another episode, Betty's impotence is evident in her fury after Henry sends Elsa Kittredge, a (female) proxy, to speak on his behalf at a fundraiser (*Wee Small Hours*, 3.9).

Henry is shown to be among the few genuinely decent characters in *Mad Men*—he does not use his power inappropriately, "fixing" tickets by paying them (*The Doorway*, 6.1), is loyal to Betty, and is a more stable father to Sally and Bobby than Don could ever be. And yet as he moves up the rungs of government, he is also shown to be an exemplary representative of the political elite. Sally had long wanted him to run for office (*Man with a Plan*, 6.7), and he decides to throw his hat in the ring on the heels of MLK's assassination. Unlike other metropolises like Washington, DC and Chicago, New York escaped civil unrest thanks in large part to the mayoral administration's earlier outreach to radicals, and Mayor Lindsay famously walked the streets of Harlem the evening of King's murder with community leaders.[56] To Henry, accompanying Lindsay was "exhilarating," but the cost of avoiding riots was "police corruption, disrespect for authority, [and] negotiating with hoodlums" (*To Have and To Hold*, 6.4). Thinking he "would do it differently," Henry accepts an appointment to a vacant State Senate seat, a stepping-stone to Attorney General and higher offices (*To Have and To Hold*, 6.4).[57] The insularity and authoritarian conservatism Mills saw in the consolidation of the elite is reflected in how this move both marks Henry and Betty as a power couple and creates tension in their relationship itself. On the one hand, Henry's newfound power grants the distinction of superiority: Betty complains to him that everyone "gets so tongue-tied around us; they can only pretend for so long that we're just regular neighbors," yet reminds Sally she's lucky Henry is important enough to get a doctor to fix her broken nose over a weekend (*The Runaways*, 7.5). On the other hand, full membership in the political class demands the renunciation of independent reasoning. This is true especially for Betty, who weathers petty humiliations from Henry when she voices her mind and opinions, which Henry too apparently holds as a private citizen. After Henry, at their neighborhood cocktail party, opines that "wildness in the kids" is a "national disease", Betty agrees and draws a link to her support for the Vietnam War: "First the kids start off protesting, and the next thing you know, every authority is up for grabs … I mean if they learned how to support their country, sacrifice in hard times, we'd have the morale to win the War." Henry first tries to change the subject, and then, to Betty's utter shock, contradicts her and defers to their neighbor (and President Nixon): "I think it's too costly. It has to be done on the right terms, but I think we should get out while the getting's good." When Betty incredulously asks "Since when?" Henry definitively (and falsely) replies, "I've always supported the President, honey" (*The Runaways*, 7.5). When Henry and Betty are preparing to retire that night, he is livid, explaining that "I'm not a dinner companion— I'm their elected representative!" and telling her to "keep your conversation to how much you hate getting toast crumbs in the butter, and leave the thinking to me!" True to form, Betty plays the good wife and apologizes. Their conversation the next morning reinforces the political elite's privilege all the more, as Henry tells Betty he doesn't want "to sit in the kitchen like the help," a phrase that manages in one fell swoop to sound classist, racist, masculinist, and paternalist in its overtones.[58] The self-opacity of the political elite is also expressed in Henry's biological description of youth unrest as a disease, as he pathologizes dissent instead of understanding it as a response to the perceived democratic deficit resulting from the elite domination of American politics.

The last and most diffuse aspect of the political order worth noting in a Millsian regard bleeds over into the power elite of the military order: the ambient terror of the Cold War and Vietnam. This theme is not foregrounded at the show's outset, yet it becomes an increasingly unmistakable background frequency as *Mad Men* progresses into the sixties, in chronological lockstep with the shift from a bomber-based nuclear strike force to the even more consuming and uncertain terror of Intercontinental Ballistic Missiles, which are practically impossible to intercept.[59] This terror manifests in various ways, all of which stress the enormous power the political elite hold over humanity as the keepers of the nuclear keys.[60] Crab Colson, for instance, a minor figure who claims to have been part of the team that provided agitprop for Kennedy in the Bay of Pigs, tells Don that he's building a bomb shelter (*Maidenform*, 2.6), foreshadowing season two's culmination in the Cuban Missile Crisis. We get an intimate glimpse of the military industrial complex when Don and Pete attend a presentation by Space Technology Laboratories on MIRV (multiple independently targetable reentry vehicle) missiles (*The Jet Set*, 2.11), and the "total annihilation" promised affects Don profoundly (Pete, on the other hand—in another acknowledgement of the economic power of the political elite—is excited by "gold rush" possible in landing a defense account, noting that a single contractor spends more annually in media than three Lucky Strikes). Similarly, season four finds Sterling Cooper Draper Pryce desperately seeking North American Aviation as a client, as their Minuteman II missile promises to be the US's primary arm against the Soviets (*Hands and*

Knees, 4.10), and they only withdraw themselves from consideration when it becomes clear that Don's past might be unearthed during the process of granting security clearance. The virtual impotence of *Mad Men*'s characters in light of nuclear annihilation is the central theme of season two's final episode (*Meditations in an Emergency*, 2.13): in it, Don anxiously watches President Kennedy's press conference announcing the discovery of Soviet missiles in Cuba, Peggy's parish priest Father Gil sermonizes about "Khrushchev and Castro" forcing JFK's hand and urges preparation for "the most important summit meeting of all," i.e. with God in the afterlife, and Roger complains, on the heels of the Sterling Cooper's lucrative sale, that "Kennedy's daring them to bomb us, right when I get a second chance." Don's response could serve as a motto for *Mad Men*'s characters' relationship to the elites in the command posts: "We don't know what's really going on—you know that." The fate of the world lies in the hands of an inscrutable minority of political power elites.

Stepping away from nuclear Armageddon, *Mad Men* also reflects the close imbrication of military and business elites in light of the quotidian violence in Vietnam. When Don and Roger score a meeting with Dow Chemical, a $20 million account that would replace the similar billings lost with Lucky Strike's departure, the executives ask in particular how Sterling Cooper Draper Pryce would aid in strengthening the company's brand given that they produce napalm and hence were a primary corporate target of street protests.[61] Don replies, "the important thing is, when our boys are fighting and they need it—when America needs it—Dow makes it, and it works," linking business success with military victory (*The Other Woman*, 5.11). In a similar manner, Peggy's campaign for Koss Headphones (which includes a planned Superbowl spot) has to be scuttled for fear of reminding its audience about Vietnam. After a joke on *The Tonight Show* mentions the practice of American soldiers making necklaces out of ears cut off dead Viet Cong, Koss determines the Shakespearean tag line "Lend Me Your Ears" to be inappropriate (*The Doorway*, 6.1), and creative must start over. Peggy's frustration at the wasted effort leads her to curse *The Tonight Show*, and her colleague Burt Peterson reminds her of the more important culprit: "I think it's the Army that's really at fault here."

c. The military order

Having just mentioned the ambient terror of war as a partial reflection of the military power elite in the *Mad Men* universe, I want to now turn to a more basic (if still ambient) aspect of the military elite's capacity to make decisions shaping opportunities for those further down the social hierarchy: its various characters' wartime experiences. Roger and Don are deeply marked by their service in World War II and Korea, respectively, and both fought— like all enlisted men—at the behest of those manning command posts (now) far removed from the battlefield. The impotence of soldiers *vis-à-vis* their superiors is a common trope in war memoirs, and even though *Mad Men's* veterans do not voice the indignation at being used as cannon fodder expressed variously by Gabriel Chevallier (*Fear*, 1930), Erich Maria Remarque (*All Quiet on the Western Front*, 1929), Norman Mailer (*The Naked and the Dead*, 1948), Philip Caputo (*A Rumor of War*, 1977), and John Del Vecchio (*The 13th Valley*, 1982), the stress of battle is no less traumatic for Don and Roger.[62] Roger, who served in the Pacific theater, is apoplectic at the thought of working for Honda (*The Chrysanthemum and the Sword*, 4.5), demonstrating a surprising vitriol out of character for a man who otherwise appears to be master of his domain. In this instance, the cooler head of Bert Cooper prevails. As Sterling Cooper Draper Pryce's resident power elitist, he appreciates that the profit motive presents an incentive outweighing any feelings of discomfort: decades before, the military power elite had put Roger in the line of fire, leaving psychic wounds quelled only by a business elite's insistence on rational material self-interest. Roger admits, furthermore, that he plunged headlong into business in order to escape the horrors he experienced, always looking forward so as to forget the past. Roger is not alone, of course, as other characters' memories of this conflict surface on occasion as a reminder of a world better left behind: when his mettle is challenged, Duck mentions that he killed seventeen men at Okinawa (*The Suitcase*, 4.7).[63]

War, of course, shaped Don in an even more evident fashion, presenting him with an opportunity literally to reinvent himself, and it too is a memory he struggles to overcome.[64] Don/Dick's arrival at Lieutenant Don Draper's Korean outpost as the sole reinforcement for what was meant to be a platoon of twenty men is a result of the tactical miscalculation of the military elites, whose understanding of what is transpiring on the ground is inadequate, to put it mildly. When Whitman steps off the transport truck, Draper protests to its driver that he needs more men, only to be told "This is it ... You're whining to the wrong guy, sir" (*Nixon vs. Kennedy*, 1.12): the military order had spoken, and one soldier is all he'll get. Needless to say, the consequences of this elite decision are far-reaching for both Dick and Don, for had more troops arrived, it is likely that fortifications would have been completed within the intended forty-eight hours rather than a month, potentially saving Lieutenant Draper's life and thereby making Whitman's metamorphosis moot. Instead, Draper and Whitman are thrown together, alone, and Whitman-cum-Draper's identity is made possible thanks to the decisions of a military–political elite they neither know nor understand.[65] It is noteworthy, moreover, that just as this military–political elite gave Dick the chance to refashion himself, it also threatens to expose his charade when the need for security clearance leads federal investigators to begin asking Don's intimates if they have any reason to think "he's not the person he says he is." Perhaps even more noteworthy is the excuse Pete gives his colleagues for the abrupt end of their courting dance with North American Aviation, an excuse the plausibility of which rests on a power elite vision of American society: "a general was insulted" and put the kibosh on the collaboration. Bert, true to form, asks "which general?"—perhaps he can use his own network to combat this affront—and Pete simply changes the subject (*Hands and Knees*, 4.10).

Modern American democracy and the semi-sovereign self

If the characters of *Mad Men* exist in a world not of their own making, in which the decisions of power elites from the business, political, and military orders set events in motion that deeply inform the possibility of agency in modern American mass society, why is it that they seem to only vaguely discern their limitations? Bert again can be taken as a case in point, for he never seems to appreciate the irony of suggesting his underlings become John Galts, acting as if anything actually depended on their wishes or actions.[66]

The sovereignty of practically every character—even Bert—is severely limited by the choices of those occupying the command posts, and yet they all, like Bert, fantasize about genuine autonomy. Indeed, the myth of sovereign control appears to be a necessary illusion for navigating the bewildering structural constraints of corporatized, industrialized America. Business and advertising rely on the myth of sovereign consumers making informed decisions about distinct commodities, when they may be more reasonably and realistically construed as predicates of an economic structure. In an early episode, Don tells Midge's friend Roy that "there is no system," and he appears actually to believe himself (*The Hobo Code*, 1.8). The stability of the democratic political order is likewise predicated on the myth of sovereign citizens exerting formal control over the mechanisms of public power, where (formally at least) Betty Draper, Peggy Olson, and Hollis the elevator operator are as powerful as Henry Francis or Bert Cooper. Finally, the American patriotic imaginary requires that the military is a neutral tool for peace, a band of brothers fighting injustice wherever it arises, without petty politics, practical interests, or ulterior motives.

The myth of sovereignty may be necessary not merely because it plays a functional role in the stability of our social structures. For one, it is easy to overlook historical social structures as limiting agency because they appear natural to those inhabiting them. To experience a hierarchical social structure as a limitation requires some sense of what could be otherwise, and the alternative experiences many of *Mad Men*'s central characters have had are of a significantly worse situation: war. The choice between becoming an organization man and resisting structural imperatives is a no-brainer if the latter recalls the prospect of death, the ultimate dissolution of the self. In this sense, the myth of sovereignty is a defense mechanism against the uncertainty of alterity, and it would be uncharitable to begrudge those who embrace it. Another reason may be that humans are narrative beings, and that in concrete experience the meaning of existence is linked to what Paul Ricoeur called "emplotment":[67] Each of us is, after all, the principal player in our own life's drama. Indeed, even Marx's *Capital*, a work about economic structures and little else, approximates a *Bildungsroman* whose protagonist is capital itself. At a more philosophically technical level, it may also be the case that humans require what Kant called "regulative ideas" for practical purposes—the idea of free will, for example, is necessary for moral consciousness even though there is no scientific evidence for it[68]—and that the possibility of sovereign control itself is something of a requirement for effective action, especially given an earlier experience of complete impotence. Less philosophically, we should not forget that *Mad Men* is a television production, with all the genre's limitations. On the consumption side of things, it is meant to appeal to a wide audience, and socially analytical pedantry does not obviously translate into solid Nielsen ratings; it is easier to simply put Jon Hamm and Christina Hendricks in the frame.[69] Furthermore, on the production side, *Mad Men* is a show written by elites for elites (Matthew Weiner boasts degrees from Wesleyan and USC Film School, top-tier institutions) and the limitations on agency experienced by those with less privilege may not take on the emphasis they would were the show made by subalterns.[70]

That said, Bert Cooper's exit from the show (and life) marks both the culmination and collapse of his happy acceptance of elitism, leading us to question the wisdom of his complacency as a captain of industry against the shifting sands of power in post-war America. He passes, poignantly, after watching the first lunar landing on television,[71] the moment when the rocket technology that gave rise to so much despair in the form of imagined nuclear bombardment is harnessed for a hopeful symbol of humanity's capacity for natality, for literally transcending the worldly, habitual frame we take to be true.[72] Bert's magical closing song and dance (*Waterloo*, 7.7), seen only by Don (whom Bert hails as "my boy"), is at once a heartfelt paean to his simplicity and an ironic undermining of everything for which his ad agency stands: "The stars in the sky, the moon on high, they're great for you and me because they're free."[73] If it is fair to accept that Bert believes the best things in life are free, it is worth noting that Bert's success in a domain predicated on fungibility enables him to declare his transcendence of basic concerns for material comfort: he is able to sing his song because he can afford to. An even greater irony exists, of course, in the fact that his epiphany only comes after his earthly life, in which he strove for costly appurtenances like Rothkos and bonsai trees, has ended. The primary lesson that viewers are meant to take home, however, appears to be the surface one, as the sequence concludes with Don, finished with his reverie, standing utterly alone in the sterile office environment that once enabled him to refashion Dick into his present self. The emptiness of the room is deafening, as if Don is reflecting on the ultimate emptiness of the life he once had so desired. In many regards, Bert's death marks a transfigurative moment for the show. With him gone, Don will almost certainly lose his job as the firm restructures, something foreshadowed in his offer to commit professional *seppuku* for the sake of Philip Morris. It also signifies rebirth, however; in the same episode, Don symbolically passes the creative torch to Peggy when he asks her to take over his Burger Chef pitch and Sally falls in love for the first time. At the margins, Bert's death and his last refrain might suggest that hope abides for a more democratic culture, forged and symbolized by the social movements churning below the elite's command posts, and inspired in part by Mills' critiques.[74] Given institutional inertia and the continuing stratification of power today, however, we might doubt that Bert's death truly marks the demise of what he represented.

In any event, for whatever its characters think, the representation of the power structure in *Mad Men* suggests that we take these myths to be true at our peril, unmasking the idea of sovereign control over our lives as so much projective piffle. It does not, however, tend towards the opposite conclusion, namely that we remain *completely* unable to affect our surroundings—such grand theoretical interpretations that reduce individuals to *nothing more than* epiphenomena of systemic economic imperatives or childhood psychic trauma belie the agency possible in the options afforded us in everyday life. *Mad Men* illuminates instead what we can call, following E. E. Schattschneider, another contemporary commentator, the *semi-sovereign self*.[75] Its characters' aspirations to have genuine control of their lives notwithstanding; their agency is always already circumscribed by real and only partly tractable social structures.

Notes

1   See the assorted essays in James B. South, Rod Carveth, and William Irwin: *Mad Men and Philosophy* (Hoboken, NJ: John Wiley & Sons, 2010), especially George A. Dunn, "'People Want to be Told What to Do So Badly That They'll

Listen to Anyone': Mimetic Madness at Sterling Cooper," pp. 20–33, and Ada
Jaarsma, "An Existential Look at *Mad Men*: Don Draper, Advertising, and the
Promise of Happiness," pp. 95–109.

2   *Mad Men*'s audience also plays the being/seeming game, as viewers are invited
to match its historically fictional characters with real persons (Jimmy Barrett
as pseudo-Don Rickles, for example), and the show's writers place fictional
firms like Sterling Cooper and Putnam, Powell, & Lowe amidst real advertising
agencies like McCann Erickson.

3   The beat, "A Beautiful Mine," produced by RJD2, samples Enoch Light's 1958
recording of "Autumn Leaves," and originally appeared (with lyrics) on rapper
Aceyalone's *Magnificent City* (Decon Records, 2006). Attention to music,
particularly for the purposes of irony, is another impressive aspect of *Mad
Men*'s production design; consider, for example, the remarkable juxtaposition of
Nancy Sinatra's "You Only Live Twice" (also with descending strings, and with
James Bond associations, to boot!) with the tableau of Don leaving the set of
Megan's first commercial (5.12).

4   Erving Goffman's notions of "performance" and "front" in *The Presentation
of Self in Everyday Life*, Rousseau's idea of *amour propre* in his *Discourse on
Inequality*, and James Scott's description of "hidden" and "official" transcripts in
Domination and the Arts of Resistance all have rich potential application to *Mad
Men*.

5   Played by Robert Morse, who starred as J. Pierrepont Finch in the Broadway
and film productions of *How to Succeed in Business Without Really Trying*, one
of *Mad Men*'s inspirations.

6   C. Wright Mills, *The Sociological Imagination* (New York: Oxford University
Press, 1959), p. 21.

7   Mills explains that "[t]he theory of man's history can all too readily become
distorted into a trans-historical strait-jacket into which the materials of human
history are forced and out of which issue prophetic views (usually gloomy ones)
of the future" (ibid., pp. 22–3).

8   Ibid., p. 23.

9   Ibid.

10   Ibid.

11   On Grand Theory and Abstracted Empiricism, see ibid., Chapters 2 and 3
respectively.

12   Ibid., p. 21.

13   Professor Emile Calvet's heavy-handed Marxist rhetoric, a pastiche of actual

Marxism, can be heard in *At the Codfish Ball*, 5.7. In *To Have and To Hold*, 6.4, Megan declares that she's sick of his "Marxist bullshit" (6.4).

14   To this list, one might also add Ginsberg's literally insane technophobia.

15   Given the fact that the Port Huron Statement was inspired by Mills' "independent radicalism," Don's unwillingness to read it is doubly ironic in light of this essay's focus. On the SDS and Mills, see Tom Hayden, *Radical Nomad: C. Wright Mills and His Times* (Boulder, CO: Paradigm Publishers, 2006), p. 55; Stanley Aronowitz, *Taking it Big: C. Wright Mills and the Making of Political Intellectuals* (New York: Columbia University Press, 2012), p. 18; but note also Daniel Geary, *Radical Ambition: C. Wright Mills, the Left, and American Social Thought* (Berkeley: University of California Press, 2009), pp. 255–6, note 8. Hayden laments that Mills' insight into social structures did not extend to questions of ethnic or gender identity. Mills explained in a letter that "I have never been interested in what is called 'the Negro problem.' Perhaps I should have been and should be now. The truth is, I've never looked into it as a researcher. I have a feeling that if I did it would turn out to be a 'white problem' and I've got enough of those on my hands just now … The US of A is a white tyranny. It will remain so until there is no distinction whatsoever drawn in marriages between the races." See C. Wright Mills, *Letters and Autobiographical Writings* (Berkeley: University of California Press, 2000), p. 314; Hayden cites excerpts from this letter in *Radical Nomad*, p. 59.

16   On the commodification of youth rebellion, see Thomas Frank, *The Conquest of Cool* (Chicago: University of Chicago Press, 1997) and Thomas Frank and Matt Weiland, eds, *Commodify Your Dissent: Salvos from the Baffler* (New York: Norton, 1997), parts 1 and 2; more specifically with regard to *Mad Men*, see George Teschner and Gabrielle Teschner, "Creating the Need for the New: 'It's Not the Wheel. It's the Carousel,'" in *Mad Men and Philosophy* (Hoboken, NJ: Wiley-Blackwell, 2010), pp. 126–40.

17   On Mills in general, see Hayden, *Radical Nomad*, Geary, *Radical Ambition*, and Aronowitz, *Taking it Big*.

18   As Mills writes: "In what period have so many men been so totally exposed at so fast a pace to such earthquakes of change? That Americans have not known such catastrophic changes as have the men and women of other societies is due to historical facts that are now becoming 'merely history.' The history that now affects every man is world history. Within this scene and this period, in the course of a single generation, one sixth of mankind is transformed from all that is feudal and backward into all that is modern, advanced, and fearful.

Political colonies are freed; new and less visible forms of imperialism installed. Revolutions occur; men feel the intimate grip of new kinds of authority. Totalitarian societies rise, and are smashed to bits—or succeed fabulously. After two centuries of ascendancy, capitalism is shown up as only one way to make society into an industrial apparatus. After two centuries of hope, even formal democracy is restricted to a quite small portion of mankind. Everywhere in the underdeveloped world, ancient ways of life are broken up and vague expectations become urgent demands. Everywhere in the overdeveloped world, the means of authority and of violence become total in scope and bureaucratic in form. Humanity itself now lies before us, the super-nation at either pole concentrating its most co-ordinated and massive efforts upon the preparation of World War Three." *The Sociological Imagination*, p. 4.

19 Mills privileges the business, political, and military elites, but he also acknowledges other important yet structurally less-consequential domains such as local power brokers, celebrities, and the very rich (see Chapters 2, 4 and 5, respectively).

20 For a contemporary pluralist analysis of democratic politics in post-war America, see Robert Dahl, *Who Governs?* (New Haven, CT: Yale University Press, 1961).

21 Mills, *The Power Elite* (New York: Oxford, 1956), pp. 7–8.

22 Ibid., p. 23.

23 Ibid.

24 Ibid.

25 In other words, the power elite framework is compatible with a variety of Grand Theories.

26 As Thomas Frank writes in his history of advertising culture, business leaders "are not dictators scheming to defraud the nation, but neither are they the mystic diviners of the public will that they claim (and that free-market theory holds them) to be." *The Conquest of Cool*, p. 31.

27 Hayden notes that Mills' earlier work from the 1940s, in contrast to his 1950s work, *did* maintain a simplistic view of class in which economic position determines the distribution of social values (*Radical Nomad*, p. 81).

28 For examples of the tendency towards conspiratorialism in the radical Left, see Noam Chomsky, *Year 501: The Conquest Continues* (Boston: South End, 1993) and David Graeber, *The Democracy Project* (New York: Spiegel & Grau, 2013).

29 Mills' conception of the elite's composition is therefore broader than the economic conception Martin Gilens and Benjamin Page employ in their widely

(mis-)reported study of influence in twenty-first-century America; see their "Testing Theories of American Politics: Elites, Interest Groups, and Average Citizens," Perspectives on Politics 12:3 (September 2014), 564–81.

30 James Scott, *Domination and the Arts of Resistance* (New Haven: Yale University Press, 1991), p. 2 and *passim*.

31 Mills, *The Power Elite*, p. 35.

32 Ibid., p. 21.

33 Ibid., p. 25.

34 Not to mention any number of recent thinkers, most prominently (albeit in very different regards) Michel Foucault and Michel de Certeau.

35 Bert's place in the power elite is underlined by Roger Sterling's LSD-induced hallucination of the former's face in place of Lincoln's on the five dollar bill (*Signal 30*, 5.5).

36 On the "Creative Revolution" in advertising, see Andrew Cracknell, *The Real Mad Men* (Philadelphia: Running Press, 2011) and, more critically, Frank, *The Conquest of Cool*, Ch. 5.

37 The viewer is given the impression that the jingle that successfully wins the Martinson's account was composed by Kurt.

38 Pointedly neglecting Duck, who did the advance work to get the Martinson's meeting in the first place.

39 This lack of cultural sophistication is further emphasized by Roger saying that the museum concerns folk "arts" rather than "art" (whether a slip or a choice by actor John Slattery—I haven't seen the script), and in Bert's animated description of whirligigs at the museum's "opening exhibit," almost certainly a misnomer given that Roger has already said that the museum itself does not yet exist. A sophisticate would presumably know the difference between a preview and an opening exhibit.

40 This statement becomes all the more true later in *Mad Men*'s run, as positive attention from the American Cancer Society saves Sterling Cooper et al. after Lucky Strike drops the agency (*Blowing Smoke*, 4.12); Bert describes the award they give Don as akin to "being dipped into gold" (*Far Away Places*, 5.6).

41 This comment is drenched in irony, of course, as we saw in season one that Bert cares not a whit about Don's real identity when Pete attempts to expose him.

42 See *The Power Elite*, Ch. 2.

43 In the same conversation, Bert justifies the war in Vietnam with recourse to the domino theory of communist contagion; while rarely political, Don, by contrast, is against the war, as he reveals in a later episode (*Collaborators*, 6.3).

44   An indication of Jim's disloyalty comes after Bert's death when he tells the staff
      that he'll open their meeting with a poem of memorial for Bert (Whitman's
      hackneyed "O Captain! My captain!"), after which they can attend to "a lot of
      pressing business here, with finalizing Don's departure and …" at which point
      Roger interrupts him with his own "urgent" business, the announcement of the
      deal for McCann to buy Sterling Cooper (*Waterloo*, 7.7).

45   By deflecting attention from the products themselves to the messages they
      convey, advertising aims at creating what linguist Michael Silverstein calls a
      "characterological aura" such that "message" is front and center. See his "The
      'Message' in the (Political) Battle," *Language and Communication* 31:3 (2011),
      p. 204. In this sense, advertising ironically reinvigorates the loss of aura Walter
      Benjamin bemoans in the age of mechanical reproduction in a manner that
      Benjamin would have felt abhorrent; see Walter Benjamin, "The Work of Art
      in an Age of Mechanical Reproduction," in *Illuminations* (New York: Shocken,
      1968), pp. 217–52.

46   See "The Culture Industry, or Enlightenment as Mass Deception," chapter 3 of
      Adorno and Horkheimer's *Dialectic of Enlightenment*. Adorno's comments from
      Minima Moralia (1946) are exemplary: "What philosophy once called life, has
      turned into the sphere of the private and then merely of consumption, which
      is dragged along as an addendum of the material production-process, without
      autonomy and without its own substance. Whoever wishes to experience the
      truth of immediate life, must investigate its alienated form, the objective powers,
      which determine the individual existence into its innermost recesses. To speak
      immediately of what is immediate, is to behave no differently from that novelist,
      who adorns their marionettes with the imitations of the passions of yesteryear
      like cheap jewelry, and who sets persons in motion, who are nothing other than
      inventory-pieces of machinery, as if they could still act as subjects, and as if
      something really depended on their actions. The gaze at life has passed over into
      ideology, which conceals the fact that it no longer exists." *Minima Moralia*, tr.
      Edmund Jephcott (London: Verso, 2005), p. 15. For applied critiques, see Thomas
      Frank and Matt Weiland, eds, *Commodify Your Dissent* (London: Norton, 1997).

47   On this topic, see Frank, *The Conquest of Cool*. Smitty and Don, incidentally, are
      impressed with the *Statement*'s countercultural implications, yet ignore its Mills-
      inspired critique of elite domination.

48   In his conversation with Hilton after the pitch, Don notes that "most ad men
      believe that clients are the thing that gets in the way of good work" (Don denies
      that he holds the same belief) (*Wee Small Hours*, 3.9).

49 Joan tells Lane that it would be a "defining moment" for Sterling Cooper (*Christmas Waltz*, 5.10).

50 Thanks to Lilly Goren for this insight.

51 The capriciousness of the industry is such that Roger worries that even the news of Lucky Strike's departure will lead other clients of Sterling Cooper to lose confidence in their abilities and do the same (*Chinese Wall*, 4.11).

52 *Mad Men*'s setting in advertising reinforces the *general* fragility of its characters' selves more effectively than Sloan Wilson's 1955 novel *The Man in the Gray Flannel Suit* (Cambridge, MA: Da Capo, 2002), in which war veteran Tom Rath (whose wife is Betsy) is a ghost writer for the head of a major television network, whose position in the power elite is unassailable.

53 The ad men's lack of integrity is reinforced by Jim's vote for selling the company back to McCann immediately after vociferously arguing against it: "It's a lot of money" he'll be making (*Waterloo*, 7.7).

54 The close relationship between business, advertising, and politics is evident throughout the series, which presents various advertising agencies working intimately with the Nixon, Johnson, and Goldwater campaigns (*Waldorf Stories*, 4.6; *A Little Kiss*, 5.1).

55 Nixon's later successful 1968 presidential campaign receives less attention in *Mad Men*; in the lead-up to the election, the show highlights its characters' concerns about violence at the Democratic Party Convention in Chicago (*A Tale of Two Cities*, 6.10). Don does watch Nixon's inaugural speech while shining his shoes, and the new President's words articulate Don's (and everyone's) anxieties about his own place beneath the command posts: "We find ourselves rich in goods, but ragged in spirit, reaching with magnificent precision for the moon, falling into raucous discord on earth. We are caught in war, wanting peace. We are torn by division, wanting unity. We see around us empty lives, wanting fulfillment. We see tasks that need doing, waiting for hands to do them." Nixon's lofty rhetoric contrasts strikingly with Don's quotidian activity, one that reinforces his obsession with image and reminds viewers of the effort that goes into appearances.

56 See the lively account in Michael Muhammad Knight, *The Five Percenters: Islam, Hip Hop and the Gods of New York* (Oxford: Oneworld, 2007), pp. 107–9.

57 Henry appears to be a politico in the nationalist, law-and-order mold; in addition to complaining of Lindsay's weakness in inviting dialogue with radicals, he thinks Sally should join the student congress rather than the Model United Nations club, for "the UN is a joke" (*A Tale of Two Cities*, 6.10). In *Field*

Trip, 7.3, Betty tells a friend that due to a conflict with Governor Rockefeller Henry had missed the shortlist for AG.

58   Betty's apparent feminism in this scene should not mask the fact that her feminist inclinations are liminal, and her fantasy offer for Henry to rape Sally's friend Sandy at a sleepover reveals a problematic relationship with male domination (*The Doorway*, 6.1).

59   For a critical history of the US nuclear weapons program, see Eric Schlosser's magisterial *Command and Control: Nuclear Weapons, the Damascus Accident, and the Illusion of Safety* (New York: Penguin, 2013).

60   In the political philosophy of the *Mad Men* era, the threat of nuclear annihilation was a guiding thread in a number of works by prominent theorists; see, for example, the opening pages of Hannah Arendt's *The Human Condition* (1958) and the entirety of Karl Jaspers' *The Atom Bomb and the Future of Mankind* (1961). Nowadays, contemporary political philosophers rarely dedicate volumes to such quotidian concerns.

61   To contemporary ears, Don's words implicitly rebuke Dow, for of the three products he names to demonstrate the company's consumer prowess (Zip Tape, Styrofoam, Rovana), the second is an environmental disaster and the other two are no longer common.

62   Chevallier's Dartemont describes the onset of the Great War from the French soldier's point of view in *Fear*: "In Berlin those who wanted all this make an appearance on the palace balconies, in their finest uniforms, in postures suitable for the immortalizing of famous conquerors ... Those who are unleashing on us two million fanatics, armed with rapid-fire artillery, machine guns, repeater rifles, hand grenades, aeroplanes, chemicals and electricity, shine with pride. Those who gave the signal for the massacre are smiling at their coming glory ... This is the moment when the first—and last—machine gun should have done its work, emptied its belt of bullets on to that emperor and his advisors, men who believe themselves to be strong, superhuman, arbiters of our destinies, and who are nothing but miserable imbeciles. Their cretinous vanity is destroying the world" (London: Serpent's Tail, 2011), p. 9. Such generalized disgust for armed conflict is common but not ubiquitous in war memoirs; for an enthusiastic endorsement of war, see Ernst Jünger, *Storm of Steel* (1920), and compare the call to authenticity Heidegger discerns in the prospect of death for a greater cause in *Die Selbstbehauptung der Deutschen Universität* (1933; Frankfurt: Klostermann, 1990).

63   In this, Duck echoes Tom Rath (see the following note). For more examples, Heinz's representative rejects the idea of waltzing kidney beans because they

look slimy and bloody—and "not just to fellows like me who saw things in Korea" (*A Little Kiss*, 5.1)—and we learn in a later episode that Jim Cutler flew bombers over Dresden during the Second World War (*Waterloo*, 7.7).

64 In *The Man in the Gray Flannel Suit*, war's traumatic experience is represented in Tom Rath's burning desire to escape the memory of killing men during World War II; Rath wants never again to think of his victims, just as Don wants to leave Dick Whitman in Korea.

65 The Korean War, incidentally, reflects the apex of conflict *between* political and military elites, seen in President Truman's relieving of General Douglas MacArthur from command for insubordination. For a memoir telling of the inadequate preparation of troops in the Korean War due to elite miscalculation, see Joseph Owen, *Colder than Hell: A Marine Rifle Company at Chosin Reservoir* (New York: Ballantine, 1996).

66 See the Adorno citation in n. 36 above.

67 Here I follow Ricoeur's *Time and Narrative*, vol. 1, *passim*. Jürgen Habermas, in like fashion, remarks that the narrative structure of thought is expressed in the "lifeworld" of symbolic reproduction and is absent from the "system" of material reproduction; see Habermas, "The Concept of the Lifeworld and the Hermeneutic Idealism of Interpretive Sociology," in Steven Seidman, ed., *Jürgen Habermas on Society and Politics* (Boston: Beacon, 1989), p. 165ff. Mills also claims that in order to be comprehensible, sociology must intersect with biography: *The Sociological Imagination*, Ch. 1.

68 On this topic, see my "In Defense of Blinders: On Kant, Political Hope, and the Need for Practical Belief," *Political Theory* 40:4 (August 2012), pp. 497–523.

69 Anybody who doubts that television as a business requires narrative structure need only watch anything by Stan Brakhage and (futilely) imagine it being screened during prime time on a major network.

70 I make this point not to impugn the show but as a suggestion as to why *Mad Men*'s gaze does not always match its representations.

71 Our last glimpse of Bert alive finds him impressed with Neil Armstrong's famous "one small step for a man" comment. "Bravo!" he remarks (*Waterloo*, 7.7).

72 Ginsberg's mental breakdown, his conviction that Sterling Cooper's computer is controlling him, also reflects a deep (and not entirely unreasonable) anxiety over the rise of the technological age.

73 "The Best Things in Life are Free," written in 1927 by Buddy De Sylva and Lew Brown; Bert's song is an implicit challenge to the last words Roger says to him,

"Let's have another cup of coffee, let's have another piece of pie," from a 1932 musical by Irving Berlin. As a Kant scholar, it would be remiss of me not to note the echoes of (one half of) Kant's celebrated comment that "Two things fill the mind with ever new and increasing admiration and awe, the more often and steadily we reflect upon them: *the starry heavens above me and the moral law within me*"; *Critique of Practical Reason*, tr. Mary Gregor, in *Practical Philosophy* (Cambridge: Cambridge University Press, 1999), p. 269.

74   See n. 11 above.

75   E. E. Schattschneider, *The Semisovereign People* (New York: Holt, Rinehart and Winston, 1960).

4

Cash or Credit? Sex and the Pursuit of Happiness

Laurie Naranch

What if we think of sex as a privileged site through which *Mad Men* works out anxieties about self-invention, sexism, security, and commerce in the 1960s as well as in our present age? Sex—as intimate activity, desire, and identity—structures the world of *Mad Men*.[1] The 1960s are often depicted as a joyous time of sexual liberation and experimentation. *Mad Men*, however, takes us beyond the countercultural clichés that sex was more fun and liberated back then. In fact, *Mad Men*'s characters don't seem to really enjoy all the sex they are having.[2] Viewers of the series often remark on the painful feelings the show invokes. In an interview with *The Chicago Sun-Times*, former President Bill Clinton (a fan of the show) said:

> You ever watch that TV series *Mad Men*? If I keep watching this program, will I ever find a happy person? Great television. Good drama. But a lot of really painful reminders in that show about how black people were supposed to run the elevators … were supposed to ask permission before they get on an elevator. The way women were treated is appalling, and only occasionally funny to me.[3]

Although it is unclear when the appalling treatment of women is "occasionally funny," it is clear that Clinton is tapping into an unhappy feeling generated by the series. That feeling of unhappiness can be used as an example of what to avoid. President Obama in his 2014 State of the Union address mentioned workplace inequalities still faced by women, saying: "It's time to do away with workplace policies that belong in a *Mad Men* episode."[4] Both presidents rely on unpleasant feelings associated with workplace and social inequalities in relation to sexism and racism to point out political failures in the quest for gender and racial equality.

We can productively read the politics of sex in *Mad Men* if we see these unhappy instances of sex as an "unhappiness archive."[5] For Sara Ahmed, tracking unhappiness is crucial to uncovering how charges to "just be happy" are often depoliticizing. Just be the happy housewife! Or, aren't you lucky to have a job! Not being able to express unhappiness, she suggests, denies a voice to women, other marginalized groups, or to those who point out problems of inequality or injustice. Ahmed suggests that unhappiness can be a political resource for critique by revealing what is politically unfair through a feeling of discomfort. *Mad Men* may likewise tune us in to what unhappiness might teach about the limits of the American promise of "life, liberty and the pursuit of happiness" famously declared in the Declaration of Independence. Paradoxically, this does not mean that it is unpleasant to watch the show. Instead, revealing unhappiness leaves open the possibility of happiness that can be taken up in political struggle.[6] Rather, a feeling of unhappiness illustrates the constraints of inequality in the workplace, particularly in terms of sex and sexuality.

An unhappiness archive can teach us about what it means for ethics and politics to be in crisis. After all, happiness is equated with living the good life. Ahmed writes, "If we do not assume that happiness is what we must defend, if we start questioning the happiness we are defending, then we can ask other questions about life, about what we want from life, or what we want life to become."[7] While *Mad Men* doesn't engage in explicit consciousness raising in the same way as feminist and anti-racist struggles do, nor does it reveal the collective political actions of the time of feminists, civil rights activists, student groups, anti-war activists, or the emerging evangelical movement, it does tap into a feeling of unhappiness that illustrates a sadness around inequalities based on those identity categories politicized in the 1960s, especially around gender and sexuality. Though the show takes place in a specific setting with a narrow band of characters, those characters illustrate how unhappy the situation is for women, and for men, in differently constrained sexual exchanges. That a feeling of unhappiness persists today in terms of sex, despite more equitable laws and social norms in relation to women, gay, lesbian, and transgender individuals, reveals that meeting the conditions for liberal equality is an ongoing political project. *Mad Men* situates sex as "not happy" to show an ethical and a political crisis of inequality in the workplace and at home.

The past is not really past

This interpretation of *Mad Men* relies on reading sex as an unhappiness archive within the frame of the drama itself; I couple this with knowledge of what is outside the frame in terms of political history both then and now. This approach tracks sensibilities rather than reading the series as social realism (this did or didn't really happen), in terms of moralism (the 1960s are a sinful fall from grace which explains why the main characters are unhappy and divorced or unmarried), or in terms of simple ideological critiques from across the political spectrum.[8]

However, because an unhappiness archive is generative of critical possibilities, it can be subject to many different interpretive readings across the political spectrum and across disciplines. For some, *Mad Men* is "TV's most feminist show" for how it portrays the realism of women's experiences similar to those featured on the series.[9] For Caroline Levine, it offers a progressive message not so much by making us feel superior to the behavior of the 1960s as depicted in the show than to subtly "honor the social movements of the late 1960s, which rise up between our present and the past" to create "the shock of historical difference" with our present moment.[10] The "shock of the banal" has potentially progressive effects as we see that we have made social, cultural, and legal transformations in our ordinary life from the environment to discrimination. However, Kent Ono claims that the historical portrayal of *Mad Men* is limited and racist in presenting the view of elite white men.[11] He finds this to be the case when looking at the few African-American characters and the even fewer Asians and Asian Americans.[12] Natasha Simons, writing in *The National Review*, observes that conservatives and liberals view the show differently.[13] Conservatives see the show as one of generational decay, confirming a hedonistic counter-culture and shallow consumerist society devoid of a moral compass. Liberals see the show not as presaging the "me generation" as much as anticipating deliverance from the restrictive social strictures of the time. In all of these scenarios, sex in the above senses features prominently. While we experience a lack of enjoyment in many examples of sex in the series we are led to feel that something is missing or something is wrong. Rather than celebrate the success of the 1960s in terms of greater gender equity and changing patterns of sexual violence, goals that are shared in general today across the political spectrum, what the unhappiness archive can reveal instead is places where we may still feel unhappiness in terms of inequalities in the workplace and in the persistence of intimate partner violence and sexual assault.

As Thomas Laqueur argues, there is a history to sex.[14] Sex as we know it, he says, is "a response to the epochal shifts of the early modern period."[15] Those shifts involved separating sex from reproduction and loosening the ways in which sex could be an exchange in which individuals acted in morally acceptable roles outside of those of virgin, wife, husband. In the 1960s these modern conditions remain and then some. Sex is severed from reproduction through both the rise of sex as pleasure in mainstream culture, scientific studies, and feminist activism. Drugs to treat sexually transmitted diseases such as gonorrhea and syphilis along with the approval of the birth control pill by the FDA have made sex "without danger" (or with these dangers less of a possibility).[16] Finally, there is the rise of a postwar consumer economy, shifting gender and race relations with civil rights and radical social movements to claim more independence for minorities and women, transformative movements making arguments for freedom from sexual violence and racial and sexual discrimination,[17] as well as an affirmative right to sexual health.[18] More philosophically, in light of these contingent historical changes, Judith Butler suggests that sex is a manifestation of norms that materialize bodies into dominant and often rigid gender structures of the proper behavior and desires of women and men.[19] That is, sex circulates and is circulated; it is rearranged and rearranges social relations. What we can see by viewing the ways that sex circulates in *Mad Men* is a simple point: that by tracking sex we can see wider social and political forces as work, forces that constrain men and women in different ways.

From the beginning, Don Draper gets around

Sex has shaped the world of *Mad Men* from the beginning of the series. In the premier episode we meet Don Draper, the creative director for the advertising firm Sterling Cooper. Don has both sex appeal—as a slim, square-jawed white man with dark hair and a sense of the mysterious about him—and a lot of sexual encounters (*Smoke Gets in Your Eyes*, 1.1). Early in the first episode, Don knocks on a door in a bohemian New York City neighborhood to visit Midge, an artist. Don wants to talk about work, while Midge wants something else. "Despite her flirtations, he's all business. The trade commission has cracked down on tobacco health claims, and Don's without a plan for tomorrow's meeting to keep the Lucky Strike account from leaving the agency ... He asks to run some ideas past her but when she unbuttons her white blouse to reveal a lacy black bra, he decides to take a break from work for a while."[20] As the official episode recap above suggests, things are not simply black and white in *Mad Men* when it comes to sex. As the first episode continues, Don meets a new client, Rachel Menken. After a testy beginning, they later start an affair. It's not until the end of the episode that we see Don arriving at a suburban house, opening the door, and going into a bedroom where we meet Betty, his wife. Don, the character who drives the show, has a complex sex life. Yet, we don't see Don as a happy swinger in this first episode or first season. Don as the central protagonist drives the series. In this regard it's important to note that Don is the character who isn't morally judgmental about sex in terms of one's identity, e.g. sexuality. Moreover, he is realistic about the consequences of sex for women as he recognizes the limitations faced by his secretary (later copywriter) Peggy, and the office manager (later partner) Joan, who are more constrained by cultural and political expectations in terms of pregnancy and being able to survive economically by having the merit of their work recognized. This isn't to say that Don is always in control of his life and the support he may give to other social outsiders (quite the contrary), but rather that his accepting attitude, if not advocacy, towards sexuality, desire, and intimate acts is a practical act of treating others decently as individuals.

The main male characters in the advertising agency have all been married, had extramarital affairs both paid and unpaid, been divorced, and often remarried. They fit squarely into cultural expectations of dominant, white masculinity of conquest and heterosexuality, but they don't appear very happy. Don has sexual encounters with many women, from a stewardess (this is before the term flight attendants),[21] to a psychiatrist, a teacher, secretaries, ethnically coded women (identified by being Jewish or Catholic), one-night stands with women who are both named and unnamed in the show, even a joyless *ménage a trois* with his second wife Megan and her acting-class friend.[22] Even after winning a CLIO award for his creative work, Don hooks up with two women, waking up without much memory in the bed of a waitress from a diner (*Waldorf Stories*, 4.6). Despite this male privilege of access to women's bodies in ways that they aren't condemned morally (the classic double-standard that men can sleep around and be virile whereas women are labeled whores), and the economic means to do so when paying prostitutes, *Mad Men* doesn't engage in a celebration of this privilege; instead it points to a lack of intimacy for someone like Don as a frustration. While this certainly has to do with the personal story of his character, that it recurs in unhappy marriages and sexual encounters of other Sterling Cooper executives reveals that multiple sexual partners does not lead to happiness for men, and that even in this privileged position, there is a social and political alienation at work.

Prostitution, selling, and economic survival

As the television critic Emily Nussbaum remarks, "Prostitution is to *Mad Men* what vampirism is to *True Blood*, a metaphor that sloshes in everywhere, juicing the most innocent interactions. It blurs the boundaries between every power dynamic: between men and women, secretaries and bosses, clients and 'creative.'"[23] Certainly, prostitution—literal and metaphorical since, after all, this is a show set in an advertising agency—is part of the dynamics of sex in the show. Here, economic survival is at stake. Prostitution also constitutes evidence of the unequal social distinctions of gender and class in terms of who buys and who sells sex. Whether it's a brothel in Hershey, Pennsylvania, or on Madison Avenue in Manhattan, men seek women for sex and women sell access to their bodies for money.

Season four finds Don commanding "Do it," and "harder" (*Public Relations*, 4.1). After his separation and divorce from Betty, we find him with a call girl named Candace. Outfitted in a red pointed bra, she sits astride Don. He commands her to slap him. And she does. This is an encounter with a "working girl" when Don is at a low point in his life after his divorce and as his work life is falling apart. What does Don seek? It may be a kind of punishment to be able to feel a way to "snap out of it"—his past, his lies, his trouble at work—but it also reveals that the idea that individual self-invention is simply a matter of hard work on the part of the individual is fantasy. That is, the scene can reveal Don's unhappiness with himself and an unhappiness that is shaped by the social and political forces in his own life.

Don certainly knows the economy of prostitution from his childhood experience and as a man in a white-collar firm in New York City. His colleagues and their clients frequent prostitutes as their expected prerogative. It's a location for heterosexual male bonding. For example, when the rather insecure Lane Pryce's marriage is falling to pieces, he and Don get drunk and pick up prostitutes on New Year's Eve, and Don pays. Lane insists the next day on paying his fair share (*The Good News*, 4.3). Rather than present this as a "bro code" male-bonding experience in their use of women for sex, the show produces a solemn, rather sad scene of the two of them in this exchange. The sadness reveals not only a challenge in male friendship or collegiality at work when dealing with family troubles, but also taps into a broader sense of social alienation when one's sense of self as a man—husband, breadwinner, stud—is undercut and unavailable. After all, it is Lane who commits suicide in the office when the circumstances of his life are too much to bear. Unhappiness reveals distinct pressure on men to conform to social expectations as well.

Besides dominant expectations for men to spend money for sex, we also see prostitution from a less privileged position, albeit still through Don's eyes. We learn that Don's mother was a prostitute who died in childbirth. Don's original identity is that of Dick Whitman, who grew up in an abusive household, overwhelmed by poverty. Dick comes of age in a whorehouse in Hershey, Pennsylvania, where his stepmother Abigail moves him and his half-brother Adam after Don's father dies. Here Dick witnesses the domestic abuse of Abigail by "Uncle Mac" as he peers through a doorway. He also has his first sexual encounter in the awkward, constrained sex Aimee gives him. This scene is not presented as every boy's fantasy but a "necessary gift" to which Dick acquiesces, and in exchange he steals change from her clients' pockets.

Don recalls this experience when he revises (destructively for his career) his pitch to Hershey's chocolate executives in the season six finale. At first, he tells clients a story about how his dad would buy him a Hershey bar for mowing the lawn, his father tousling his hair as dad's love and chocolate became inextricably intertwined as "the currency of affection" (*In Care Of*, 6.13). As the clients chuckle with delight at the heartwarming story, Don's smile freezes and his hand begins to tremble. In actuality, the object of the Hershey bar conjures up not the fantasy of the happy childhood, but the reality of the unhappy one. Don says "I grew up in Pennsylvania, in a whorehouse," his voice a bit unsteady. "Closest I got to feeling wanted was from a girl who made me go through her johns' pockets. If I collected more than a dollar, she bought me a Hershey bar … It was the only sweet thing in my life." This is not a vision that the executives want to sell Hershey's bars. What Don's unhappy memory of sex shows is the trauma of economic necessity and an abusive childhood relieved, if only temporarily, by a Hershey's bar.

Don, however, is not someone who is free of sexist attitudes as a result of these experiences. While he is attuned to the reality of constraints on individual life choices in terms of sex and class, he does use sexist insults in relation to Betty. It was Don's stepmother who continually reminded him of the "whore" his mother was. Whore is also what Don calls Betty when she asks for a divorce and as she begins a new relationship with Henry Francis, who will become her second husband (*Shut the Door. Have a Seat*, 3.13). "Whore" was famously what Othello called Desdemona, a false claim, but one with the harshness of shame and a male (often female) prerogative of punishment that Shakespeare exploited well in his intimate tragedy of manipulated treachery on the part of the advisor Iago and the inflexibility of Othello's male pride. *Mad Men* isn't a tragedy in this sense. Rather, it's an ordinary level exploration in these scenes of how the term "whore" is used to illustrate economic hardships experienced differently by women and how whore can be used to shame women. In the case of the label being applied to Betty, it doesn't seem to stick, given Don's own extramarital affairs and that viewers' sympathy lies with Betty on this point.

Rather than present women sex workers as simply whores in a moralistic fashion as fallen women or as women who are innocents simply exploited at the hands of male sex traffickers, *Mad Men* presents prostitution as an enterprise of economic survival in the context of an unequal, gendered, and raced world where structures of inequality constrain the choice. This recognition also allows us to read Joan Harris's constrained choice to have sex with a client as prostitution. Herb Rennet wants to sleep with Joan in order to offer the Jaguar car account for the firm; this is a pimped arrangement on the part of the partners, but also one in which she has some limited agency or capacity to choose (*The Other Woman*, 5.11). Pete presents the proposal to Joan; she is initially repulsed. The partners—Bert, Roger, Don, Pete, and Lane—meet to discuss "selling" Joan for the contract with Jaguar. Don walks out in disgust. The others discuss details. Roger, Joan's on and off lover, boss, and father of her child (although little Kevin is passed off as her then-husband Greg's son) is not her advocate. Lane proposes to give Joan a five-percent stake in the company and a voting partnership instead of a lump sum payment if she agrees to this exchange (although this isn't a fully altruistic offer since he has mismanaged funds and she knows it).

When presented with this proposal, Joan finally agrees. Economic independence is at stake for her: the choices are so narrow for women, even one who is clearly as talented in business and management as Joan is. Don goes to Joan's apartment later to say that she doesn't have to do this; but she already has. We see how distasteful the sex is for her; but she plays the part of the seduced woman, wearing a black dress and allowing the velvet-robe-clad Herb to put an emerald necklace around her neck, a necklace she takes off the moment she gets home. Joan's choice reveals some agency or capacity to choose on her part, but it's hardly a choice freely entered into. Instead, through the feelings of unhappiness presented, we see an illustration of the structures of sexism that won't allow Joan to rise in the corporate world and achieve economic security for her son on her considerable talent alone.

Sex known and unknown, seen and unseen: Sexuality

From the outset of the series we see closeted gay men. While there are a few lesbian hints (Joan's roommate Carol confesses her attraction to her in season one; Joyce Ramsey is a butch lesbian creative consultant who challenges Peggy's heterosexuality in season four), the focus, not surprisingly in a series that revolves around an advertising office where men dominate the creative and executive worlds, is on men. Salvatore "Sal" Romano, an art director at Sterling Cooper during the first three seasons, is the original closeted gay character on the show. He is married but there is apparently little sex there and no children in the works. He also admits to being too afraid to take up the offer of Eliot Lawrence of Belle Jolie cosmetics to go to his hotel room. When Sal does risk a sexual encounter it is with a bellhop from the hotel where he and Don are staying for work. Sal is "caught" by Don as a fire alarm empties all the rooms onto the street. Don, however, doesn't say anything.

But it's in Sal's refusal of the advances of the very important client, Lee Garner, Jr. of Lucky Strike, who appears coded as bisexual, that his fate is sealed. He didn't "take one for the team" as Don put it, and Garner insists that Sal be fired which is what happens.[24] How frustrating, we might say. After all, Sal is a sweet character. He is creative and kind. The unhappiness feeling shows not only a frustration that he can't be himself as a gay man, but also that he refuses a quid pro quo form of sexual harassment (one that Joan put up with) when he refuses to flirt or have sex with Garner to get the account.

In more recent episodes, we meet Bob Benson (introduced in season six). He has a thing for Pete Campbell that leads to an awkward pass at him, and Pete's response of repulsion. In the office, Bob becomes friends with Joan. In the first half of season seven he is called to bail out an executive from Chevy who was arrested for trying to fellate an undercover officer (*The Strategy*, 7.6). Bob gets him out of jail, to gay-baiting taunts to both of them by the officer on duty. The executive assumes rightly, although Bob denies it, that Bob is a fellow traveler. Giving Bob some inside information that the firm will lose the Chevy account, but get Buick, he says Bob should expect to get a call to come work directly for General Motors. Bob tries to conform to the executive "ideal" by proposing a marriage of convenience to Joan. She says to him, with a bit of commonsense and sadness, that he doesn't prefer women and she deserves love (7.6).

It appears that even transgressive group sex or a bit of sado-masochistic role-playing doesn't fill the happiness void. Roger Sterling looks exhausted in the opening of season seven as he rolls out a bedroom with many bodies draped around it (*Time Zones*, 7.1). Don is enticed by Megan and her friend Amy into a three-way sexual encounter when he visits her in California, but this won't save their marriage or renew their sexual and intimate spark. Don's affair with Sylvia Rosen, the wife of a neighbor in the building where he and Megan have their New York apartment, involves some role-play. He entices her to a hotel room, lays out a beautiful dress, and asks her to be ready for him. When he arrives in the room, she is coiffed and ready for what she thinks will be a night out. But Don commands her to stay put. This isn't what Sylvia has in mind and she leaves, refusing Don's attempt to control their exchange. Transgressive heterosexual sex also does not appear to be a path to liberation or individual fulfillment.

Finally, while spouses and co-workers may eventually find out with whom you've been sleeping, it is the gaze of children that has a more disruptive impact. Echoing Don's glimpse of his stepmother being forced into sex by "Uncle Mac," Don's daughter Sally inadvertently catches Don and Sylvia having sex when she enters their apartment looking for an "I Like You" letter she left for the Rosens' son (*Favors*, 6.11). This seeing is what ultimately ends Sylvia and Don's relationship and it strains the relationship between Don and Sally. Relationships with one's children are also at stake, as this piece of the unhappiness archive shows.

Sex and consequences: Pregnancy

Besides the consequences of failed marriages, closeted sexuality, the risk of arrest for same-sex exchanges, and having the children know about your sexual imbroglios, there are other consequences to sex that *Mad Men* presents with starkness. One of these consequences is the fear of pregnancy for unmarried women. In season one, voluptuous office manager Joan instructs Don's new secretary Peggy. In addition to giving her insight into in her office duties, Joan also refers her to a gynecologist from whom she can get a birth control prescription. Peggy is presented as innocent and unstylish. She comes from a Catholic family in Brooklyn, so her naiveté and the religious background set the stage for her initial undoing. First, arrogant young account executive Pete Campbell insults her for her appearance. Yet later that night he appears at her door, drunk from his bachelor party. They start an affair and Peggy gets pregnant. She remains in denial about her pregnancy, and to other characters she just appears to be getting fat. One day, thinking she's having abdominal pain, she goes to St. Mary's Hospital where it becomes evident that she is in labor. Peggy will give her child up for adoption. It will be Don who visits her at the hospital and urges her to close the door on this experience and come back to work. The unhappiness of being in denial about being pregnant and not having many options in light of that situation is at stake here.

People of a certain era may remember homes for wayward girls. Pregnant women weren't allowed in high school and were typically socially shunned. Adoption was a typical choice for unmarried mothers. Abortion was illegal. It wasn't until 1970 that New York state passed what was then the most permissive abortion legislation in the US, and not until 1973 that the Supreme Court decision *Roe v. Wade* legalized abortion in the first two trimesters. Although single mothers are more socially accepted now and there are services for young adult women who become pregnant, the challenges of raising a child alone and at a young age remain. Anxieties, not just hopes, about becoming pregnant if engaging in sex still shape the social experiences of women whether inside or outside a marriage contract.

Abortion does present itself as an option for women with unwanted pregnancies in the series. Don's two wives both contemplate abortion. Betty finds herself pregnant with their third child as the marriage is falling apart. Megan is unsure about her pregnancy given her career goals and her increasingly shaky marriage with Don. But neither character undertakes this action. Betty's doctor doesn't advise her about an underground abortion provider since a woman of her class and race shouldn't want an abortion. Megan miscarries, an experience she relates to Sylvia Rosen along with her thoughts about ending the pregnancy. Finally, Joan finds herself pregnant with Roger's child as a result of their cathartic sex after being mugged on the street. However, Joan is still married to Greg, who is in on a tour of duty in Vietnam. Joan tells Roger she is pregnant and they agree to "take care of it." Once she is at the clinic, she's reminded of her age (not that old!) when a woman in the waiting room asks if she's there with her daughter. She decides to keep the child and say Greg has fathered it rather than risk being too old to conceive. She doesn't want her shot at motherhood to be lost and so a deception is put in place. The unhappiness of wanting a child but not knowing if you will be too old or unable to conceive is an anxiety that remains and is perhaps even more prevalent today as many women delay pregnancy in relation to a career or other life circumstances.

The risks of sex in terms of both unwanted pregnancies and anxieties about pregnancy/childbirth are borne by women. The show doesn't address sexually transmitted diseases (STDs). This may be due to the fact that public consciousness about STDs is at a lull: the setting is after the post-Second World War gonorrhea and syphilis treatments and prior to the HIV/AIDS crisis of the 1980s. Rather, sex and reproduction are tied together in pregnancy—a consequence that does not go away, although it can be ameliorated, by birth control measures. Unhappiness is revealed through worry about unwanted pregnancy as well as in ambivalence and trepidation in the desire for a child.

Sexual violence: The specter and reality of rape

Betty and her second husband Henry Francis talk while Sally enjoys a visit with her friend Sandy, a violin prodigy. Henry has enjoyed hearing Sandy play violin. Later that evening Betty, having noticed his admiration of Sandy, says that the girl is just in the next room: "Why don't you go in there and rape her? … I'll hold her arms down" (*The Doorway*, 6.1). Well, isn't that uncomfortable? Betty, never a warm mother but a selfish, vain, and often childish woman, crosses a line in verbalizing this collective assault of a child and passing it off as "spicing things up" for her and Henry sexually. And Betty pushes it. She says she'll leave with Sally so Henry can have his way with Sandy; he could even gag her so the boys won't hear. There's an unhappiness check for you.

In no way does this suggestion come across as titillating or acceptable, and Henry finds the suggestion repulsive. It is a casual presentation of a violent fantasy that reveals Betty's unhappiness in her marriage and her inability to make an ethical distinction between exciting sex and assault. As a call for attention, this conversation reveals how violent sexist ideas of domination shape the imaginative life of both men and women.

But it is Joan who is raped, by her fiancé, Greg. This isn't sex but violence; a sexual assault. Greg, presented as jealous and insecure, senses something intimate between Joan and Roger. As Joan goes into Don's office to close up for the night, Greg locks the door, pushes her down, and rapes her (*The Mountain King*, 2.12). It's a fundamental premise of liberalism that you can't make a choice or consent if there is no exit or option to say no. The presentation of the assault in the confines of the office shows Joan's distressed reaction to the attack, yet many fan comments afterwards didn't read the scene as one of rape. The actress who plays Joan, Christina Hendricks, offered her surprise at this interpretation saying: "What's astounding is when people say things like, 'Well, you know that episode where Joan sort of got raped?' Or they say rape and use quotation marks with their fingers. I'm like, 'What is that you are doing? Joan got raped!' It illustrates how similar people are today, because we're still questioning whether it's a rape. It's almost like, 'Why didn't you just say bad date?'"[25] Joan does go on to marry Greg. It is not a happy marriage but it provides a cover of respectability for Joan. The marriage finally comes undone when Greg reveals to Joan that he has voluntarily reenlisted to return to Vietnam, without consulting her.

Besides rape "jokes" and actual representations of rape, *Mad Men* also exposes sexual harassment in the workplace through feelings of unhappiness in other scenes. When Joan is subjected to a sexist cartoon by the freelancer Joey, Peggy fires him. Thinking that Joan will be pleased by this, Peggy enters the elevator with her and says, "I don't know if you heard, but I fired Joey." Joan responds: "I did. Good for you." She claims that now everyone in the office will know that Peggy solved the problem for Joan. Peggy says "I defended you." Joan retorts "You defended yourself," and closes the scene saying "You want to be a big shot … but no matter how powerful we get around here they can still draw a cartoon. All you've proved to them is that I'm a meaningless secretary and you're a humorless bitch" (*The Summer Man*, 4.8). While this opens up a debate for different strategies for how women negotiate sexist and hostile behavior in the workplace (even with legal and policy protections) it clearly reveals the confined nature of their choices—dramatized by the elevator setting—to go it alone without recognition of the other's experiences or that the insult was shared.[26]

Sex sells … or does it?

"Sex sells" is a cliché about advertising in a modern age. Yet in the series *Mad Men* this notion is dismissed as simplistic and naïve by the main character Don Draper. In the episode *For Those Who Think Young* (2.14), Peggy and Salvatore come into Don's office with a draft drawing for a Mohawk Airline campaign. Peggy reads the tag line: "Where are you going?" We cut to the ad on Don's desk. The ad depicts a slim Anglo-looking man in a business suit stepping off the plane on to the tarmac with a slim Anglo woman facing him in a short skirt, her backside and stiletto heels in the center of the drawing. Don responds: "Are you going to underline 'you'? For half the people it will be 'Where are you going?'" he says with a flat affect. Peggy notes that they also have the tag: "Come away with us." Not impressed with the mockup, Don continues, "Sure. Fine." Peggy, getting a bit exasperated, says: "It's what we talked about." Don: "It's obvious. I'm uninvolved." Grabbing a pen from Sal's suit pocket, Don draws a red box around a small girl in the picture and asks "What about that?" Peggy sees this as sentimental. Don says that she's right, but that sentiment doesn't mean sentimental and, as he says, we're talking about businessmen. Peggy responds: "Right. Businessmen who like short skirts. Sex sells."

"Says who?" queries Don as we cut to Peggy looking down and Sal taking out a cigarette to light. Don then offers the striking claim: "Just so you know, people who say that think monkeys can do this." After riffing a bit more, Don picks up a pink homemade valentine which says "I love you Daddy" on it and tosses it on top of the mockup. Looking at Peggy he says, "You are the product. You feeling something. That's what sells. Not them. Not sex. They can't do what we do. And they hate us for it." Peggy tries another option: "Welcome back, Daddy?" Her voice lilts up at the end. Don: "Is that a question?" Peggy:

"What did you bring me, Daddy?" Don pauses and says "You can put that in your book" as he pulls out a cigarette (ironically, often an indication of a successful sexual encounter that occurred off screen in television and film of the era, and sometimes product placement for the industry).

According to mainstream business knowledge, sex does sell, but it depends on the product. In *Mad Men*, however, what Sterling Cooper wants to sell is a vision of the happy family. It's a family more nostalgic than real, from the bittersweet images in season one's Kodak slide carousel to season seven's grappling with the notion of family dinner and fast food, and we see that through the unhappiness archives of sex in the series. Season seven has a return to this pitch when Peggy is the lead on the Burger Chef account. In discussion with Don, Peggy wonders if such a happy family really exists (*Waterloo*, 7.7). She asks, "Are there people who eat dinner and smile at each other instead of watching TV? Did you ever do that with your family?" Don sighs sadly: "I don't remember." The days of idyllic suburban family life, before the sexual revolution, teen pregnancy, working mothers with no time to cook, and sons being drafted to Vietnam that Peggy ruefully mentions seem impossible for Don—or any of us—to remember, perhaps because what he (and we) are nostalgic for is a 1950s illusion that was never fully real, or built on repression and restriction as much as freedom and desire. The longing for contentment in the happy family is an inversion of the unhappiness archives around sex. While the happy family image is sold, existing families can never measure up; when we feel unhappiness around sex we might feel happiness in not being in that historical environment anymore, or hopeful that there are still other possibilities for equality and individuality than what we currently have. Our awareness of what could and should be done can rise with an unhappy moment.

Sex and other exchanges

Mad Men is savvy in presenting sex in myriad forms. There is an aesthetic pleasure when watching the series that is indeed sexy.[27] In many ways sex is presented as exchange and consumption in the context of power, privilege, and individual desire for connection with others. As many commentators and scholars have mentioned, in *Mad Men* the past is not really past. Jeremy Varon writes: "in my view the show is more plausible as the staging of a fantasy than the rendering of history."[28] For Varon *Mad Men* implies the 1960s failed before they even "happen." While the show has been accused of being too favorable to the 1960s, he suggests rather that "the problem may be just the opposite: that fearful of indulging in 1960s sanctimony the show makes its leading characters' detachment and cynicism its own."[29] While I am sympathetic to the view that *Mad Men* is constructed with the present in mind, I disagree with Varon that the series abandons any sort of critical political purchase for fear of being sanctimonious. If we trace the unhappy moments of sex in the series, we see not detachment or cynicism but a lack of enjoyment. This lack of enjoyment in sex provides a feeling for what is wrong and opens up some possibility of what might be better.

Thinking of *Mad Men* in a political register, the categories of choice and constraint are central as individuals function in ordinary work and personal life. These are central categories of political modernity in a liberal tradition. This is a tradition that revolves around the individual who equally and freely contracts with others to secure the political and social world (the social contract) in the interest of securing worldly goods through rights. Yet as critics of liberalism rightly point out, freedom and equality are only secured in relation to shared social resources and are fundamentally dependent on others for the enjoyment of rights. If a critical liberal legacy is attuned to the importance of what supports "life, liberty and the pursuit of happiness," we see that the playing field of opportunity is not as open or even as we might hope. As an archive of unhappiness around sex, *Mad Men* offers us the possibility of thinking and doing otherwise, as we continue to recognize ourselves, our experiences, and unequal power dynamics still at work.

Notes

1   Thanks to Lilly Goren, Linda Beail, Lori Marso, and Wendy Pojmann for comments on earlier drafts. Thanks also to Michelle Tirado for her deep knowledge of *Man Men* episodes and interest in cultural criticism.

2   See for example J. M. Tyree's article, "No fun: debunking the 1960s in *Mad Men*
    and *A Serious Man*," *Film Quarterly* 63 (2010), p. 4.

3   Lynn Sweet, "Bill Clinton Pitches Health Care; Muses on 'Mad Men,'" *Chicago
    Sun-Times*, November 11, 2009, http://blogs.suntimes.com/sweet/2009/11/
    bill_clinton_in_chicago_pitche.html (accessed August 2, 2014).

4   Thanks to Linda Beail for the reference. See http://www.mediaite.com/tv/
    president-obamas-2014-state-of-the-union-address-full-transcript/ or http://
    www.whitehouse.gov/the-press-office/2014/01/28/president-barack-obamas-
    state-union-address (accessed August 2, 2014).

5   I take this term from Sara Ahmed but use it a bit unfaithfully. Ahmed
    constructs an unhappiness archive from feminists, queers, and migrants to
    illustrate the normalizing dangers of calls just to be happy and not complain.
    Finding political and cultural resources in "killing joy" is a mode of critique that
    Ahmed wants to recover for critical politics. See her *The Promise of Happiness*
    (Durham, NC: Duke University Press, 2010).

6   Ibid., p. 222.

7   Ibid., p. 218. For instance, for Ahmed, the image of the "happy housewife" is
    rendered unhappy by feminists who are said to be a "killjoy" by pointing out
    the sexism of limiting women's choices solely to happiness in a heterosexual
    marriage with children (see Chapter 2).

8   I took inspiration for this formulation from Anthony Lane's review of François
    Ozon's film *Young and Beautiful*. Ozon is well known for his complex portraits
    of female sexuality and uncomfortable presentations of sex in contemporary
    society, usually France. *The New Yorker*, May 5, 2014.

9   Stephanie Coontz, "Why 'Mad Men' is TV's Most Feminist Show." *The
    Washington Post*, October 10, 2010.

10 Caroline Levine, 'The Shock of the Banal: *Mad Men*'s Progressive Realism,' in
    Lauren M. E. Goodlad, Lilya Kaganovsky, and Robert A. Rushing (eds), *Mad
    Men, Mad World: Sex, Politics, Style & the 1960s* (Durham, NC: Duke University
    Press, 2013), p. 144.

11 Kent Ono, "*Mad Men*'s Postracial Figuration of a Racial Past" in ibid., pp. 300–19.

12 As viewers, we are well aware of the raced, gendered, and sexed discrimination
    present in the show in this very time period. As reported by Lisa Chow,
    advertising agencies have not changed all that much in terms of diversity in
    the office, even if the three-Martini lunch is a thing of the past. For instance,
    Chow reports that the New York City Commission on Human Rights in
    2006 found that blacks make up 2.5 percent of the managers of several large

advertising firms. Only 18.5 percent of the United States Congress are women while three women (from Guam, the US Virgin Islands, and Washington, DC) serve as Delegates to the House; of these 99 women, 30 are women of color (30.3 percent overall). Corporate boards remain predominantly white and male. Lisa Chow, "'Mad Men' Haven't Changed Much Since the 1960s," *NPR*, January 14, 2010, http://www.npr.org/templates/story/story.php?storyId=122545036 (accessed November 29, 2014).

13 Natasha Simons, "*Mad Men* and the Paradox of the Past," *National Review*, July 19, 2010, http://www.nationalreview.com/articles/243490/i-mad-men-i-and-paradox-past-natasha-simons (accessed August 2, 2014).

14 Thomas Laqueur, "The rise of sex in the eighteenth century: historical context and historiographical implications," *Signs* 37: 4, *Sex: A Thematic Issue* (Summer 2012), pp. 802–13.

15 Laqueur notes that the Industrial Revolution starts the story whereby heterosexuality "came to be freed from both reproduction and from the scarcity of resources"—a worry for a population control advocate like Thomas Malthus in the nineteenth century and read by political radicals interested in birth control as a way to sever reproduction from sex. Ibid., p. 806.

16 For a good analysis of women's reproductive politics and experiences see Leslie J. Reagan, "After Sex What?: A Feminist Reading of Reproductive History in *Mad Men*," in Goodlad et al. (eds), *Man Men, Mad World*, pp. 92–110. Also, as reported by PBS: "1957 The FDA approves the pill, but only for severe menstrual disorders, not as a contraceptive. An unusually large number of women report severe menstrual disorders. 1960 The pill is approved for contraceptive use. 1962 It's an instant hit. After two years, 1.2 million Americans women are on the pill; after three years, the number almost doubles, to 2.3 million. In 1964 ... the pill is still controversial: It remains illegal in eight states. The Pope convenes the Commission on Population, the Family and Natality; many within the Catholic Church are in favor. 1965 Five years after the FDA approval, 6.5 million American women are on pill, making it the most popular form of birth control in the U.S." http://www.pbs.org/wnet/need-to-know/health/a-brief-history-of-the-birth-control-pill/480/ (accessed August 2, 2014).

17 "Sex" became a protected category in the 1964 Civil Rights Act prohibiting discrimination at the workplace. In the mid-1960s, as historian Alice Kessler-Harris points out, "two of every five women workers were single, widowed, or divorced; more than half of them supported other family members, and especially children." *In Pursuit of Equity: Women, Men and the Quest for*

Economic Citizenship in 20th-Century America (Oxford: Oxford University Press, 2001). Yet the Equal Employment Opportunity Commission (EEOC), created in 1965 to implement Title VII of the 1964 Civil Rights act prohibiting discrimination on the basis of race, creed, color, national origin or sex, did not take a strong position to end discrimination on the basis of sex until the end of the 1960s. The Justice Department did not prosecute a single case of discrimination against women until 1970, while it had by that time taken 45 claims of racial bias to court.

18   There was activism within the Civil Rights Movements and radical political social movements around sexual violence and sexual autonomy, for example Rosa Parks was an anti-rape activist before she refused to give up her seat on the bus. Groups such as the Boston Women's Health Collective, authors of *Our Bodies, Our Selves* and activists in women's health, were founded in 1969, as was Redstockings, a radical feminist group committed to women's liberation in New York City, to mention only two. There was also activism for mainstream sex fairness at work and against violence in the home and street. For instance, the National Organization for Women (NOW) was founded in 1966. Among the tasks it took on were violence against women, representations in the media, and equal employment. The President of NOW in New York wrote to the *New York Times* in 1968 asking for sex-segregated job ads to be eliminated, in keeping with EEOC guidelines. See letter from Janet Farset, Taimement Collection, New York University.

19   Judith Butler, *Bodies That Matter: On the Discursive Limits of Sex* (New York: Routledge, 1993).

20   This is the description from the AMC website description of the episode called "Smoke Gets in Your Eyes." See http://www.amctv.com/shows/mad-men/episodes/season-1/smoke-gets-in-your-eyes (accessed August 8, 2014).

21   The cases brought by women stewardesses were some of the first to test the EEOC's enforcement of the anti-discrimination provisions of Title VII of the Civil Rights Act. This both challenged sex discrimination of women stewardesses, dress, weight, age, and paved the way for men to have these jobs also in the mid-1960s.

22   There are many sites that trace Don Draper's sexual encounters and the women with whom he's involved, such as http://www.thedailybeast.com/articles/2014/04/13/every-woman-don-draper-s-hooked-up-with-on-mad-men.html (accessed August 8, 2014).

23   Emily Nussbaum, "Working the Street," *New York Magazine*, August 11, 2010, http://nymag.com/arts/tv/reviews/67491/ (accessed August 8, 2014).

24 *Out* magazine has a nice, short rendition of Sal's character and outrage at how homophobia closeted this sweet character's life: http://www.out.com/entertainment/popnography/2013/06/25/mad-men-queer-gay-lesbian-characters-confirmed-speculated (accessed August 8, 2014).

25 This quote is from the online feminist magazine *Jezebel* in an article by Latoya Peterson (2009), at http://jezebel.com/5374654/on-mad-men-when-is-it-rape (accessed November 29, 2014).

26 And while there are mechanisms in place for combating discrimination at work, as the recent report about New York State Senator Democrat Vito Lopez reveals, his intimidation and harassment of female employees shows how the norms and structures of masculine privilege shut down many complaints and actions meant to protect women who want to advance in state politics. My thanks to Shannon O'Neill for pointing out the report to me, which you can find at http://www.nytimes.com/interactive/2013/05/16/nyregion/20130516-lopez-jcope-report.html?ref=nyregion&_r=1& (accessed August 2, 2014). Moreover, sexual assault continues to be a lived reality for women, and men, in intimate settings. For example, 37.4 percent of female rape survivors were attacked between the ages of 18 and 24; 90 percent of women know the person who sexually assaulted or raped them; 95 percent of sexual assaults are unreported. While nine out of every ten rape victims in 2003 were female, one in every ten was male and about 3 percent of American men, or one in thirty-three, have experienced rape or attempted rape in their lifetime—Aauw.org, "Sexual Assault Statistics." The United States military is also currently addressing a widening scandal on the persistent and pervasive sexual assault in the military primarily targeting women even as women are now legally allowed to serve in combat roles; this violence also encompasses men as victims and survivors of sexual assault.

27 That style is marketed well by AMC and corporations who tie into the show. Banana Republic has a *Mad Men* clothing line tied into seasons four, five, and six. Moreover, while you are deciding if you are a skirt or a suit as you "Mad Men yourself" in the avatar game section, you may also decide "Which of Don's Women are You?" Television, after all, is a business itself funded in large part by advertising dollars, as is the web presence of the channel and show. Sarah Kelsey, "Banana Republic's 'Mad Men' is Back: A Preview of the New Spring Collection," *The Huffington Post* Canada, February 21, 2012.

28 Jeremy Varon, "History Gets in Your Eyes: *Mad Men*, Misrecognition, and the Masculine Mystique," in Goodlad et al. (eds), *Mad Men, Mad World*, p. 258.

29 Ibid., p. 274.

Part Two

Business and Identity

5

Appearances, Social Norms, and Life in Modern America: Nationalism and Patriotism in *Mad Men*

Lawrence Heyman

Introduction

"Nostalgia is the concept that we're never happy; we just THINK we USED to be happy." This is a concept that first arose during a late-night conversation in a college; theater students in the 1980s were trying to figure out why plays set in the 1940s and 1950s and musical revivals were popular among theater-going audiences. There is a sense that people want to see a time in their lives that felt happy; they want to relive theater that came from a "happier time." As sardonic as it sounds, there is a thread of truth to this adage. Both published commentary and casual conversations indicate that, in fact, nostalgia is a powerful draw for many *Mad Men* viewers. Given that the show is set in the not-too-recent past, we, the audience, are allowed glimpses of American life as it was, and in some cases we are reminded of how things once were in our lives or in the way in which our parents lived. Critic Adam Gopnik has noted that value of nostalgia as a plotting component, explaining:

> When the new season of "Mad Men" began, just a few weeks ago, it carried with it an argument about whether the spell it casts is largely a product of its beautifully detailed early-sixties setting or whether, as Matthew Weiner, its creator, insisted, it's not backward-looking at all but a product of character, story line, and theme.[1]

Gopnik expands upon this idea with his "forty-year" rule, which roughly states that in terms of nostalgia there is a forty-year threshold for looking back; this magic number sets the standard for nostalgia in modern scripted drama. Gopnik's quote also highlights the appeal of the beautifully detailed settings and costumes. If plot, time period, character, and setting are the foremost elements in the show's construction, it could easily be argued that nostalgia, costumes, and art direction play very strong ancillary roles. One should not make the mistake of assuming that the show is in any way an actual documentary of historic events. As scripted drama, *Mad Men* is constructed with real-life events that serve two purposes: as "mile marker" references to where we are in the era, and also as dramatic tools. Viewers may not always be aware of the way in which nationalism and patriotism are woven into the narrative, but Matthew Weiner and the writers of *Mad Men* are able to carefully slip back and forth in what some might call a selective reality. While the show's principal setting, Sterling Cooper in its various incarnations, is fictitious (as is a rival firm with which it eventually merges, Cutler, Gleason and Chaough), the other firms discussed on the show are real. McCann Erickson still exists, as does BBDO (Cooper refers to this firm as Batten, Barton, Durstine and Osbourne in a cryptic moment that cements him as part of the "old-guard establishment"). In other episodes there are conversations about Young and Rubicam (they send over the African statue at the end of *A Little Kiss*, 5.1). J. Walter Thompson, Leo Burnett, and Ogilvy and Mather are also mentioned, and both Roger Sterling and "Ho Ho" make reference to Ogilvy's book (a comic moment occurs when "Ho Ho" mispronounces Ogilvy's name and Don corrects him). The series also features episodes that contain the iconic historical events that outline the 1960s, from the Nixon–Kennedy election, the death of Marilyn Monroe, to the Cuban Missile Crisis and the assassinations of John F. Kennedy, Dr. Martin Luther King Jr., and Robert F. Kennedy, as well as the 1968 Democratic National Convention riots and the moon landing. These moments provide contextual annotations of the real time in which the fiction is set. They also establish and reinforce the massive cultural changes occurring all around the main characters and the context in which the ad campaigns are being pitched and mounted by the agency.

In setting the work environment for *Mad Men* in a Madison Avenue advertising agency during the decade of the 1960s, Matthew Weiner creates a microcosm in which to examine and develop storylines that are based in a reality to which the viewer can relate nostalgically. In the latter half of the twentieth century, advertising became the tapestry that has signified and validated the modern American identity. Advertising is of metaphoric significance in both plot and character development. The place and time in which the show is set allows Weiner and the other writers to create a pastiche of visual, historic, and metaphoric references as the show evolves. In examining the show in search of themes of nationalism and the American national identity during the cultural shift of the sixties, one conclusion is that many of the characters are no more aware of these themes than is the contemporary American viewer in his or her everyday moments. If the viewer examines the boardroom conversations and pitch meetings at Sterling Cooper more closely, he or she begins to realize that significant emotional events were carefully woven into the fabric of the ads produced by Madison Avenue during the time in which the show is set, and the conversations among the characters on *Mad Men* are, in fact, discussions of these shifting understandings of national identity and patriotism during the Cold War, social unrest, and American involvement in Vietnam. Nationalism, patriotism, and our American identity are tied up in the advertising we consume and in some cases may actually be sold as products unto themselves. It is no secret that advertising is a form of manipulation. In order to manipulate buyers, ad men and women must first understand what motivates us. In constructing the decade-long drama that is *Mad Men*, Weiner and the show's other writers illustrate the massive cultural and political change that took place on a large scale by viewing it through the microcosm of the ad agency. Themes, storylines, and events were selected and crafted for dramatic effect, but they were also used to illustrate how life in America changed from the cool gray conformity of the early 1960s to the multi-colored, broad-patterned brightness of the late 1960s. From the Kodak pitch that focuses on nostalgia and how we cling to the way we once were, to the Burger Chef pitch that focuses on how we can find places to exist together, in the face of the changing, shifting model of what constitutes a family, the show addresses, in a very real way, who we were, how we viewed ourselves, and how we changed during this time in our history. The characters on the show are depicted as they navigate the landscape of historic events, and a portion of the show's drama derives not only from their reactions to the events but to the inevitable progress and change that takes place, whether they want it to or not. Nationalism and patriotism can operate as constructs that allow us to cope with, manage, and impose our views, opinions, and values on the change that comes with progress.

American exceptionalism: Appearances and reality

Contextual analysis of the show must consider the thought processes that drive the characters forward in the pursuit of whatever it is they see as success. Geoff Martin and Erin Steuter's *Pop Culture Goes to War: Enlisting and Resisting Militarism in the War on Terror* makes this observation: "American exceptionalism is a deep-seated cultural value shared by many in the United States that leads them to overblown self-confidence and a sense of the special virtue of the United States."[2] This arrogance, this sense of self-entitlement, has much earlier origins than the War on Terror. At the end of World War II, Henry Luce, writing for *Life* magazine, proposed the idea that the next era of history would be the "'American Century' ... that now America must assume the leadership of the world."[3] The world in 1960, at the beginning of *Mad Men*, is very much the world of the American century. Visually and contextually the show is firmly rooted in the serious business of the time. The first shot of *Smoke Gets in Your Eyes*, the pilot episode, tracks carefully through a dimly lit, smoky bar in midtown Manhattan. When the camera comes to rest on the main character, it is not from the front; we don't see his face initially. Instead the camera stops at a slight angle behind him; he wears a crisp white dress shirt, and works in shirtsleeves, hunched over, writing slogans, thoughts, and ad copy on a napkin. He's broad shouldered, square jawed, and his hair neatly groomed. Before we meet him or he delivers his first self-assured line we recognize him as the archetype of the American businessman. Don Draper stands out amid all of the men and women who press shoulder to shoulder in the crowded bar. We, the viewers, do not yet know why he stands out, but the ease with which he addresses the white-coated, older, African American busboy gives some insight. His conversation is natural, so much so that the busboy is silent, looking around nervously as though wondering why he's being addressed. When a Caucasian waiter, also in a white jacket, intervenes to ask if the man is bothering Draper, he is dismissed out of hand with the same ease and directness used to quiz the busboy about his smoking choices. Don Draper is a man very much in command of whatever room he inhabits. During a pivotal scene in "Nixon Versus Kennedy" (1.12), in which Pete Campbell attempts to expose Don Draper's true identity to the senior partner of Sterling Cooper, Bert Cooper tells him as much. After Campbell's grand revelation that Draper is not who he seems, Cooper's response to Campbell is simple and direct. In what has become one of the show's most memorable lines Cooper says simply, "Mr. Campbell, who cares?" He goes on, "The Japanese have a saying, a man is whatever room he inhabits, and right now Donald Draper is in this room." His final piece of advice to Campbell is that there may be more profit in recognizing that fact than not.

Donald Draper moves undaunted through the staid and subdued interiors of 1960 but is equally at ease, at least to all outward appearances, as the sixties progress and his surroundings shift. Nothing about him is accidental. He is very much an invention; a façade used to interact with others in a meaningful way. Bert Cooper's function in the office seems superfluous before the scene with Campbell and Draper. Perhaps Draper's façade represents American business and the idea that appearance may be more important than substance, or even a metaphor for US national identity of the time. Bert Cooper, then, represents older establishment practices and how business was done in the past. Throughout the series, indeed right up to his final soft shoe in season seven, Bert Cooper's function is to provide both characters and viewers with glimpses into the way things "really work," though he himself acknowledges that it's not always the way things should work, but rather the hidden realities behind the business that is done daily within their firm.[4] Pete Campbell crosses a line and breaks one of the unwritten rules of advertising by pitching copy to a client in a bar. When Draper wants to fire him and Roger Sterling agrees (there are just things that are not done), Bert Cooper clarifies Campbell's importance to the firm not as an account man, but because of his lineage. Later in the episode, it is revealed that Campbell's mother's family was among the earliest inhabitants of New York City as farmers. Cooper's comment about firing Campbell has nothing to do with business and everything to do with appearances; he wouldn't want anyone at the New York Yacht Club to be talking about how Campbell was fired by Sterling Cooper (*New Amsterdam*, 1.4). Appearances matter.

If the scope and power of American business is repeated through visual metaphors, then so is the conformity of Cold War America. The work setting of the show's first seasons is in the offices of Sterling Cooper. These are presumably the same offices that were occupied by Roger Sterling's father when he and Bertram Cooper founded the business before the war. Though technically modern, there is a dated quality in the offices and corridors of the place. The rows of Herman Miller and Steelcase desks, chairs, and file cabinets line up neatly with executive offices at the perimeter. Each of these offices is separated from the secretarial pool by doors, but also by walls of diffusion glass. Those office interiors—which are lined with dark paneling and illuminated by indirect light, as in the case of Don Draper's corner office—are not the offices of the present. The sparse furniture, lamps, and abstract wall hangings all echo a bygone era. These are late 1950s offices, home to serious business, where captains of industry roll up their sleeves and make the decisions that shape the way we buy the things consumers of the period buy. These offices are part of the place that Luce referred to as the "greatest and most powerful nation in the world."[5] But they are also in some ways the offices of the past. It is no coincidence that the exterior shots of the Sterling Cooper building are all from a low angle almost against the base of the building looking skyward. The gray, steel, and glass structure stands as a monument to American industry. As described in a pitch later in the series, this is the city that Bethlehem steel built.

The visual shift as the series moves forward is subtle but unmistakable. If Bertram Cooper is The Establishment in context of the show, then the offices occupied by the firm in seasons one through three are very much his domain. He occupies an office in a point of prominence in the agency; an office that is not only centrally located, large and luxurious, but also a few steps up from the rest of the offices. It's not clear that Cooper does more than eat meals and "hold court" in this office, and there is the added eccentricity that he works in his stocking feet and requires employees to remove their shoes ceremonially before entering. There is a powerful symbolism then when, at the end of season three, as Sterling Cooper plans a mutiny prior to being bought out, Cooper loses his office as the firm moves into the Time Life building. It is a loss that is never rectified. For the remainder of the series, Bertram Cooper, whose name is on the letterhead, who started the firm and built it from the ground up, and who *is* The Establishment in the firm, becomes superfluous if not completely irrelevant. One must wonder, if a named partner can become irrelevant, is there anything permanent about the business depicted in this series, or Sterling Cooper itself?

The second episode of the series, "The Ladies' Room", opens in an upscale restaurant as a Caesar salad is prepared tableside. The Sterlings and Drapers are out to dinner, smoking and enjoying cocktails as the salad is plated and distributed. They sit in a high booth with lush tufted upholstery. The walls are decorated with elegant maroon and gold silk and velour. The linen covered tables contain full silver place settings and all of the accessories that one might equate with a much more formal dinner. The restaurant is opulent, the service is beyond detailed as three jacketed men hover, serving, clearing, and attending while Roger orders more drinks. With all the smoking and conversation, the food goes untouched through the entire scene at the table. The subtext of the scene visually is that what's being served and where they are is taken for granted; this is where they belong, it is the way of the world as they know it. In moments such as these, the viewer understands the mindset of the elite men and women who populated this period in our history. But these moments also serve another, subtler purpose—they provide the viewer with context for the change that will happen throughout the decade of the show's progress.

The business of America

Mad Men is about doing business in 1960s corporate America. The posture and attitude of the main characters are inseparable from the settings they inhabit. Confidence (or the appearance thereof) and attitude almost supersede content or relevance in meetings that are driven more by the ego of the men running them than by other, more relevant information. The self-assured arrogance of the men in the executive level is unparalleled. And yet there are flaws and shortcomings in spite of the illusion that the men in power are in control of their surroundings and situation. In *The Marriage of Figaro* (1.3) Draper and his creative team meet with Rachel Menken to discuss possible changes that can be made in a campaign to modernize her family's department store and help bring it more into line with competitors. Draper, Pete Campbell, Harry Crane, and Ken Cosgrove convene in what appears as a typical lunch meeting with sandwiches and drinks on the table. Also present is the British researcher who ostensibly has compiled the data contained in the report. As the conversation progresses and Miss Menken thumbs through the report, it becomes clear that Sterling Cooper has thoroughly researched and evaluated the competitors, but nobody has actually visited Menken's department store. This becomes clear when Menken observes that several of the "innovations" attributed to her competitors are already present in her store. When she asks directly if anyone has visited her store, all but Don Draper look sheepishly away. Finally Draper intervenes, forthright and direct: "Miss Menken, I can assure you that no one at this table has ever been to your store, a wrong I will personally correct this afternoon." He proceeds to escort her out of the meeting, as she comments, "It's nice the way you handled that; it's hard to get caught in a lie." He responds, "It wasn't a lie, it was ineptitude with insufficient cover." She laughs, "Something about the way you talk always restores my confidence." He brushes it off and says "I have a deep voice." But there is more going on in this interlude. It is first and foremost a flirtation, as we witness what Pete Campbell describes as Don "turning it on". But as a political metaphor, that ability to calmly reassure others is a large part of the appeal of nationalism. Nationalistic ideology is based in the idea that we know what's right, we will do what's right, and when we are wrong, we will simply fix it. It's an oversimplification, clearly, but significant for its simplicity and directness.

Similarly, in the episode entitled *Babylon* (1.6), Roger Sterling and Don Draper meet Nick Rodis from Olympic Cruise Lines and members of the Israeli tourism board in order to explore the possibilities of an ad campaign. The meeting is awkward at best; it's clear that none of the partners in the room has done any research about Israel or the prospects for tourism. From mispronunciation of names to general lack of understanding of how to address the campaign, the meeting goes virtually nowhere. But throughout their interactions with the prospective clients, there is the prevailing sense that Don and Roger are so self-assured that they either can't imagine being wrong, or they don't care if they are—it doesn't matter. Later, Pete Campbell thumbs through the Israel tourism brochure and is of the opinion that Israel sounds "downright red …" based on his interpretation that Kibbutz living is communism. Taken together, these moments present the audience with the idea that despite the outward confidence and arrogance that is the ethos of the period, these post-war Americans are, at times, unclear on the details of their own nationalistic views. In his discussion of what he knows about Judaism, Don comments lightly that he's "read the Bible, but that's about it." He says it with a smile on his face, though viewers may likely cringe at the off-handed insult. It is one of the examples of the sort of American business hubris that dominates much of the early episodes of *Mad Men*. It is as though the client and campaign are secondary, but the implicit question remains—to what?

In another episode, when Don is informed that they've lost an account, he goes to Roger Sterling with the news. Roger's response is to recall what his father said about client relationships: "You know what my father used to say? Being with a client is like being in a marriage. Sometimes you get into it for the wrong reasons, and eventually, they hit you in the face" (*Long Weekend*, 1.10). The clients that they serve are little more than a nuisance with which they must deal. It is a strikingly naïve take on the nature of their business, but the characters act in these situations as if they do what they do simply because it is what they are supposed to do. In the gray, conformist offices of this post-Cold War environment, business happens because that is the way it has always been, that having drinks with a client is as important as actually producing work. If Henry Luce was right, then who we were as a nation at this point in time was, in the minds of men like Roger Sterling, Pete Campbell, Bert Cooper, and, to a degree, Don Draper, somehow predestined and "as it should be." What takes place as "business" in the context of the *Mad Men*'s early 1960s bears only a passing resemblance to business in the show's late 1960s and even less so to the contemporary eye.

During the presentation to Belle Jolie lipstick executives in *The Hobo Code* (1.8) the more senior of the two lipstick executives expresses that he's unsure of the approach Sterling Cooper is proposing. The idea was Peggy's, but Don feels sure that it is the right campaign, so much so that he stands, thanks the executives for their time, and prepares to leave the meeting. As he does so he reminds them that they've been offered a new approach, yet seem inclined to continue as they have with a product that is currently number four in the marketplace. The senior executive asks him to sit back down, but he flatly refuses without the assurance that his campaign will be considered seriously. Later in the episode, copywriter Freddy Rumsen describes the situation: "Don circled the village three times and then set it on fire ..." Donald Draper has difficulty managing a room that he does not "own," and so he forces executives to see things his way and place their trust in him, or ignore his opinion at their own peril. In the early seasons of the series this works. A stubbornly set square jaw is perceived as confident; arrogance is valued as a sort of character strength. It isn't until after season three that we, the viewer, and the characters themselves begin to see the flaws in this approach.

Unlike Don Draper, Roger Sterling has inherited his reputation and possesses the arrogance of someone who has been told from a very early age that the world is his to do with as he wishes. It's not that Roger Sterling does not understand the business in which he works; he understands it very well. Roger's asides, his off-the-cuff commentary and quips, provide comic relief, but they also establish context. They reveal to the audience that although Roger may be acutely aware of the ways in which business works, he simply doesn't care. While having lunch with Roger in *Red in the Face* (1.7), Don checks his watch and suggests that they need to get back to the offices for a meeting with Richard Nixon's campaign and PR team. Roger's reply is simple: "My name is on the building, and nobody's going to start a meeting without me." But we know it is not really Roger's name on the building—it is his father's name. Roger occupies a position of power and privilege because of who he is and not necessarily what he has done. It isn't until season three's *Shut the Door. Have a Seat* (3.13) that, while sitting in a bar with Don, Roger delivers the line, "I've acted like I started a business my whole life, but I inherited it." Equally important is the pivotal moment during season seven episode seven, when Bert Cooper explains to Roger that people never followed him because he never acted like a leader. It is only later that the viewer discovers that this is Bert Cooper's final challenge to that little boy who sits, frozen in time, on Bert's lap in a photograph that Cooper kept in his office.

The real world of fictitious advertising

Sterling Cooper is a relatively small shop that functions among much larger competitors. One choice that the show's creators made was to set this fictitious agency in the landscape of many Madison Avenue's real agencies: McCann Erickson, Young and Rubicam, BBDO (Batten, Barton, Durstine and Osbourne, as Cooper refers to them), and other named agencies give viewers a real background against which to compare Sterling Cooper. McCann Erickson recurs as a looming behemoth, a huge agency with international reach and massive resources. The firm is referred to on numerous occasions—at one point Draper calls it a "sausage factory." In another moment, while discussing a client comparing McCann Erickson to Sterling Cooper, Don notes that they have "six floors of creative." McCann Erickson reappears throughout the series because of the company's initial interest in trying to lure Draper away from Sterling Cooper, but also as an acknowledgment that some businesses flourish by their ability to acquire their rivals and control competition. In *Shoot* (1.9) Jim Hobart, the CEO of McCann, attempts to hire Don away from Sterling Cooper in part by hiring Betty, Don's wife, as a model for a Coca Cola campaign. He also sends gifts of golf clubs and club memberships to Don in an attempt to entice him with the promise being a member of a larger, more exclusive "club." Draper ultimately resists, opting to stay at Sterling Cooper, and, in turn, destroying Betty's re-emerging modeling career.[6]

It may seem odd to think of Donald Draper as being principled, but he seems to be the one guy at Sterling Cooper who operates with a code of honor. Regular viewers of the series know that he is a deeply flawed character and an unfaithful, philandering husband. Given all of his damaged relationships, and his deeply troubled past, he is an unlikely hero. At one point, while having dinner with Pete Campbell and aspiring jai alai entrepreneur Horace (Ho Ho) Cook Jr. (*The Arrangements*, 3.4), Don attempts to offer Ho Ho some advice as Pete looks on uncomfortably. He suggests that although Cook has a lot of money, which Sterling Cooper will gladly take, jai alai might not be the venture to back; that he should, instead, find a better one. Ho Ho mistakes the genuine piece of advice for a sales tactic, and goes on to suggest that if jai alai fails, it will be Don's and Sterling Cooper's fault. The viewer senses the honesty in Don's words, and knows that the advice comes from a place in which Draper is trying to do the right thing for a somewhat misguided rich kid. Another interpretation of this interlude is also possible, notably that Don Draper's business principles may be viewed as "quaint" rather than successful as the show progresses. The fact that Sterling Cooper is a fictitious agency existing among other real-world agencies can also be a representation of the not-so-subtle idea that the Sterling Coopers of the world ceased to exist in the face of the progress and "success" of places like McCann Erickson or Young & Rubicam. In addressing the concept of competing with Young & Rubicam, Don notes this company's "overwhelming force": "Y&R has six floors of creative. They can throw bodies at this account for weeks. We don't have that kind of firepower." Sterling Cooper begins its journey in this series as a successful and well-established firm. It is when the landscape begins to change, when the industry begins to develop, and when firms begin buying other firms in seasons two and three that the landscape becomes less stable for Sterling Cooper.[7] In the play *Inherit the Wind* by Jerome Lawrence and Robert Edwin Lee, the lawyer Henry Drummond, one of the principal characters, delivers a speech to the jury about progress: "Gentlemen," he says:

> progress has never been a bargain. You've got to pay for it. Sometimes I think there's a man behind a counter who says, "All right, you can have a telephone; but you'll have to give up privacy, the charm of distance. Madam, you may vote; but at a price; you lose the right to retreat behind a powder puff or a petticoat. Mister, you may conquer the air; but the birds will lose their wonder, and the clouds will smell of gasoline!"[8]

It's possible that Matthew Weiner is saying the cost of progress is that the "good guy" ceases to exist in the presence of the good businessman. In *The Other Woman* (5.10) when the other partners vote, in Don's absence, to offer Joan Harris a five-percent partnership and voting rights in exchange for sleeping with a Jaguar executive in order to get the account, Don not only objects to the decision but goes to her apartment in an attempt to intervene. Don's line is poignant when one considers that a car account is a crown jewel for an ad agency: "it's not worth it, and if we don't get Jaguar so what, who wants to be in business with people like that?" Joan replies, "You're one of the good ones, aren't you?" It's true, as odd as it may seem in the compartmentalized life of Don Draper the businessman, that dealing with unprincipled people is truly beneath him, an idea that Pete Campbell struggles with throughout the series and one that becomes more obsolete as the series progresses. Fear of the loss of independence or to a larger degree the loss of "self" for sleeping with a Jaguar executive in order to get an account may be why many viewers can relate to Don's apparent fear of progress, but there may also be a part of Don Draper that resists becoming the "people like that."

Contemporary viewers live in an age of globalization and faceless corporate behemoths. Part of the allure of *Mad Men* is the nostalgia for the seeming simplicity of a place like Sterling Cooper. One of the recurring tropes throughout the series is the repetition of the requirements for a good client portfolio. To modern audiences it seems quaint that success rides on three relatively simple accounts. In the atmosphere of the show, all firms need airline, tobacco, and car accounts in order to be considered successful. These three products all promise campaigns that will appeal to men—individuals who are, after all, the ones tasked with creating, accounting for and managing much if not all of the industry in the world of the show. In advertising, though, the average consumer is the "woman of the house" and where the products' campaigns are designed to appeal to the person who will be buying them, these three items represent masculinity. Airlines signify international reach and business travel, almost all of which was done by men; Peggy admits to Don that she's never been on a plane in *The Suitcase* (4.7). Tobacco companies are important clients due to the sheer size of tobacco accounts, and because such accounts provide seemingly unlimited cash flow. Tobacco *needs* advertising to lure new customers (Don states this in his season four, episode twelve meeting with the American Cancer Society). Automobiles matter because they were and to some degree still are a major part of American industry. In the world in which Sterling Cooper exists, in order to be considered successful by prospective clients and by the competition, a firm must have a client portfolio that contains those three items.

Early in the series, Herman "Duck" Phillips is hired as the new head of accounts. In season two he helps to orchestrate the takeover/merger of Sterling Cooper by Putnam, Powell, and Lowe, a British firm with which he had previously worked. The merger will benefit the partners financially, and will benefit Phillips professionally; he will become the president of the firm and therefore able to assert control over the creative team and Don Draper, with whom he's been at odds since his hiring. The ongoing battle between Draper and Phillips originates from the competing perspectives that each holds about what area of the firm actually drives business. What is not clear is the strategic advantage of allowing the takeover/merger to occur. Roger Sterling, Bert Cooper, Cooper's sister Alice, and Don all stand to gain financially, but what will the firm gain from the merger? In *Love Among the Ruins* (3.2), after a lunch to secure the account for the yet-to-be-built Madison Square Garden, Don is told not to take the account because Lane Pryce has been instructed that it will be too costly a venture. Don asks Pryce, sent from the UK by Putman, Powell and Lowe to "manage" Sterling Cooper, "Why the hell did you buy us?" Pryce's response is, "I don't know." It isn't until the end of season three, when the partners discover that Sterling Cooper and Putnam, Powell, and Lowe are being bought by McCann Erickson, that this is revealed as the plan for Putnam, Powell, and Lowe all along. Lane Pryce's first official act on behalf of Putnam, Powell, & Lowe is to fire a third of the employees at Sterling Cooper. The firm's workforce is streamlined and any new business that threatens to cost too much, such as the Madison Square Garden campaign, is rejected. A takeover by Putnam, Powell, & Lowe yields short-term gain for the executives at Sterling Cooper but little else, but in buying Sterling Cooper, Putnam, Powell, & Lowe makes itself a very desirable acquisition for McCann Erickson. The apparent lapse in understanding the details and nuances of managing business in an international market where competition is fierce seems to be a failing of Sterling Cooper. When Don has his final meeting with Conrad Hilton in *Shut the Door. Have a Seat* (3.13), Hilton asks Don why he doesn't just go work for McCann. Hilton refers to Don as a "prize pig."[9] Don rejects the idea and again likens McCann Erickson as a sausage factory. It isn't until Don is trying to convince a burned-out Ted Chaough, in the seventh-season episode *Waterloo*, that the work is what really matters that Don articulates for Ted the potential value of the trade-off inherent in a McCann Erickson takeover: they won't have to worry about running a business or being responsible for accounts; they simply have to come to work and run their creative department. "Or so it would seem" might be the unwritten portion of Don's conversation with Ted. Can a firm like Sterling Cooper continue to exist as the 1960s move beyond Don Draper's "quaint" notions of professional and business ethics?

The American way

If progress and change are inevitable, then patriotism and, to a larger degree, nationalism are concepts that allow a nation of individuals to maintain a sense of control in the face of a rapidly shifting world. For a business like advertising, nationalism and patriotism are useful because they create or project a sense of stability. Conrad Hilton articulates the idea of American nationalism as good business in *The Wee Small Hours* (3.9). In a phone conversation in the middle of the night, Connie tells Don "America is wherever you look, even on the moon, that's where we're going." The topic comes up later in a face to face meeting when Hilton says "It's my purpose in life to bring America to the world whether they like it or not … We are a force of good, because we have God. Communists don't, it's their most important belief, did you know that?" He goes on, "Generosity and the Marshall Plan, everyone who saw our ways wanted to be us …" Hilton tells Don that he doesn't want any politics in his campaign, but there should be goodness and confidence. In this moment, Conrad Hilton elucidates the idea that America represents all that is noble and right in the world and that everyone needs to know that, whether they want to or not. For this post-war business titan, this idea of America is somehow beyond mere politics. It is America's manifest destiny writ global, prefiguring Ronald Reagan's notion of the United States as the shining city on a hill, beacon of freedom, and virtue to the world. Lee Garner Sr., one of the Lucky Strike owners, simply says that "we might as well be living in Russia" when complaining about new federal guidelines for what can and cannot be said in advertising campaigns for tobacco. This comment, more than Hilton's, describes the level of understanding and the context in which most Americans think of the Soviets—as a vaguely defined and distant threat of constraint and conformity. It's particularly apropos that a commentary on the idea of freedom and the American way comes from a tobacco executive, in a meeting that is rife with retrospective irony, as the men alternatively suffer fits of coughing in the smoke-filled room and discuss the "myth" perpetuated by the government and *Reader's Digest* that their product is somehow bad for one's health. For Lee Garner, the "American way" is the ability to sell his product in whatever way he sees fit, without interference from the government or any other outside forces.

The fear of the unknown, and the unspoken threat of missiles, is also discussed in the second episode of season one, *The Ladies' Room*. The campaign is for Right Guard antiperspirant. It marks the first time that such a product has been marketed in aerosol cans. During a brainstorming session with Don, the copywriters and art director pitch ideas for graphics and tags for the product. All of the imagery seems to involve the space theme. We, the viewers, are reminded that space travel is still a new and unexplored concept that will materialize during the Kennedy administration, a fact that the characters on the show do not yet realize. As copywriter Paul Kinsey pitches idea after idea featuring astronauts, space suits, and rockets, his prose is dreamy and idealistic, speaking of how near we are to "the future." It is in this moment that the viewer experiences the wonder of space travel and the idea of future civilizations popularized in science fiction literature, television, and advertising of the period. Don Draper is unmoved and indifferent as he interrupts Kinsey, noting that "some people think of the future and it scares them. People see a rocket and they build a bomb shelter … I don't think it's ridiculous to think that we're looking for other planets because this one will end." The room goes completely silent as the art director, copywriter, and account man try to follow Don's stream of consciousness. He goes on to examine the ad and ask, "Who buys this?" He continues to examine the thought process of the target buyer. "Who is this moron in the space suit?"

The scene serves two purposes. It allows us to see Don's creative process, what Kinsey in a later episode describes as his *magic*, but it also focuses on what people at that time feared most—bombs and missiles and, on some level, progress itself. The occasional political references, which are less rare than we perceive them to be, provide the "shading in" of the characters' perspectives, their points of view, and the way in which they see themselves as citizens, and as individuals. There is yet another dimension to Don's mediation about the future; it is the idea that some may resist progress in order to cling to the past. The theme of space travel and exploration of new frontiers recurs throughout the show, reminding viewers of the novelty of it all. Bert Cooper's epitaph for his secretary and former lover Ida Blankenship points to this recurring trope: "She was born in 1898 in a barn. She died on the thirty-seventh floor of a skyscraper. She's an astronaut" (*The Beautiful Girls*, 4.9). Cooper's comment elucidates the massive cultural shift experienced over the span of the twentieth century, but it also highlights how surreal it must have been to live in the 1960s and actually witness the development of the space program.

Season seven episode seven, *Waterloo*, captures the wonder described in abstraction by Paul Kinsey in his Right Guard pitch in a particularly moving vignette as the camera discovers and lingers on each of the show's respective "families" sitting, transfixed, as they watch Neil Armstrong and the Apollo 11 moon landing. In this particularly elegant moment we are quietly reminded that our national identity at the time was very much tied to where we were going, and what we were capable of doing. The scene is so lovely because it is shot without the benefit or distractions of dialog; the only commentary we hear is that of the real soundtrack from the mission. The characters are lit by the glow of their television sets as they sit, rapt, watching the vision of a man walking on the moon. Don, Peggy, and Pete are together in a hotel room; Roger, his ex-wife Mona, and son-in-law Brooks sit together on a couch with little Ellory nearby, wearing a toy space helmet; Betty, Henry, Sally, Bobby, Gene, and their house guests are all seen sitting together and watching in the family room. The message is clear: no matter your social status, family situation, or place in the country at that moment, nationally, we watched together in awe. The show captures other moments such as this, but none with such clarity or elegance. Even Conrad Hilton sees the moon as the new frontier when he tells Don that he wants a Hilton on the moon because "that's where we're going." When Don pitches the Hilton campaign, Connie leaves, upset because Don did not include the moon. There is, of course, the metaphor that Hilton asks for the moon and expects it to be delivered to him, but there is also the concept of the moon as it exists in the collective consciousness of all Americans at the time. In a historical moment of national optimism and confidence, it is the newly minted superpower's next challenge to conquer and frontier to explore.

If space exists as a theoretical frontier in the zeitgeist of the show then California is the actual frontier for many of *Mad Men*'s characters and indeed for many Americans at the time. California of the 1960s is introduced to viewers in the fittingly surreal episode entitled *The Jet Set* (2.11). Pete Campbell and Don Draper fly to LA for a conference of defense and aerospace contractors. Shot through a filter of hazy, blistering sunshine, these scenes visually present California more as a dream than an actual place. The LA hotel lobby and foyer are wide and airy. Shortly after arriving and attending a few meetings, Don abandons Campbell to spend time with a group of jet-setting European aristocrats. Don's wardrobe shifts from New York, steel gray suits and slick hair, to soft, white casual trousers, relaxed golf shirts, and dry, windblown hair. We see this iteration of Don Draper in the *The Mountain King* (2.12), the episode in which we learn of and eventually meet Anna Draper. We see Don transformed further in *The Mountain King* as he re-becomes Dick Whitman. Walking home from the grocery store, he is wearing a cotton windbreaker, casual slacks, a short-sleeved shirt. He smiles easily and makes small talk with a group of men building hot rods in Anna's neighborhood. The transformative effect is undeniable, but it isn't long lasting. In California, Don more fluidly toggles between his two personas, Don and Dick. There are differing opinions on the strength of *Mad Men*'s "California" episodes, with critics often less positive in their analysis of these narratives than the general audience. At the same time, there are ways in which these episodes are distinct. Earlier in the series, Draper/Whitman is much more at ease with himself in California, his being seems lighter, he is relaxed and smiling, the scenes themselves are brightly light and have an openness about them—that is, until Anna Draper dies. The trips to California after Anna's death have a different cast to them; they are darker (both in style and substance), and Don no longer embodies his Whitman persona while there.

California affects Pete Campbell too. A scene from *The Jet Set* (2.11) provides some foreshadowing as Pete sits near the hotel pool in a swim outfit and white shoes, conducting business on a hotel phone and arranging poolside meetings. In season seven, Pete will relocate to California with Ted Chaough to open a West Coast office of Sterling Cooper and Partners. Don flees to California to shed his Draper persona and re-inhabit Dick Whitman while connecting with Anna Draper, who he perceives as "the only person who really knew" him. Campbell comes to California after his marriage to Trudy ends. The California of the early episodes is very much the California that lived in the imaginations of New Yorkers and Midwesterners in the 1960s. Orange groves, bright sunshine, vast and beautiful hotels all existed alongside crisp, elegant modern homes in the collective imaginations of people who hoped for the promise of another frontier. The characters who go there do so to reinvent themselves. Megan Draper heads west because she thinks Don is going there too, but when that changes, she goes to pursue her dream of becoming an actress.

By the time Megan moves to California in 1969 (which transpires between the end of season six and the start of season seven), the "dream" of California is starting to fade. As for the rest of the country, shifting cultural and political dynamics are clearly present in this perpetual frontier. Megan lives in the Hollywood Hills, has parties with her Bohemian friends, and lurches awkwardly through visits from her husband. Indeed, during what will be his last visit to California, in season seven's episode *The Runaways*, Megan, Don, and one of Megan's actress friends engage in what can only be described as a rather awkward threesome. The audience knows that California will not deliver on all of the promises imagined by the characters. Some of the most pronounced blog chatter of the final few seasons has consisted of speculation about whether Megan Draper will, through some plot twist, end up a victim of Charles Manson. Viewers know what is in store for Californians: the Manson murders, drought, fires, mudslides, earthquakes, political corruption, and the commodification of Hollywood. We know, too, about the pollution, overcrowding, decline of California schools, and all of the realities that exist and overtake the dream California of the early episodes.

We see the shift in California's portrayal, separate from Don/Dick's shift, when Don and Roger fly to LA to connect with Harry Crane and meet with

Carnation executives during the summer of 1968 in season six's *A Tale of Two Cities* (6.10). Don and Megan talk on the phone as each watches the riots at the Democratic National Convention on national television. Megan is visibly shaken by the events as Don tries to calm her by changing the subject. The next day, in the Carnation boardroom, Don, Harry, Roger, and a Carnation executive make small talk and discuss politics. When the CEO enters, Roger laughs about how the riots gave Nixon the 1968 election. It seems as though everyone is on stable ground, joking and bantering about politics, when the CEO interrupts, attempts to draw the conversation back to business, and then pounds the table angrily commenting on the protesters: "Those long-haired fools disgrace this country." When asked to describe the meetings later, Roger notes that "it was a series of busts, and not the kind I like" (6.10). Roger's strategy to be glib and Don's trademark deep-voiced surety both fall flat, leaving them in an unfamiliar landscape of a new frontier for which they were not prepared—one in which they don't have all the answers, and where talking confidently through the noise doesn't help. For better or worse, in prior meetings Roger and Don had always commanded and held the room. The CEO's outburst and anger are notable because Don and Roger couldn't predict the outcome. Both men were thrown off and bothered by a situation in which they were normally in control (or at least working in concert with the client, as in the conversations about government controls with Lee Garner). In this situation, they *should* theoretically agree with the Carnation CEO, but they don't, and that is not what they would have expected.

Shifting ground

Navigating in complex social and political environments is not new to Don, but the later episodes reveal circumstances that appear familiar but are actually fraught with a degree of uncertainty. One of the conflicts that is presented early in the series involves the interplay between characters who are part of the early 1960s post-beatnik, pre-hippie counter culture, and the business establishment. One might expect the group of pseudo-intellectual beatniks to create a situation in which Don Draper might falter as they calmly and cynically mock the advertising profession and establishment as a whole. Toward the end of *The Hobo Code* (1.8), Don visits his lover Midge Daniels in her Greenwich Village loft as she, her friend Roy, and a few other friends plan to get high and listen to Miles Davis. As Don is preparing to leave, they mockingly tell him that he "creates the lie, that he makes *want*." The typical counterculture versus establishment argument ensues in which Don tells them to stop talking and to "make something of yourselves," and goes on to explain that there is no big lie, no grand plan, that "the universe is indifferent." In a rare comic moment, one of the beatniks seems deflated by this concept, replying, "Why'd you have to go and say that?" Don turns, and straightens his tie, takes his hat and prepares to leave. Roy reminds him that the police are in the building, ostensibly to settle a domestic dispute, and that Don can't leave with the cops outside. Don gestures with his hat before placing it on his head and flicking the brim, "No, *you* can't go out there …" and with that he leaves, nodding to the officers in the hallway as he makes his exit. Even if Don isn't exactly who he seems to be, he understands that his privileged position affords him a certain casual comfort that sets him apart and insulates him.

That Don Draper moves from season to season without significantly changing his appearance is noteworthy. Virtually all of the other characters shift and adapt to the times, changing their wardrobe, hair, and style. While Don's surroundings change and update (he moves from a stuffy and dated suburban house to a rundown apartment in the Village, and finally ends up in a classic mid-sixties penthouse loft), physically, the character does not change. Don is the constant, he is the American businessman, and his presence is almost iconic. Don is acutely aware of how he's perceived by others—this is what makes him such a good ad man. Don knows how to present himself in a way to put others at ease. He knows that advertising is about telling people what they want to hear, and meeting their needs by telling them that what they are doing or how they are feeling is okay. In the final episode of season three (*Close the Door. Take a Seat*, 3.13) as he is trying to convince Peggy to come with him to the new firm being established by the partners fleeing the Putnam, Powell, & Lowe sale to McCann Erickson, Draper explains both Peggy's value and the braiding of advertising and nostalgia: "Because there are people out there who buy things, people like you and me. And something happened, something terrible, and the way that they saw themselves is gone. And nobody understands that. But you do. And that's very valuable." In this moment, he acknowledges Peggy as his protégée, and may even be acknowledging that Peggy sees things differently from the other creative team members with whom they have worked. Moreover, the conversation articulates something about Don, Peggy, and advertising itself: that the important thing is knowing what people want to hear or feel and then carefully tailoring a message to meet that need. If how Americans "saw themselves is gone" in a way that few but Don and Peggy understand, then their success in advertising is not due merely to manufacturing or feeding false consumer desires. *Mad Men* seems to be suggesting that the illusions ads create are real ways of grappling with a world in flux and identities that are tumbling free of old moorings. The stories Don and Peggy are able to tell for clients and products are most successful when they also tap into these changing identities: drawing on the nostalgia for what one yearns for, personally and politically, or what one may now have the imagination or ironic knowledge to aspire to. Their most compelling work speaks to the deep hopes, desires, and fears of Americans who are redefining themselves in this new post-war, Cold War, civil rights era. Their success in advertising comes as both Don and Peggy don't just listen or understand, but *embody* the limits and possibilities of America in the 1960s. Don's rural poverty, wartime psychic wounds, and reinvention as confident, self-made business genius embody much of what Americans are running from and toward in this decade. Peggy's working-class, white ethnic roots and her stumbling forward through doors just opening to women express the norms and changes happening for so many Americans at this moment. As Don says to Peggy later in *The Strategy* (7.6), "You can't tell people what they want. It has to be what *you* want." Their intuition into what will connect with consumers comes best from their identification and personification of American character and identity itself.

If Don's observation during the Right Guard pitch is true, and some people look warily to the future with fear and trepidation, that fact is brought into sharp focus with the much-heralded arrival of an IBM computer in season seven, episode four, *The Monolith*. Early in the episode we hear both Jim Cutler and Harry Crane describe the new computer that will be installed (taking over the art department lounge) as "the future." Following the death of Bert Cooper, Roger observes that Jim Cutler won't be happy until the firm consists of himself, Harry Crane, and the computer. During *The Monolith*, Don watches as the installation proceeds, and he becomes friendly with the project manager. The manager confides in Don that many who are threatened by the computer see it on a cosmic level. He points out that the computer is capable of storing and managing infinite amounts of information, while human existence is finite; the computer can store the numbers of more stars than a human being might see in a lifetime. Don replies by noting that a man lying on his back looking at the stars isn't thinking about numbers. He understands both the cosmic and immediate real-life implications of a machine that is literally displacing the human beings in the art department by eliminating the lounge and work area, dispersing them to their various offices, and there is a creation of both space and isolation that did not exist before the computer arrived.

Late in the episode, as the installation of the computer continues, Don stops to talk to the project manager again. He is drunk and is being escorted out by Freddy Rumsen, but stops and says cryptically, "I know what you're doing here, I know who you are ... your name ... you go by many names ..." The scene is unsettling because of the sinister overtones, the idea that installing the machine is somehow evil. But Don is not the one most traumatized by the presence of the computer. Michael Ginsberg is troubled by its arrival, installation, and constant use, constant state of operation. He becomes paranoid, imagining that Cutler and Lou Avery are having secret meetings of some sort in the computer room. Ginsberg visits Peggy's apartment fearful that the machine is somehow causing him to become gay; ultimately, after a psychotic break, he mutilates himself by cutting off his own nipple and is last seen being taken out of the office on a gurney (*The Runaways*, 7.6). While no one may seriously imagine that he was predicting the future, this may be the fear of progress and the future that Don Draper imagined in that faraway moment in season one. Given the twenty-first-century context in which viewers watch the show, in which citizens are under surveillance by the government and worry about privacy when identity data is mined for profit, where every interaction can be filmed with cellphone cameras and youthful indiscretions never disappear from the internet, Ginsberg's paranoia about the power and prevalence of technology to take over our lives in even the most personal or intimate aspects may resonate eerily rather than simply be dismissed as insane.

As with the Carnation meeting, there are moments in the show where the shifting nationalistic viewpoint and the standard class, cultural, and regional divisions are blurred and characters only realize that they're treading on unfamiliar or unsafe ground after the fact. Such is the case with a conversation that is ostensibly about patriotism, the military, and the draft. The conversation takes place over dinner with GM execs. For personal reasons, Don is in a position in which he's attempting to find either a deferment or some other method to circumvent the fact that his neighbor and former lover's son has dropped out of school and become eligible for the draft. As the partners look on uncomfortably, Don attempts to feel his way through the conversation in search of a possible deferment for Mitchell (*Favors*, 6.10). As he awkwardly broaches the topic and presents the possibility of the young man being drafted, it's clear that it is not a conversation that anyone at the table wants to be having, a reality that nobody wants to consider. And when Don suggests that there are "things people can do about it ..." the conversation takes a turn for the worse, and sours further as one of the two executives responds that it makes him sick. It's difficult to imagine that the Don Draper from the Belle Jolie meeting, the Carousel pitch, or who corrected professional ineptitude in handling the Menken account, would ever make the mistake that was made at the dinner with the GM executives. This has nothing to do with Don or his confidence but speaks to a much larger issue. Modern-day viewers realize that this shift was occurring on a national scope and not simply in uncomfortable dinner conversations. The vantage point of patriotism in the US had never before confronted a war that divided the nation as Vietnam did. Previous wars impacted our nation and the men who fought them. Roger's reaction to doing business with a Japanese client in *The Chrysanthemum and the Sword* is an example of the lasting damage of World War II. Conversations on the subject of war in the 1960s varied significantly from previous conversations about previous wars, especially if those 1960s conversations were taking place in the latter half of the decade. One such conversation occurs in a party setting, in *A Little Kiss* (5.1), where Stan Rizzo, Stan's cousin, Bert Cooper, and Abe Drexler (Peggy's boyfriend) discuss Vietnam and the threat of communism. Abe, talking to Bert, describes the war as a civil war and explains that there is no huge monolithic threat of communism. Stan interjects, "Bombs are the perfect product, they cost a fortune and you can only use them once." The conversation is a brief aside in the party setting, but one gets the sense of the scope of such conversations, at parties and over awkward dinners, where one could no longer make assumptions about the views of one's companions due to the immense shift in the collective American consciousness of the period.

Progress is inevitable and often the change it begets is real in a very permanent way. It is this permanence and inevitability that necessitates that if we wish for something—a new technology, a different way of doing business, a partnership, merger or innovation, or the influx of wealth that accompanies successful business dealings—we must be prepared to use it or live with it forever. When Roger Sterling comes to Bert Cooper to announce that Putnam, Powell, & Lowe has made an offer to "Put a lot of marmalade on your toast," Bert's response is that he doesn't want to sell out his life's work simply because Roger has had an "increase in overhead" given his recent divorce from his first wife, Mona. With each sale and merger between Sterling Cooper and other firms, each of the partners gains a little more wealth while at the same time becoming a little less unique and a little more like their competitors.

Matthew Weiner, the show's creator, was born in 1965. Like many of the show's viewers (this writer included) he may have vague recollections of the way things were in the US at that time without necessarily remembering specifics. As mentioned earlier, the attraction for many viewers is being able to see, capture, and reimagine some of the details from a time in which they grew up, but may not have been aware of their surroundings or the events as they would if they were adults. We are able to look back from our modern vantage point with our post-millennial sensibility and see places that we know: the ultra-clean, mod designs of Howard Johnsons, the cavernous department stores we visited with our mothers or grandmothers, the coffee shops, and backyards, and even roadside picnics that we experienced but don't fully remember are all pulled into careful focus and lovingly recreated by producers and designers. For these viewers, nostalgia is less of a desire to return to the way things were than it is a desire to see the carefully shaded-in details that we don't quite remember. In a twist of dramatic irony, the show that sparks feelings of nostalgia in its viewers also addresses the concept of nostalgia in its characters. In his pitch for the carousel projector, Don describes the device not as a space ship, but as a time machine that takes us back to places we want to go again (*The Wheel*, 1.13). Like nostalgia, nationalism is a construct, a mechanism that allows us to cope with change. The two concepts are at times intertwined in a sort of irony. In the case of Roger Sterling, moving through multiple iterations of mergers, acquisitions, and reinventions of his father's agency, is an effort to return somehow to the way things were, when they were "good." At the end of season three, upon leaving Sterling Cooper's offices for the last time as they embark on Sterling Cooper Draper & Pryce, Roger asks Don how long it will be before they're in a place like 'this' again. Draper replies, "I never imagined myself working in a place like this." Nationalism is in part the idea that we will be able to face whatever change or adversity befalls us and succeed because of who we are as a nation. Nostalgia is the idea that part of that success is a product of who we were. Weiner recognizes that by examining who we were, combined with our prevailing attitudes at the time in which the show takes place, may actually provide us with answers to who we are now and perhaps offer a roadmap of sorts. In recalling a time when many successful businesses bore the names of the men who created them and in some cases continued to work there, Weiner presents us with what might be learned from nostalgia moving forward. In large part, nationalism is nostalgia: an idea of the way we once were, and for who we are as told through the narrative of that history. For the twenty-first-century viewer seeking to reinvent the landscape once again, to move away from the faceless, corporate environment populated by franchises designed to appear unique, this nostalgia is marked less by a sense of loss than by a framework for progress as we examine, explore, and re-imagine our past.

Weiner's decision to set the show in the 1960s presents viewers with American nationalism that is (over)confident in the wake of victory in World War II and the US emerging as one of two superpower poles in Cold War global politics. The arrogance and power of admen who wine and dine clients at Manhattan's most elegant spots, view women as existing for their visual (and sexual) pleasure in the office, and even challenge or correct their own clients symbolizes the sense of unlimited prosperity, privilege, and possibility of that moment, perhaps the climax of "the American century." However, over the course of the decade that *Mad Men* chronicles, that confidence erodes and American identity is complicated. Postmodernity has offered us an understanding of ourselves as multiple and fragmented identities, no longer the modern autonomous self. Postmodern global and economic realities of the twenty-first century are foreshadowed as our faith in modern, rational politics is shaken. From the Bay of Pigs to the Vietnam War and the movements for civil rights and women's equality, we see the characters of *Mad Men* grappling with a world where the foundational assumptions of American goodness and moral authority are shaken. Don's forced leave of absence from the firm, the failure of his marriages, even the aforementioned desperate conversation in which he tries to find a draft deferment for Mitchell Rosen—all of these demonstrate the demise of that jaunty self-made striding in the world. Don Draper personifies the self-doubting, duplicitous side of US power-wielding that Americans grew increasingly aware of as the Vietnam war dragged on, followed by Watergate and Iran-Contra, the invasion of Iraq on unsupported evidence of weapons of mass destruction, Abu Ghraib, and perpetual secret drone strikes. Conrad Hilton's certainty that America occupied the moral high ground, offering the hope of freedom and democracy to the world, became challenged in our own minds. Both the appeal and the interrogation of American superiority resonate across the decades as we watch the unfolding of the 1960s and feel the echoes of those dilemmas even now.

Over the course of the series, Don Draper's identity and power are challenged. He loses his position of authority at Sterling Cooper, and when he does return, has the humbling experience of reporting to his former protégée Peggy. Those who might formerly have had less voice and access to power, such as Peggy Olson, Joan Holloway, Michael Ginsberg, or Dawn Chambers, gain opportunity and status. Don's loss is not just one of masculine white privilege: it is a loss of bravado that systems of privilege enable. After admitting, as he does to his daughter Sally, that he "told the truth to the wrong people in the wrong place at the wrong time," Don Draper has to reinvent his own identity and sense of self yet again—as did we in the 1960s, and as we are now.

Notes

1   Adam Gopnik, "The Forty Year Itch," *The New Yorker*, April 23, 2012, http://www.newyorker.com/magazine/2012/04/23/the-forty-year-itch (accessed May 9, 2014).

2   Geoff Martin and Erin Steuter's *Pop Culture Goes to War: Enlisting and Resisting Militarism in the War on Terror* (Lanham, MD: Lexington, 2010), p. 37.

3   Terry Anderson, *The Sixties* (Boston: Pearson, 1998).

4   See Loren Goldman's chapter, "The Power Elite and Semi-Sovereign Selfhood in Post-War America," for a much more in-depth discussion of Bert Cooper in particular, and advertising agencies in general in the business environment of the 1960s.

5   Anderson, *The Sixties*, p. 2.

6   Natalie Fuehrer Taylor, in Chapter 8, has a much more intricate analysis of Betty, her desire for a career, and her role in McCann Erickson's quest for Don.

7   See Kate Edenborg's chapter, "Going Groovy or Nostalgic," on the shifting landscape and business practices in advertising during the tumultuous 1960s for more details on how approaches to advertising and consumers reflected this shifts.

8   Jerome Lawrence and Robert Edwin Lee, *Inherit the Wind*, 12th edn, vol. 8 (New York: Random House, 1955), Act II, Scene 2, p. 83.

9   Pete Campbell also characterizes Don in a similar way, as "a very sensitive piece of horseflesh," in season seven's *Waterloo*, as members of the Sterling Cooper team are preparing for the Burger Chef pitch meeting, and Pete is concerned about distracting or disturbing Don before the pitch.

6

Going Groovy or Nostalgic: *Mad Men* and Advertising, Business, and Social Movements

Kate Edenborg

When considering the 1960s, we often think about the conflict between the ideals of consumerism and the ideals of the era's cultural revolutions. We hear stories of those involved in these revolutions, those who countered the nation's established institutions and demanded change. Less often do we hear the stories of those whose daily lives were focused on clients and consumers, who worked in offices for companies that sold products. This chapter explores *Mad Men*'s portrayals of these cultural shifts, the changing nature of the nostalgic "free market" as it mixed with groovy "free love" and other social movements that dominated the 1960s.

Mad Men provides us with an angle into the business world of post-war American industry, through the perspective provided by the Sterling Cooper advertising agency, a fictional Madison Avenue firm jockeying for accounts and in competition with other advertising agencies. Those who were not considered members of the social movements and revolutions of the 1960s were not necessarily uninterested or uninvolved in the changes. Historical narratives often demand an "us-versus-them" approach to create an engaging story. But *Mad Men* engages viewers with an innovative story about a time many of us think we already know everything about. It uses the cultural grasp of nostalgia to focus on the realities of the 1960s. The show weaves in national historic events to provide context for the more intimate portraits it draws of individuals as they engage with the larger cultural shifts around them. This historical grounding gives us something familiar to connect with while we watch a world with which many of us are less familiar: the business world of the decade.

Social movements swirled around corporations and companies. Race, gender, and social issues were discussed, debated, and sometimes dismissed throughout the 1960s. Civil rights, women's liberation, anti-war groups, and the sexual revolution were all independent but intertwined movements. The younger generation took the lead in making social change happen as they moved into adulthood. At the same time, the "kids" were becoming consumers, the youth market. Consumers were changing, and brand-new consumers were identified as business grew domestically and globally. Clients started demanding ways to reach audiences in these new markets. These changes in the social and cultural expectations and audiences ultimately meant a changing approach to advertising.

As journalist Thomas Frank writes in his book, *Conquest of Cool*, most histories of the 1960s youth culture describe it as "a reaction to the stultifying economic and cultural environment of the postwar years."[1] Yet few scholars examine how older generations and the worlds of business and middle-class traditions were themselves changing. The 1960s "was the high watermark of American prosperity and a time of fantastic ferment in managerial thought and corporate practice."[2] But we don't hear that story. Instead we hear about how "business was the monolithic bad guy who had caused America to become a place of puritanical conformity and empty consumerism."[3] Business was the "them" that needed to be countered and changed. While the business world had power and influence, it wasn't moving as one giant monolithic institution. The show highlights the inconsistent and scattered decisions and strategies within the business world.[4] There were many factors that influenced business decisions and strategies, including personal issues.

Mad Men shows how work life and personal life intersected and inter-twined in an era when they were much more segregated than today. The connection between these two worlds is often overlooked in other histories and representations in popular culture. Yes, there is a nostalgic element to what *Mad Men* shows present-day viewers and what the agency presents to 1960s consumers. But this nostalgia is not escapist or regressive; it is "a complex and nuanced form of historical narration that constructs itself as collective and recuperative."[5] If there is romantic nostalgia for the 1960s—the movements, the sit-ins, the sex, drugs and rock 'n' roll—this nostalgia likely excludes the reality of daily work life. Yet business, capitalism, consumerism, and advertising were also changing. This is showcased in the series' first episode, when the agency becomes aware of governmental regulations that will impact the cigarette industry. And this would be just the beginning. The Equal Employment Opportunity Commission, which was created following the Civil Rights legislation of the 1960s, contributed to establishing a number of standards affecting businesses. These changes in product safety, environment and energy use, and worker health and safety were connected to concepts of equality and quality of life.[6] The social movements of the time influenced how offices and industries functioned in these subtle but significant ways.

Although politics is explicitly discussed in a number of episodes of *Mad Men*, especially around the topics of elections and particular presidents, the show helps illuminate the uneasy partnership that occurs between business and politics. This mutually beneficial and dependent relationship between government and business has always been a contentious part of America. As Kim McQuaid explains,

> Big business and the federal government in modern America are like two people who have been living together much longer than either cares to admit. They are not married and they never will be but they maintain a close symbiotic relation because they need each other.[7]

Regulatory changes and shifts in the economy both impact this "symbiotic" relationship. In the 1960s the economy expanded at a faster rate than any time since the 1880s:[8]

> An era of managerial, scientific, and technical innovations; corporate labor and business–government accommodations; cheap energy and other natural resources, international economic expansion by United States firms and economic stabilizers like cold-war military spending and New Deal social insurance programs replaced the anxious years.[9]

For the advertising world and for Sterling Cooper & Partners, this meant logistical challenges brought forth by capital expansion, including trying to deal with problematic phones during conference calls between New York and

Los Angeles offices, and the displacement of the creative team's lounge with a monolithic computer. *Mad Men*, with its focus on workplaces and office lives, gives viewers a more fully realized understanding of the 1960s.

We tend to assume that businesses are "a static, unchanging body of faiths, goals and practices" and that American business culture was merely peripheral to all that was going on in the 1960s.[10] According to Frank, "Virtually nobody has shown much interest in telling the story of the executives or suburbanites who awoke one day to find their authority challenged and paradigms problematized."[11] But *Mad Men* is interested in exploring just these subtle challenges to (and shifts in) authority, and many viewers have found this particular interrogation of shifting power and position quite engaging.

The 1960s is often depicted as a decade when ideas about shared values instantly changed, yet much was in motion before the decade began. "Mainstream culture was tepid, mechanical and uniform" and young people challenged that mainstream culture.[12] But it was not only the young who countered the cultural norms of post-war America: many older Americans agreed with the direction the movements were taking. While there were fissures between young and old, between "the establishment" and the challenges to the status quo, perhaps the gulf between these two groups was not as deep as has been retrospectively assumed. Much of this can be attributed to what Frank calls "hip consumerism." And while businesses saw value in promoting rebellion for business reasons and often co-opted the concept, there was also the "enthusiasm of ordinary, suburban Americans for cultural revolution."[13]

Advertising of the era

As a television show, *Mad Men* is a piece of popular culture that shows an audience how another type of popular culture was created. The series illuminates the complex processes within (and outside of) an ad agency—the interactions among the employees, the impact of national and international events, people's pasts, and, of course, the needs of clients. The history of the times, the assassinations, celebrity deaths, cultural events, and elections are the backdrop for the characters on *Mad Men* and they experience these happenings during the course of seven seasons. But these cultural and political events are background and not the center of the story that *Mad Men* is telling. The series' writers and directors are quite aware of the audience's knowledge of the iconic events of this decade. While to some it might seem the series underplays the 1960s' historic events, it instead provides a unique window into the lives of these ad agency employees (and others).

Madison Avenue advertising agencies, in the early 1960s, were clinging to traditional approaches, structures, and ways of working, in part due to client demands. Yet they needed to create content for a large, young, and flush audience. The consumers themselves were also becoming more diverse. In addition, there were changing activities in the home, and some changes among those who were at home. Companies who made products and services were hesitant to recognize and react to these changes. The ad agency, itself a somewhat new creation, took on the role of "middle man," determining how to address generational shifts as well as the race and gender revolutions, all of which contributed to the change in who the consumer was and what kind of purchasing decisions he or she made.

The idea that American advertising not only mirrors but shapes society is a commonly accepted concept.[14] It provides a nice, clean explanation of how advertising content connects with culture and cultural change. While an advertisement doesn't always convince a consumer to buy a product, we know that a great deal of thought is put into the creation of the advertising content itself. According to Juliann Sivulka, advertisers are cultural mediators who encourage consumption as both a material and cultural process.[15] Often overlooked is the way that ad makers' own lives and experiences are also intertwined in the cultural processes. Sivulka notes that the advertising "process evolved as a business science—some would say art—as marketing applied new theories of economics, sociology and psychology to the complexity of advertising."[16] This recognizes the intricacy of the field, as well as the tendency to want to make it something more quantifiable and predictable.

These shifts in how business was done are revealed in the *Mad Men* offices. Business leaders were still figuring out how to navigate the new corporate order of managerial capitalism that developed in the 1950s.[17] Before World War II, companies were led by a chief executive officer and sub-executives who reported directly and informally to each other and the chief executive.[18] By the 1960s, decentralized management was a better fit. A more diverse range of products and services for wider and wider markets meant the development of more new industries. Many industries expanded into new areas. The leaders of these new, diversified companies, now corporations, had expertise in finance, marketing, or law. The managers worked in offices, not on shop floors.[19]

The fluctuation in the economy, development of new technologies, and shifts of cultural ideals, especially related to what was deemed appropriate for men and women, all shaped how products and services were manufactured, marketed, and advertised. Advertisers needed to interpret the meanings that individuals and groups attach to products and to create markets for them.[20] In the 1950s advertising messages were often based on concepts connected to the ideals of the American dream. By the early 1960s both the civil rights movement and the women's movement were gaining momentum and shifting what the American dream meant. These revolutions also overlapped with the emergence of a significant number of politically engaged young people who would become part of a new and relevant advertising audience. These developments led to "new ways of doing business, a revitalized creative approach, and an emerging social consciousness."[21] None of this happened overnight. And *Mad Men*, through a fictional lens, helps to show the subtle shifts within the United States, in the lives of ordinary citizens, and within business and industry. The series profiles how one ad agency experienced "the creative revolution" in advertising.

The typical and traditional ad agency during this era had a staff that included account executives, researchers, copywriters, art directors, and media buyers. In the late 1950s and early 1960s many agencies leaned heavily on appeals to post-war tranquility and suburban ideals in their ads. At the same time, many agencies started to realize that "fantasy-filled advertising no longer seemed appropriate for a young and more skeptical audience."[22] These old-fashioned appeals were replaced by approaches that emphasized inspiration, intuition, and creativity. 1957 saw the publication of *The Hidden Persuaders*, by Vance Packard, a book about ad firms using psychological methods to sell to their customers. Most major firms were using these approaches by the 1960s. In the early seasons of *Mad Men* the agency looks to expertise in the social sciences, such as Dr. Greta Guttmann's report in the pilot episode, *Smoke Gets in Your Eyes*. She presents the idea that people who smoke have a death wish, and that this angle can be utilized in an ad campaign. Don ignores the report and then flips its logic. (Guttman has a doctorate in psychology.) Another psychologist, Dr. Faye Miller, is featured throughout season four as a strategist for a consumer-research consulting company. She uses focus groups to develop ideas for ad campaigns, mostly for beauty products. The campaign Don develops for the cold cream doesn't draw from the research. He tells Faye, "A new idea is something they don't know yet, so of course it's not going to show up as an option." Still, these approaches acknowledge the resources the agency commonly relied on in deciding pitches and targeting audiences or markets.

Don and Peggy move away from these scientifically-based efforts in later seasons, often with successful results. In the fourth season Don develops the Glo-Coat floor wax advertisement with Peggy. The knowingly nostalgic ad is based in inspiration and intuition. The collaboration and childhoods of these two creatives leads to the ad's approach. Don wins an advertising award for this work (yet ultimately loses the account). In season seven, the initial approach to the Burger Chef pitch was dependent on an old-fashioned and romantic ideal of the nuclear family at the dinner table (*Waterloo*, 7.7). The ad aimed at making mothers feel comfortable with fast food as an option for that dinner table. Peggy developed this approach after talking to hundreds of mothers in station wagons at Burger Chefs across the Midwest. On one level, Peggy has a strong desire to be one of these mothers, even though the families don't seem ideal. All along, Peggy was unsatisfied with this direction for the Burger Chef campaign, and she realizes the concept of family *itself* has changed and adapts the advertising pitch to reflect that shift. The campaign re-defines family and re-imagines the dinner table: friends, strangers, co-workers who meet and connect at this bright, public place, and "break bread" together. She taps into a shifted sense of community that is brought about by the social changes that surround the agency, rather than what consumers say they want.

At the same time, agencies started recruiting new, unconventional employees, sometimes of different ethnicities, or of different generations and perspectives. Don promoted Peggy to copywriter, the agency's first female in that role, during season one. At the beginning of the second season, Don was compelled to hire two younger creatives—Kurt and Smitty. The young copywriter/art director team always worked together. Not only were they part of the youth culture (they were fans of Bob Dylan), but Kurt was openly gay. The talented and ambitious Jewish copywriter Michael Ginsberg was hired by Sterling Cooper Draper Pryce in 1967.

Those that came to the creative team needed to come with inspiration rather than a specific set of educational or business credentials. With each of these recruits there is a sense that the creatives have something both intangible and necessary. For example, in *Close the Door. Take a Seat*, (3.13) when Don comes to Peggy's apartment and explains why he wants to hire her, he notes that it is because she "understands" consumers from a unique perspective. Creative talent became the primary credential that mattered.

This creative revolution in advertising was led by Bill Bernbach of Doyle Dane Bernbach (DDB). His approach was to insert cultural criticism, not marketing methods, into the ads.[23] Bernbach is credited with changing the look, language, and tone of American advertising, starting with Volkswagen, with direct text and simple layout. The print ad included much more "empty space" and focused on the car, not the idea of luxury. Even *Mad Men*'s Don Draper is affected by the ad's approach in the series' third episode (*Marriage of Figaro*, 1.3). Pete appreciates the power of the famous Volkswagen "Lemon" ad, part of a larger ad campaign. It seems to challenge Don's false connection to his "past" and "present" ideals. He examines the ad and comments on how it got everyone in the office talking. But Don doesn't compliment the work; he is publically dismissive of it, saying "I don't know what I hate about it most."

Privately, Don spent time trying to figure out why it worked, and especially why everyone in the industry and in the office was talking about it. He started to realize that effective advertising was becoming more about getting attention than promoting the product itself. Don's advertising mantra, "If you don't like what's being said, change the conversation"—another form of getting attention re-focused—inspired his ad in the *New York Times* after the agency lost Lucky Strike in season four. Don also advocates for this approach to his creative team while reviewing taglines for oven cleaner in the first episode of season six—he lectures his team on wearing out the word "love," saying "We want that electric jolt to the body." He illustrates his point by posing this scenario:

"What's the difference between a husband knocking on a door and a sailor getting off a ship? About 10,000 volts." Don and Peggy often seem to strive for authenticity as a form of creativity in the workplace, even while facing static and constructed realities in the home.

During the 1960s, the ad agency structure became less corporate and less willing to solely follow clients' preferences, no matter how strong they were.[24] *Men Men* highlights these changes in a number of instances, including when Don treats the executives from Jantzen with contempt at the start of season four because they won't follow through with their inclinations towards a more "sexy" approach to selling women's swimsuits, and when he fires Jaguar during season six. Peggy, like Don, is seen battling with corporate executives from Heinz in season five after they dismiss her idea and she defends it, noting that "It's young and it's beautiful, and no one else is going to figure out how to say that about beans" (*Far Away Places*, 5.6). Reflecting the tension between the ad agency creatives and the companies they are working to serve, as well as institutional sexism, Heinz requests that Peggy be dismissed from the baked beans account.

Creatives trump clients

As the decade progressed, ad men (and women) took consumers' assumed skepticism into account and made it part of their advertising approach. In fact, Frank said that the best product pitch was "Buy this to escape consumerism."[25] A field that had been steeped in romantic or idealized messaging needed to be relevant to a different kind of consumer, and that meant not being "your father's ad agency" but being groovy and hip. We see this repeatedly over the course of the seven seasons of *Mad Men*. As Don Draper's creative "genius" ages, Peggy Olson's younger perspective takes center stage, not so much replacing Don's capacities, but creating ads alongside him. Both of them, in the first seven episodes of the final season, are set in contrast to the pedestrian and "square" capacity of Lou Avery, who replaces Don as head of Creative at Sterling Cooper & Partners when Don is put on leave by the partners. In season seven, episode four (*The Monolith*), when the new computer is installed in the creative lounge, Peggy explains that Lou didn't fight for their space since "he doesn't believe in creative because he doesn't know how to do it." Some of the differences are generational (and political) as Lou angrily defends himself at one point, calling the creatives "a bunch of flag-burning snots."

Sterling Cooper struggles with how to figure out what exactly a "groovy" message looks like. The agency's attempts come in fits and starts, a path that was close to the reality for most in the field at that time. Many advertisers and their advertising agencies, though conservative by the nature of their interests, also recognized the need to be responsive to consumers. These consumers were changing dramatically. Larry Dobrow, a writer for *Advertising Age*, explains: "Change in the sixties was different. It was more abrupt. For many it was not easy to handle or understand."[26] Leo Burnett, famously one of the premier ad men of the 1950s, had a style that was "homespun straightforward and familiar."[27] In many ways, this is Don Draper's style at the beginning of the series. In the first scene of the first episode of *Mad Men*, Don is scribbling words on a cocktail napkin, likely drawing from familiar stories and images from his past to incorporate into an ad message. As we move later into the decade, this kind of "old-fashioned" approach to coming up with ad campaigns was not effective, but neither was listening to your clients. Peggy's St. Joseph's aspirin ad in season six (which references to the box-office hit *Rosemary's Baby*) and the Burger Chef new "family" ad in season seven are both examples of how to make traditional products or themes "groovy." The intertextual reference to popular culture in the aspirin ad and the redefinition of family and community via Burger Chef speak to changing times and new consumers. What would audiences and consumers see as being relevant to them? Authenticity and truth. What would clients and companies want? Profits and promotion.

Up to this point, pleasing the client had been the focus for ad agencies. Pete tells Don they lost the Dr. Scholl's account because, according to Pete, they were disappointed with the creative. Don's upset, but he and Roger have the same response: "The day you sign a client is the day you start to lose them" (*Long Weekend*, 1.10) Only Roger is serious about the statement. Don sees it as an offhanded remark, but Roger sees it as the reality. He and

Pete are the liaisons between client and creative, and they have to straddle that divide. Roger, in season four, begs Lucky Strike to reconsider leaving Sterling Cooper in *Christmas Comes But Once a Year* (4.2); Pete, in a number of instances, negotiates with his own father-in-law, who represents Clearasil at Richardson-Vicks. Pete was ordered to end Sterling Cooper Draper Pryce's relationship with the company, but instead he shoots for a bigger goal and says that they want to keep Clearasil if it includes the parent company, Richardson-Vicks (*The Rejected*, 4.4) Neither Pete nor Roger is successful in these battles.

Duck Phillips, who was head of Sterling Cooper account services for a time, explained that "[g]ood creative is important but can't run the show" (*Tomorrowland*, 4.13). Duck has a vested interest in diminishing the value of the creative department at Sterling Cooper, since he is trying to position himself as the head of the agency itself. But while account executives always fear the loss of clients and companies, the creative approaches of copywriters and art directors were increasingly valued, sometimes even at the expense of the client preference. Jane Maas, who worked at Ogilvy & Mather in the 1960s, said, "The product was no longer the holy grail."[28] There was always tension between account work and the creative departments/teams, and many on the account side were reluctant to cede to the rising importance of the creative wings of ad agencies. This tension is seen not only in the clash between Duck Phillips and Don Draper through many of the early episodes, but also throughout season three when Lane Pryce arrives to "manage" Sterling Cooper for Putnam, Powell, & Lowe. As we move into the most recent season, creative has a new adversary, the monolithic computer that Harry Crane and Jim Cutler decide they need, but of which the creative team remains quite skeptical.

The advertising industry's reaction to youth culture was complex and went beyond just co-opting messages.[29] In some cases advertisers saw these new values as consistent with the ways they'd started to or wanted to manage their businesses. According to Frank, "hip became central to the way American capitalism understood itself and explained itself to the public."[30] In fact, in one episode, Pete Campbell talks about an opportunity where he'll be interviewed about "hip ad agencies." This was for an actual 1966 *New York Times* article,

"Advertising is: A Science? An Art? A Business?" by Victor S. Navasky (*Dark Shadows*, 5.9)

Social movement messages seem to be created to appeal to a youth market yet, as Frank states, images of youth were not appropriate for the youth market. "These consumers already knew they were young. Youthfulness was best used as an appeal to older consumers."[31] Many of the *Mad Men* characters seem to understand this, especially, ironically, the oldest member of the agency, Bert Cooper. While Cooper follows the newest trends in design and art, is taken with the space race, and recommends that others read the contemporary fiction like Ayn Rand, he tends not to be particularly romantic about either the past or the future. He sees them as useful to the business he is in—advertising.

Effective 1960s advertising messages hinted or suggested non-conformity and a number of the campaigns developed at Sterling Cooper reflect these hints. According to Frank, the ads often avoided the traditional use of a spokesman, and turned to unexpected persuaders to make the pitch in the advertisements.[32] The Sterling Cooper creative team is seen pursuing this avenue of approach as they brainstorm Sno Ball cake treats taglines with "Hit me in the face with a Sno Ball" or "Yes, even me," showing a devil eating a Sno Ball (*Dark Shadows*, 5.9), or when Ginsberg successfully pitches Butler footwear on the Cinderella concept (*Mystery Date*, 5.4).

Subtle revolutions

While the social revolutions of the 1960s were significant, we see subtle shifts in the Sterling Cooper office. Not surprisingly, business interests drove substantial changes in advertising agencies, and this is reflected in the various incarnations of Sterling Cooper over the course of five seasons: the company faced a buyout, was broken up, went independent, merged with another company, and was then on the brink of being enveloped by another conglomerate. Profitability and survival often subsumed any potential changes related to race or gender that an ad agency might make. At the same time, we have seen throughout the multiple seasons the casual racism and sexism that dominated corporate offices during this era. In retrospect we know that certain things were changing when it came to gender and race, but the impact of these larger changes often lagged in reality.[33]

The agency itself often tended to stumble when it came to race. Sterling Cooper is compelled to hire an African-American secretary in season five after an incident with a competing ad agency. Often the consumer interests were of overriding concern, such as when Pete wanted to market Admiral television sets to African Americans, but the Admiral executives refused this campaign outright, even when Pete had evidence to support his proposal (*The Fog*, 3.5). Peggy tries to inject race consciousness into her pitch for the Goodyear Tire account with her suggestion to feature Harry Belafonte in the ad. This, too, is immediately rejected (4.9). According to Maurice Isserman, black Americans at the start of the 1960s realized that even those who supported them wouldn't put forth the effort unless the movement had a big enough impact.[34] In the case of an ad agency, the impact needed to be financial. Each of the agency's efforts are more motivated by the bottom line than a commitment to civil rights.

Although many agencies during this era employed women, most did not allow them to serve in management positions or have much responsibility within the office. This was acceptable to most women in those positions. According to Gail Collins, "for those [women] who did venture into the public world, the mere fact of being allowed to take part was so exciting that the details scarcely mattered."[35] Peggy Olson's career path is quite realistic to women like Jane Maas, who came into advertising in the 1960s. Peggy started out as a secretary who was asked to join an office-based focus group on the Belle Jolie lipstick account. Her comments, not during the focus group but as the area was being cleaned up, sparked interest among the male account and creative team members, who see her capacity to come up with and write some copy for female-oriented products. After Don hears how Peggy called a trashcan full of blotted tissues a "basket of kisses," she is asked to come up with some copy for the campaign. Subsequently Don gives her more assignments on a variety of campaigns, and, over the course of the entire series, he cultivates her creative capacity and ultimately works alongside her. Her career developed because she was interested in the work, she worked diligently and successfully, and often, though not always, found Don to be a supportive mentor. Other women, most specifically office manager (and eventual partner) Joan Harris, also have substantive responsibilities. Joan was given interesting and appealing work to do in reading scripts for potential advertisement conflict, but that work was quickly taken back from her by Harry Crane, who hires an untrained and inexperienced man to take over this task, highlighting the overarching disrespect directed towards many women in the workplace in the early 1960s. While the external historical shifts seemed to happen quickly, the progress in the reality of life in an office was much more plodding.

Sexism, feminism, and static advertising campaigns

Advertising changed little with regard to what modern audiences would see as sexist ad content until the end of the 1960s. Ad content tended to promote stereotypes of femininity without regard for female tastes, and in many ways conformed to and reinforced the lived reality of many middle-class women in the United States. According to Maas, "For most of my career I was writing advertising for brands that sold to women, brands that were generally meant to clean your house or feed your family." Mass explains further that "[i]n the world of the sixties there was only one person doing the cleaning and the cooking. It was SHE."[36]

There are myriad examples throughout all seven seasons of *Mad Men* of this kind of pitching of home-based products for the "housewife," from Betty Draper's unknowingly falling prey to the advertising for Heineken in season two (*A Night to Remember*, 2.8), to the grocery store stunt that Peggy and Pete come up with to try to save the Sugarberry Ham account in season four (*Public Relations*, 4.1), to the complicated process to determine the right pitch for the overworked housewife who wants to take her family to Burger Chef without feeling guilty in season seven (*The Strategy*, 7.6). Frank explains that much of the advertising in the 1960s was just as it is portrayed on *Mad Men*—bifurcated by gender and the kinds of products that each gender sought out and purchased (groceries vs. cars; face creams and cosmetics vs. bank accounts;

fast food for the family vs. airlines and hotels). "Sexism was one arena in which advertising made virtually no advances until the end of the decade."[37] Agencies relied on stereotypes of femininity without regard for female tastes.

The reality was that everything Americans had taken for granted about women's roles was called into question. Initially, advertisers and companies saw housewives as sources of profit for household goods.[38] Throughout the 1960s more women became working women. The changing economy put a higher value on women's skills, work conditions improved, and the birth control pill gave women confidence to take on a career.[39] The number of married women in the workforce continued to increase too. Now these working women were getting incentives to work *and* spend. Products changed to address the needs of this new consumer, but the advertising didn't necessarily shift quickly to reflect the changes.

Towards the end of the 1960s, some agencies started to use the women's movement message as key components of their ad campaigns. Frank notes that

> Feminism, as it was understood by the industry in the late sixties and early seventies, was an almost perfect product pitch, and toward the end of the decade the ads of a great number of products specifically marketed to women took on overtly liberationist themes, even when the product had clearly been developed according to less liberated notions of femininity.[40]

Even these ads tended to continue to address women in "idealized roles" rather than real-life situations.[41] Peggy questions the Patio Cola ad pitch (which riffs on Ann-Margret in *Bye Bye Birdie*) and the Playtex campaign (Are you a Marilyn or a Jackie?) because she notes that women don't situate themselves in these contexts and that trying to sell them items based on these idealized male fantasies is not a useful approach (*Love Among the Ruins*, 3.2; *Maidenform*, 2.6). Neither campaign is ultimately successful in the eyes of the client. One can see the shift in notions through the thought process Peggy has for the trajectory of the Burger Chef ad in episode four of season seven. She starts out with the traditional notions of femininity, especially women's role in the home as mother. She questions it, even though others (especially the men) in the office compliment her on the pitch. She reworks the ad, providing more of a focus on new versions of family that were more reflective of the growing reality in homes across America, comprising working women, single women, and single men, living on their own, the ever-present television set at the dinner table, and the civil unrest that was nightly projected into so many homes. Advertisers were trying to satisfy their clients (the product makers) while not necessarily paying as much attention as they should have to the actual consumer in many ways. While consumers would like to be idealized, their lived realities were fairly disassociated from the fantasy. As Peggy becomes more powerful within the agency, her voice is somewhat more respected and her perspective receives more attention. That said, the consumer herself is changing as well, and sometimes the shifts in approaches were based on their suggestions to bulk up the bottom line.

Early in the 1960s most women "grew up without ever seeing a woman doctor, lawyer, police officer or bus driver,"[42] and women were discouraged from seeking jobs men might have wanted. Yet, according to Collins, as the era started, most women wouldn't have seen themselves as being poorly treated. Inequalities went unnoticed because the economy was booming and the standard of living was generally at an unprecedented high.[43] Women compared their opportunities and achievements to those of other women, not to men. This started to change at Sterling Cooper as well. Initially, Peggy looked toward Joan for guidance on her career path, but by the final season Peggy was comparing and competing with other men, including her (former) boss, Don.

Many of the movements, especially the women's movement, owed their success to the civil rights groups. Their battles had revealed inequalities and Americans grew sensitive to questions of fairness. This opened up the way for other discriminated-against groups to demand their rights, among them women. The younger generations were more skeptical about their societal roles and especially noticed gender inequality.[44] Early leaders of what became known as second-wave feminism included Betty Friedan, who founded the National Organization of Women (NOW) to develop negotiating power in government. While NOW achieved legal and political victories, younger feminists were winning popular culture victories.[45] The office/work environment reflected the fissures within the feminist movement as this is integrated into the narrative on *Mad Men*. At the start of the series, Joan's position was coveted in that she was a leader and manager of many of the women in the office. As she expands her role, even becoming a partner, other women, Peggy included, no longer want to be Joan—they want more substantive positions, but so does Joan. Joan wants to be an "account man" but expresses fear of being "knocked off the diving board" (*A Tale of Two Cities*, 6.10).

Just as advertising tried to capitalize on the themes of the women's movement, ad campaigns also attempted to integrate aspects of youth culture. In season six, as mentioned earlier, Peggy's approach to the St. Joseph's aspirin advertisement is inspired by a popular horror film, *Rosemary's Baby*. In season five's episode *Lady Lazarus*, Ginsberg pitches a "Hard Day's Night" concept to executives from Chevalier Blanc, and the clients request music that sounds like The Beatles. The idealism of Camelot and the Kennedys, along with the freedom associated with rock'n'roll, all became ad campaign themes during the mid to later 1960s.

American historian Roxanne Dunbar-Ortiz notes in Ben Agger's book *The Sixties at 40* that this youthful energy had to do something. "Participatory democracy came about to address the alienation young people felt about their self determination as human beings." Dunbar-Ortiz indicates this was the main pillar that the civil rights movement and later movements built on.[46] *Mad Men*, in setting the work environment in a fictional Madison Avenue firm, is able to delve into many of these subtle trends and shifts as the characters work on ideas, use focus groups, create copy and advertisements for a diverse array of products, and try to figure out how consumers think and how best to appeal to these simultaneously rational and irrational individuals.

The revolution will be televised

Even as the historical events of the 1960s were upending American society in many ways, there was another, somewhat secondary, revolution going on: the expansion of television as the primary medium through which Americans experienced news, entertainment, and advertising. Television advertising was becoming increasingly relevant, given its reach, and clients began to request television ads as part of their media plan. Even so, many ad agencies did not consider television advertising nearly as instrumental as the more traditional forms of advertising (such as print, radio, billboards, etc.).

Ad agencies usually had few employees working with television advertisements, and Sterling Cooper was no exception: Harry Crane, often with a nameless assistant, leads the television accounts and is constantly clamoring for more compensation and at least a little respect from his colleagues. Yet Harry is seen as vital to Sterling Cooper's success, since the partners invite him to join the clandestine departure from Putnam, Powell, & Lowe at the end of season three in *Shut the Door. Have a Seat* (3.13) and give him the responsibility for "media" at the new Sterling Cooper Draper Pryce agency. At the same time, Harry is not the most ingratiating individual, and this, combined with the still somewhat suspect approach to television among the "old guard" at SCDP, often puts Harry at odds with many of his colleagues.

As television itself becomes more vital, the media offices at many ad agencies grew in importance and respect. Sterling Cooper and Partners decided they needed a West Coast office in part to work alongside the entertainment business in Hollywood, and Harry Crane makes a convincing case to Jim Cutler in season seven for the need to purchase a substantial computer so as to better access the media markets throughout the United States. This decision is in part due to a *New York Times* article about a competing agency's computer and in part because Harry has been lying to clients about having one. Harry says that the firm's computer will soon be able to "integrate local and national markets into one report." This also highlights the push and pull between clients' demands and the "expert opinions" of those in the advertising world. None of them knows why they need a computer.

Such mistakes also happened within television as advertising agencies like Sterling Cooper started to shift their media emphasis, sometimes without client buy-in. In season four's episode *The Chrysanthemum and the Sword*, Don suggests shooting a splashy (fake) television commercial to mislead a competing ad agency. However, the client, Honda, had set rules for the cost of the development of the ad pitches and creating a television advertisement would exceed the budget. This also highlights the expense of television, along with the fact that the agencies and the clients were still not sold on the usefulness of television advertising. Color television came to dominate electronic media in the 1960s and had an impact on post-war popular culture and political processes. Computers were a tiny part of this, only being used for data processing. These technologies were adapted to broader social purposes that could mobilize audiences as such, or as consumers.

A revolution in advertising

In the midst of the myriad social, political, cultural, and technological revolutions throughout the 1960s, the advertising industry was immersed in its own subtle revolution, a revolution in marketing practice, management thinking, and ideas about creativity.[47] By the mid-1960s this meant, among other changes, employing methods of "market segmentation." Advertisers started realizing that there were diverse consumer needs and many audiences for both their products and their advertisements. Sterling Cooper hired a consumer research company to help implement this approach in season four's *Christmas Comes But Once a Year*. Agencies, in a bid to figure out hidden desires, started to try to identify products that consumers didn't even know they wanted.[48] Early in season six Sterling Cooper and Partners is hoping to get the Koss headphone account. The first stereo headphones were invented in 1958, so this was still quite a new product. Headphones were not something consumers thought they needed until the mid-1960s: as at-home use of turntables and radios increased, so did the use of headphones.

Products with potential

The potential clients and types of products mentioned in *Mad Men* offices varied slightly throughout the first seasons, but there were some particular themes. Most of the products or items highlighted were not directly related to the social movements that were transpiring throughout the United States. Early on the agency made a pitch to work on Richard Nixon's 1960 campaign. In a venial nod to social consciousness, Don Draper wrote and published his letter regarding Lucky Strike, and his willingness to collaborate with the American Cancer Society. Most of the items advertised throughout *Mad*

Men's multiple seasons generally fall into three categories: female-/family-oriented household products and services; major industries such as aerospace, automotive, and travel; and vice/leisure.

At the start of the series most of the products advertised were the household products, such as beauty items (Belle Jolie and Clearasil) or family items (Kodak Carousel and Maytag). Yet industries such as banking and tourism were increasingly present, and Lucky Strike cigarettes played a prominent role over multiple seasons. Season two included significant family-focused ads, and the agency came to realize the importance of aerospace and airlines (Mohawk). In the third season, the ad creation turned to service industries (Hilton Hotels and Western Union) and the promotion of iconic places (Madison Square Garden and Penn Station). During this same season, the staff struggled with campaigns for some household items, including Patio Cola and Admiral Television. It was during this period that Sterling Cooper became more aware of the increasing diversity of its advertising audience. Family products became, once again, more prevalent in season four, but the agency was trying to attract entire industries instead of discrete products: for example, seeking out the entire line of Vicks' Chemical products instead of just Clearasil.

During the next two seasons fewer ads were discussed during the course of the show, but a few dominated the conversations, especially auto companies: in season five it was Jaguar; in season six, Chevrolet. During this period, a key question dominated the discussion at most companies and ad agencies, including Sterling Cooper, namely, should products be promoted as *groovy* or *nostalgic*? While the discussion of the pitches centers on whether the ad approach should be one of these or the other, it is clear that this tension is present throughout the entire series, reflecting the same tensions in the cultural struggles throughout the entire era. As the nation moved into the 1970s, the creative revolution in advertising began to falter, and *Mad Men* signals some of this with the arrival of the computer and the inclination among some of the partners to rely more on market research than on creativity.

Popular culture contested

As Frank suggests, the "sixties are more than merely the homeland of hip, they are a commercial template for our times, a historical prototype for the construction of cultural machines that transform alienation and despair into consent."[49] This is what makes a television show about the advertising world in the 1960s so powerful, especially a show that presents stories of the people who were not particularly hip or especially groovy, yet many of whom embraced social changes as they encountered them. Advertising was not fomenting the revolutions: according to Maas, "[m]ost successful advertising mirrors society; it doesn't lead the way."[50] So a television show about this industry in a time of tumult has a fascinating challenge. The characters are all surrounded by change and conflicting cultural and political messages; they are leading lives where their goals are in some flux, given the shifting social mores and expectations. And some of the characters are, themselves, creations out of whole cloth, experiencing all of these shifts as they maintain their own duality, or hide secrets that are at odds with whom they present themselves to be "in public." This sometimes makes it more difficult to figure out how to sell a product, though at other times it may prove to be an asset.

Because *Mad Men* is about advertising—a form of popular culture established and expanded in the 1960s—it can reveal some of the role that popular culture had in social change in that time.[51] The audience of the television show also learns a great deal about how advertising connected with the "dynamics of contemporary social life" in the 1960s.[52] Viewers have a perspective on how popular culture contributes to a generation's social cohesion and individual identity.[53] *Mad Men* also provides a forum for a broader understanding of these cultural revolutions and insights into how individuals may have navigated these changes. Class, race, gender, and anti-war/peace issues were clustered together as components of the social and cultural revolutions of the 1960s. As Agger describes, these were "twisted into strands that overlapped and formed a tapestry of difference within unity."[54] *Mad Men* explores this complexity over the course of seven seasons, following how the characters' lives intersect while also being impacted by the social and cultural shifts. The same could be said for the trajectory of the advertising industry and corporate world.

Media scholar Alex Bevan makes a distinction between *restorative* nostalgia that seeks to return to earlier times and *reflective* nostalgia that "suggests a flexibility and mediation regarding history, the present, and the passage of time rather than the recovery of a perceived truth."[55] *Mad Men* engages contemporary viewers in the latter, inviting us to reconsider what the 1960s mean, to us and to our politics. In the twenty-first century we have very different work and home boundaries, constant interpersonal communication, dual incomes, alongside significant shifts in home and work life. Yet *Mad Men* offers us a groovy lens through which to interpret the changes and challenges we face in this digital, global, postmodern era, and to interrogate our relationship to the values and experiences of our past.

While we aren't experiencing social movements as they were expressed in the 1960s we are experiencing some of the same intense personal and political undercurrents that leave us feeling uncertain and insecure. Sometimes reflecting on our nation's history gives us bearings to help us understand the uncertainties of the present. It informs how we might choose to navigate the future. *Mad Men* brings to light the "historical situatedness" of key concepts in our lives, such as "nation," "family," and "media." Yet it also reveals the points of fissure in the "collectively" shared narrative.[56] In the 1960s the nation went from a "heady feeling of living in a world malleable to their grasp" to facing war in Vietnam, domestic unrest, and social upheaval.[57] It seemed that the nation's leadership needed to choose between creating a Great Society and maintaining an orderly one. Changes in the business world were often overlooked due to what scholar Todd Gitlin calls a "new velocity of experience, a new vertigo"[58] that characterized the 1960s. According to Michael Pickering, when a nation experiences an "acceleration of social and cultural change" it will tend to select what to remember, and thus nostalgia becomes the lens through which memories are saved or discarded.[59]

Because "the relationship between the past and present is fragile and corruptible"[60] we need to take care when evaluating the meaning and authenticity of what we know about an era. As Agger explains, "people living in turbulent times fail to understand the convergence of their personal histories with history itself."[61] Those born after the 1960s have grown up surrounded by often polarizing messages about this decade. Yet these messages have not provided a depth of understanding; they are often seen in caricature.[62] Those polarizing messages remain with us in the present. This is part of the draw of a show like *Mad Men*, which situates its narrative in the recent past but which reflects to the viewer many of the same fissures that dominate contemporary political culture. The shifting terrain of advertising provided the writers and creators of *Mad Men* with a canvas on which to knit together the past and the present. The creative, scientific, social, and technological changes of the 1960s advertising industry prefigure and reflect our dilemmas in negotiating individual freedoms and identity in the face of changing norms and opportunities. As *Mad Men* chooses to focus on the quotidian, the everyday lives and work of Americans (elite though this Madison Avenue swath may be) rather than extraordinary historical figures and events of the time period, it presents an opportunity to notice the complex ways in which individuals and institutions interact, and how social and political change occurs in myriad ways from multiple access points. As these "Mad Men" and women negotiate new, groovy possibilities and their own nostalgic yearnings, they offer us the imaginative space to consider our own relationship to the past, and to the political possibilities of the future.

Notes

1   Thomas Frank, *The Conquest of Cool: Business Culture, Counterculture and the Rise of Hip Consumerism* (Chicago: University of Chicago Press, 1997), p. 6.

2   Ibid.

3   Of course, anyone who watches *Mad Men* would snicker at a reference of puritan notions in relation to the show.

4   Fellow authors Loren Goldman and Lawrence Heyman also explore aspects of this topic in their respective chapters within this book.

5   Alex Bevan, "Nostalgia for pre-digital media in *Mad Men*," *Television and New Media*, 14.6 (2012), p. 546.

6   Kim McQuaid, *Uneasy Partners: Big Business in American Politics 1945–1990* (Baltimore and London: Johns Hopkins University Press, 1994), p. 135.

7   Ibid., p. xi.

8   Ibid., p. 104.

9   Ibid., p. 105.

10   Frank, *Conquest of Cool*, p. 6.

11   Ibid.

12   Ibid.

13   Ibid., p. 13.

14   Juliann Sivulka, *Soap, Sex, and Cigarettes: A Cultural History of American Advertising* (Belmont, CA: Wadsworth, 2012), p. xiii.

15   Ibid.

16   Ibid.

17   See, in particular, Loren Goldman's chapter on the power elite for a rich assessment of the corporate order and who actually held power within the post-war economic landscape in the United States.

18   McQuaid, *Uneasy Partners*, p. 91.

19   Ibid., p. 92.

20   Sivulka, *Soap, Sex, and Cigarettes*, p. xiv.

21   Ibid., p. 246.

22   Ibid., p. 256

23   Frank, *Conquest of Cool*, p. 58

24   Ibid, p. 60.

25   Ibid, p. 69.

26   Larry Dobrow, *When Advertising Tried Harder. The Sixties: The Golden Age of American Advertising* (New York: Friendly Press, 1984), p. 9.

27   Ibid., p. 3.

28   Jane Maas, *Mad Women: The Other Side of Life on Madison Avenue in the 60s and Beyond* (New York: Thomas Dunne, 2012), p. 136.

29   Frank, *Conquest of Cool*, p. 27.

30   Ibid., p. 26.

31   Ibid., p. 121.

32   Ibid., pp. 141–3.

33   Please see chapters by Laurie Naranch, Natalie Fuehrer Taylor, Denise Witzig, and Linda Beail for more in-depth exploration and analysis of *Mad Men* and the issues of sexuality, feminism, masculinity, and race.

34   Maurice Isserman, *America Divided: The Civil War of the 1960s* (New York: Oxford University Press, 2000), p. 45.

35   Gail Collins, *When Everything Changed: The Amazing Journey of American Women from 1960 to the Present* (New York: Little Brown & Co., 2009), p. 25.

36 Maas, *Mad Women*, p. 157.

37 Frank, *Conquest of Cool*, p. 152.

38 Collins, *When Everything Changed*, p. 95.

39 Ibid., p. 102.

40 Frank, *Conquest of Cool*, p. 153.

41 Sivulka, *Soap, Sex, and Cigarettes*, p. 274.

42 Collins, *When Everything Changed*, p. 11.

43 Ibid., p. 25.

44 Ibid., p. 105.

45 Ibid., p. 194.

46 Ben Agger, *The Sixties at 40: Leaders and Activists Remember and Look Forward* (Boulder, CO: Paradigm Publishers, 2009), p. 81.

47 Frank, *Conquest of Cool*, p. 20.

48 Sivulka, *Soap, Sex, and Cigarettes*, p. 218.

49 Frank, *Conquest of Cool*, p. 235.

50 Mass, *Mad Women*, p. 157.

51 Dustin Kidd, "Harry Potter and the functions of popular culture," *Journal of Popular Culture*, 40 (2007), p. 81.

52 Ibid.

53 Ibid., p. 87.

54 Agger, *The Sixties at 40*, p. 207.

55 Bevan, "Nostalgia for Pre-Digital Media," p. 548.

56 Ibid., p. 557.

57 Isserman, *America Divided*, p. 124.

58 Todd Gitlin, *The Whole World is Watching: Mass Media in the Making and Unmaking of the New Left* (Berkeley: University of California Press, 1980), p. 233.

59 Michael Pickering and Emily Keightley, "The modalities of nostalgia," *Current Sociology*, 54.6 (2006), p. 922.

60 Ibid., p. 938.

61 Agger, *The Sixties at 40*, p. 1.

62 Isserman, *America Divided*, p. 297.

Part Three

Those Seen and Not Seen, Heard and Not Heard

Masculinity and its Discontents: Myth, Memory, and the Future on *Mad Men*

Denise Witzig

History and memory

As *Mad Men* and its seductive world moves from television screen to cultural memory, viewers are invited once again to interpret the AMC series as a commentary on the sixties and on a history of sexual politics that has led inexorably to the reconfiguration of gender norms for women and men. A common critical perspective is that the show bears witness to the birth of feminism and the death of masculinity in the twentieth century, at least traditional masculinity in all of its familiar hegemonic swagger. This perspective is, of course, refracted through the lens that is focused squarely on the mad man himself, Don Draper, and it is amplified through a larger narrative that interrogates the properties of time and cultural memory for the character as well as the viewer. In many ways, the show encapsulates what Daniel Halevy calls the "acceleration of history," a term, according to Pierre Nora, that refers to "the most continuous or permanent feature of the modern world [being] no longer continuity or permanence but change."[1] *Mad Men* fixes our gaze on the past and its impermanence in a way that both objectifies its power and makes it comprehendible. In this way, the viewer is encouraged to understand historical change through cultural memories activated by narrative and characterization, but also by strong visual identifications that are informed by the viewer's own desire for recognition and for meaning, a longing to know the "swiftly retreating past."[2]

In the character of Don Draper, the past is embodied in complex ways and calls upon numerous interpretive strategies addressing the role of history and popular culture in constructing masculinity, the influence of memory in the expression of individual consciousness, identity and stability, and the powers of visual representation to evoke unconscious negotiations and identifications on the part of the viewer. The story about masculinity in the twentieth century that *Mad Men* offers is one that is deeply informed by a historical unconscious that recognizes masculinity, and gender, as problematic, conflicted and divided. This fragmented identity is in itself an aspect of a collective or cultural memory produced primarily by image culture and popular representations of the hegemonic male and that figure's power. Ultimately, this is a perspective crucially informed by feminism and a feminist critical perspective.

Memory and its effect

This reading of *Mad Men* depends a great deal on interpretations rendered less through the specifics of history than through a series of cultural memories largely dependent on popular culture, its images, idioms, and totems that configure gender and its rituals. Memory—or the apprehension of memory, how we understand its shaping influence—is crucial to our experience of *Mad Men* and its interpretation of the twentieth century. This is perhaps nowhere more evident than in the consistent popular calls for the show to represent more, increasingly more, of the sixties. Where is the Civil Rights Movement? Vietnam? Shouldn't the female characters be reading, debating Friedan? Even the Manson family and its counterculture threat lurks in the shadows, as blogs about the show so frequently remind us. And the linking of big and slow-moving mechanisms of history is frequently read and assessed through the vicissitudes of fashion: Peggy's wearing a pantsuit—only a matter of time before a woman has the corner office. Megan's miniskirts remind us of the liberations of the sexual revolution. Don, clad in gray flannel among the polyester flares of younger co-workers, clean-shaven in a sea of sideburns, seems to us trapped on the page of the Arrow shirt ad, iconic of an outdated manhood. In fact, each character on *Mad Men* represents a recognizable past filtered through a projected future, one framed within the interpretive visual field of image culture. This is how history looks on *Mad Men*. Though we know the future to be complex and messy, we want the past to be imaginable. We want to see it and we want it to reflect our own fantasies about and desires for change and transformation.[3]

In Virginia Postrel's book on the machine of image culture in the twentieth century, *The Power of Glamour: Longing and the Art of Visual Persuasion*, she defines glamour as a rhetoric that focuses and objectifies unarticulated desires for "escape and transformation, grace and mystery."[4] She writes that glamour engages "displaced meanings" that resonate from complex and inchoate cultural interactions and beliefs, quoting cultural anthropologist Grant McCracken that, in order to preserve and transmit ideas about identity and values, cultures create common myths, rituals, and spectacles to portray them. "Glamour," says Postrel, "represents a way through which individuals access *personal* versions of displaced meaning … Like rituals and myths, glamour, too, makes the ideal seem available and real."[5] Glamour paradoxically encompasses the attributes of being both "timeless" and "modern."[6] In this reading, glamour's interaction with myth and spectacle, its virtue of being at once timeless and modern, explains some of the popular appeal of *Mad Men* and its relationship to viewer desire, particularly in its visualization of the ineffable nature of time and its connections to cultural transformation. We employ the rhetoric of glamour to interpret the look of history on *Mad Men*, as we use its discourse to understand gender and its appearances in the politics of social change. From this critical perspective, *Mad Men* is not so much a show about feminism or the deceased American Male as it is about the audience's desire for seeing and comprehending those identifications as historical prototypes and markers of contemporary conventional gender relations.[7] As such, within the rituals and mysteries of glamour, they represent a kind of nostalgia, like Don's Kodak Carousel pitch, representing images depicting a past that is lost but has meant something important about the viewer and his or her world. This is who we were, the collected images suggest in deference to the impulse to know who we *are*.

At the same time that the interpretations of gender history on *Mad Men* conform to a rhetoric or discourse of glamour, the nostalgia evoked in that dynamic participates in what Freud might call melancholia or what the art historian Michael Ann Holly refers to as the "unsettling" of the past. Holly acknowledges the absence, loss, and mourning that the contemplation of history provokes, particularly in the aesthetic realm so redolent of inchoate emotions and desires.[8] Historian Joan Scott locates a similar experience of melancholy in thinking about history, particularly feminist history, noting its quality as a "veil that hides the future,"[9] and she goes on to assert the difficulty of locating concretely the utopian cultural transformation that such a politics of gender proposes. The dynamic of melancholia, a process engaging loss or absence, is conveyed through these theories as a contemporary experience of time, memory, history and gender and it is a quality at the heart of *Mad Men*, its narrative and characterization. In a reciprocal relationship with the project of glamour that aspires to a personal and subjective future, the pull of melancholia that contemplates and mourns an objective past, a shared history, is key to our understanding of Don Draper and the representation of masculinity on the show.

Memory and myth

Mad Men has much to say about cultural masculinity, its relationship to memory, and to the past and future. The viewer's interpretation of Don Draper as troubled and *endangered* corresponds to the defining qualities of memory on various interrelated levels: through characterization, the narrative itself, and viewer recognition. Memory is crucial to the character of Don, presenting a backstory that serves as narrative exposition for the viewer. It also signifies the experiential growth and development of the character, as it evokes Don's rich psychological complexity and self-awareness. This is key to viewer identification with a character who is a liar, adulterer, and war deserter, and who is nevertheless emotionally and narratively compelling and sympathetic. If not exactly heroic, Don is recognizably "modern"—unquestionably divided, ambivalent, and vulnerable, as he is self-aware and driven in service to his own happiness and desire for wholeness, although it is not always clear if that is achievable. And his modernity is dramatically conveyed through the engagement of memory on multiple levels—through the forward and reverse narratives of the show, the character's consciousness of those narratives as a story of his own psychology, and the viewer's identification with and recognition of the relationship between the narratives and the character as a story about identity and, with it, a critique of historical masculinity.

If the narratives of femininity on *Mad Men* depict an ascendant or aspirational story that appear to foreground a coming feminist revolution, the story of masculinity on the show conveys crisis, loss, and an ambiguous future. The crisis is, crucially, Don's own, as the larger narrative has revealed to greater degree season after season. But crisis is also thematically representative of a historical moment of transition in the plot of hegemonic masculinity, as middle-class, white, heterosexual males become aware of the shifting grounds beneath their well-shod feet and compete just to stay upright. This transition—social, political, economic, sexual, racial—is explicitly gendered in the show, as mad men and mad women come to terms with their desires and personal dramas. And it is also gendered in the viewer's cultural memory as, in watching the sexual politics of boardroom and bedroom, we recognize "how it was" for women and for men in those days. In this, we participate in a myth of masculinity, in Roland Barthes' sense of myth as an organizing principle of collective memory. We are called into an identification with the recognizable Past that myth produces, a story of gender that is historicized as politically and socially developmental and progressive.[10] The so-called death of the hegemonic male, perhaps a foreshadowing of the "end of men" frequently declared and debated in the twenty-first century, is one of the myths at work in *Mad Men*.[11] Our understanding that Don will have to change as a man in the 1960s, to embrace an alternative masculinity, is an interpretive response to our historical memory about gender.[12] Our story of masculinity is Don's story as well, although the viewer undoubtedly has the benefit of knowing what comes next. And the organizing influence of memory that is so critical to the larger interpretive narrative is further reinforced by a cultural discourse about masculinity and modernity, as noted above. We know who Don Draper is because we have seen him before, but not for a while. And, in a way, we have missed him.

Memories of masculinity

A 2010 article on the actor Jon Hamm in *Details Magazine*, subtitled "The Last Alpha Male," by Adam Sachs, offered this perspective on Don Draper and his fans:

> What does it say about masculinity today that we've exalted such an openly divided character—the fraud who values authenticity, Cicero's ideal Orator selling Glo-Coat floor wax and reading Frank O'Hara's poetry at night, the great charmer who can't make anyone happy for long, including and especially himself?[13]

The question answers itself, of course, through its appeal to nostalgia; even the piece's title evokes a kind of lament for an endangered species. Elsewhere, the character is referred to as "a style icon who's come to help us rediscover our lost masculine cool," and "an archetype of homegrown masculinity," although this last quote refers obliquely to Hamm, who plays Draper, as a doppelganger or alter-ego of the character who is this embodiment of masculinity.

That this idealization is based on the *look* or glamour of the character and the actor who plays him is no surprise in a magazine whose editorial focus is image culture. And the relationship between the look of Don Draper and characteristics of historical masculinity is carefully constructed on *Mad Men*, as it conveys a particular visual pleasure in the viewer that is in itself nostalgic—the "masculine cool" to which the author of the article refers. The "cool" here is the look of idealized male figures on the screen in the 1950s in particular: the cool of Cary Grant or Gregory Peck or even Rock Hudson before he was gay. These are the urbane, good-looking white men of cinema who project virility, money, and class in their Savile Row suits and wield an uncomplicated masculine authority even while being chased down by crop-dusters and double-crossing blondes. That finely tailored suit that is the costume of the cinematically idealized mid-century company man is actually an extension or performance of the male body itself, a kind of armor that signifies self-discipline, confidence, and station and attests to its wearer's bona fides as a man in charge of his destiny.[14]

This is the world of advertising after all, and what you see only hints at what you get. Although the suit is a costume for Don Draper, he knows all too well that clothes make the man. The designation "man" is important to this stylized identity and to our nostalgic apprehension of it. That the suit, and its retro re-introduction to men's fashion through the popularity of *Mad Men*, signifies a cultural myth or memory about masculinity inevitably gestures to the body itself and its representation of gender and sexuality. Again, the relationship is represented as one of "style."[15] The desire implicit in this kind of pop culture nostalgia is gendered along apparently unsophisticated configurations; as the critic asserts, it is a desire for a "real man." Historical masculinity, or our cultural memory of it, corresponds with its cinematic and televisual representation(s) as an idealized organization of the law of gender that is edgy (or cool) and reassuring all at once. The man in the gray flannel suit beckons to us, perhaps not as an archetypal father, but as a model of male knowing. It is an image that invites our gaze directly, with self-assurance and implicit certitude.[16]

More to the point, it is the juxtaposition of this image of the cool and confident Don Draper, his glamour, with his story fraught with ambivalence, loss, and dread, or melancholy, that so compels the viewer of *Mad Men* and draws us to the character. This duality evokes another story about masculinity that is less idealized, one configured within the contradictions of rebellion and conformity. In mid-twentieth-century popular narratives, primarily in novels and films, we see male characters tortured by gender uncertainty and fear that their male agency is subject to an almost inherent or inevitable social castration that is represented as both professional and personal loss.[17] *Mad Men* show-runner Matthew Weiner is quick to credit the influence of the book and film *The Man in the Gray Flannel Suit* for key elements in Draper's male crisis: the lingering trauma of war, the questions of heroism, failure, flight; the social imperatives of conformity, respectability, gender role adherence, and performance.[18] And then there is the suit itself, familiar in our cultural memory on the body of Gregory Peck in the film version of the novel. "No other dress style of the modern era elicits such scorn as the gray flannel suit," says Natasha Vargas-Cooper in *Mad Men Unbuttoned*.[19] The suit is the uniform of professional class, white, mid-century America, and it is worn as a costume that performs, contains, and eventually mocks historical masculinity. As Vargas-Cooper notes, Joseph Heath and Andrew Potter write in *Nation of Rebels* that "If we regard any sort of standardized dress as uniform, then it is easy to treat the man in the gray flannel suit as equivalent to the National Guardsmen … Here come the cops, here come the suits, here comes The Man."[20]

The Man is that prototype of a certain masculinity that today we call "hegemonic," but it is also a style of and discourse about being male that produced the resistant narratives of both the Playboy "empire" and the counterculture, as Barbara Ehrenreich asserts in *The Hearts of Men*. Inevitably, as social historians suggest, Vietnam and the women's movement would add their own nails to the coffin of the gray-flannelled alpha male, "caught up short by [his] own myths."[21] Hegemonic masculinity itself—conflicted, humiliated, ambiguous—is positioned in the popular history of the 1960s as diminished and fatally flawed, even obsolete. Don Draper, in his integral duality and ambivalence seen through the cultural lens of our own myth-making resurrects and re-frames The Man, at the same time embodying his fractures, his losses, his wounds, the wound itself.[22]

The wounded or castrated white, middle-class male is at the heart of many American popular narratives, particularly as emblematic of the failure of cultural myth or "the dream" and the vicissitudes of history, the victim of contesting stories about traditional masculinity. We see him in Hemingway and Fitzgerald, the *hero manqué* who is self-aware and idealistic, but overreaching and hopelessly adrift in a newly pessimistic modern world. That this is a character who represents not only existential crisis but a crisis of masculinity, an identity narrowly constructed and defined, can be seen in a variety of genres, particularly in *film noir* and suspense thrillers consistently viewed through the lens of post-war narratives of loss and betrayal in the ruins of the hero. Images from some of these popular films attest to the dangers faced by the man-in-crisis, dangers that are made explicit by the repetition of the gray flannel suit in freefall.[23] The graphic image of the falling, suited male figure appears as an homage to this representation in the opening credits for every episode of *Mad Men* and in the poster for season five. At the beginning of each show, the image is doubled to suggest Don's dividedness—in identity and psyche—as one graphic male figure sits secure, surveying the billboard skyscraper landscape, cigarette in hand, while another falls headlong and flailing into the modernist abyss. Through these visual gestures, the viewer is invited to recall Hitchcock's film *Vertigo* and its nightmare sequence: the man in the suit suspended as in space, flailing downward, head first, arms akimbo, through the vortex. Don Draper, like Hitchcock's character in the film, is the figure caught in the act of falling, always falling, never touching the ground. As in the dream, it is depicted as a terrifying plunge into the unconscious of the dreamer, a plummet into the vortex of the psyche, but for the viewer it can also represent the drop into the past, into history. It is the dream of the hysterical male, of fetishized masculinity, falling in a ritual of loss over and over, always falling. The Man is dead. Long live The Man.

This reading relies, of course, on the representational nature of popular culture and its intrinsic relationship to Freud's theory of the unconscious, to configure and dramatize subjective fantasies and memories on the part of the viewer, translating these into recognizable interpretations of human experience.[24] But it also suggests a larger discourse about gender, its historicization, and instability, reflecting cultural fears about social change and its inevitability. Something is lost, after all, when men and women envision new futures and new selves. The exhilarating dynamic of social progress in the

Figure 1   *Mad Men*, AMC

twentieth century, its triumphs and gains particularly within the realm of sexual politics, is nevertheless accompanied by movements and gestures of loss, failure, and betrayal. But it is not feminism that strikes the death blow to hegemonic masculinity. It is history itself.

Memory and the elegiac ego

I got the feeling that Jon understood a kind of independence, and he had a wound.

Matthew Weiner[25]

As discussed earlier, the psychoanalytic theory of melancholia addressed by Michael Ann Holly can offer a critique of the interaction between aesthetic or visual culture and history, pervaded as it is by a powerful recognition of the past, the passage of time and loss. The melancholy produced as an effect on *Mad Men* is an aspect of the nostalgia that frequently characterizes responses to the show. Critics have addressed the series' narrative's focus as a mirror into the past or personal history, one that can channel emotional recognitions and resolutions.[26] The suggestion of a narrative past that is haunted or embodied by a former self or selves is crucial to an interpretation that *Mad Men* is faithful to recent history and its depiction of real lives, but it is also an integral aspect of characterization through the story of Don Draper. And Don's own relationship with his past is narratively and historically masculinized in its representation of loss and melancholia.

Integral to an understanding of how psychic processes are contextualized and gendered by cultural interpretation, Freud's influential work "Mourning and Melancholia," written in 1917, is widely recognized to be a response to the Great War. In this theory of grief, revisited and revised years later in *The Ego and the Id*, Freud posits that the loss of the object-choice, the loved person, in death results in a temporary divide in ego identification: "an object-loss was transformed into an ego-loss and the conflict between the ego and the loved person into a cleavage between the critical activity of the ego and the ego as altered by identification."[27] The condition of melancholia, which resembles mourning, is differentiated by its introduction of narcissism into the process. "It is on the one hand, like mourning, a reaction to the loss of a loved object, but over and above this, it is marked by a determinant which is absent in normal mourning or which, if it is present, transforms the latter into patho-logical mourning."[28] Furthermore, says Freud,

> If the love for the object—a love which cannot be given up though the object itself is given up—takes refuge in narcissistic identification, then the hate comes into operation on this substitutive object, abusing it, debasing it … The self-tormenting in melancholia … signifies, just like the corresponding phenomenon in obsessional neurosis, a satisfaction of trends of sadism and hate which relate to an object, and which have been turned round upon the subject's own self …[29]

The theorization of mourning as a transitional process, which inevitably recovers the healthy ego to itself, and its contrast with self-consuming and obsessive melancholia is shifted, however, in Freud's later writings on the effects of war. In *The Ego and the Id*, Freud rethinks the nature of object-loss and its relationship to grief and to memory. As Tammy Clewell says, "In grounding the formation and later development of the ego in the loss of significant others, Freud collapses the strict opposition between mourning and melancholia, making melancholy identification integral to the work of mourning."[30]

It is in this identity formation, this consciousness of the lost other as intrinsic to the self, this perpetual woundedness, that I'd like to propose we read Don Draper as a compelling figure of modernity—Freud's *elegiac ego*. "The complex of melancholia behaves like an open wound," says Freud in "Mourning and Melancholia,"[31] and Don's melancholy is dramatically repre-sented in the narrative as intrinsic and formational to the character's personal narrative—the story of a past that predetermines his future—and public or historical, as iconic of a kind of dominant masculinity configured within socio-cultural responses to transition and trauma. It suggests a wound that is psychic, sexual, intrinsic. The wound is integral to Don's identity and, as such, within the discourse of psychoanalytic theory, it creates a masculinity that is to some degree feminized through its vulnerability and pervading quality of absence.

This is a masculinity that problematizes and engages the potentially trans-formational power of memory on a number of levels. Don's memories are central to the narrative, as is his doubled and sometimes multiple story/ies and identity/ies. Memory is an organizing principle of Don's character in that it provides complexity, as well as motivation. Don's manufactured identity is made possible through the circumstances of war, like a baptism of fire. Early on we learn the secret of this masculine enigma: in Korea he traded dog tags with a dead comrade, wiping out his own traumatic history, his desperate circumstances, his grief for an unknown mother and unloving father. But, throughout the series and despite the character's charisma and success, he lives with a divided and deeply ambivalent sense of self, haunted by the knowledge of his crime—the "murder" of Dick Whitman, his true identity—and memories of that former life. In this aspect of the story, Dick is Don's uncanny Other, familiar and strange, the ghostly figure in the mirror.

Dick, of course, is never truly dead nor can he die. Don's memories about him, and about his impoverished rural upbringing, serve as the character's consciousness and motivation, while they also construct another story about modernity, acting as a memorial to a way of life split and transformed by war and the emergence of a new world. Don Draper has everything this new world can offer. But he is consumed by his elegiac ego. His consciousness is constantly paying tribute to and repressing the Past.

The Past—an idea of selfhood, a story about an integrated and knowable "self"—here instead suggests a split subjectivity and modern alienation within psychological, narrative, and historical trajectories. This notion of the Past is one that refuses fixed or recuperative interpretation; it is dynamic and constantly redefining itself as it in turn creates the Present. The ineluctability of time and its distinctive relationship to loss is key to our understanding of Don Draper as a character as it is to our understanding of hegemonic masculinity on *Mad Men*, that gender identity itself is a social construct built on competing, even false, ideas about power and self-determination. As in popular twentieth-century narratives discussed above, masculinity on *Mad Men* is in crisis by definition or default, its very characterization circumscribed by the qualities that have given it its historical power.[32]

The end of men

If we see Freud's *elegiac ego* in full dramatic force in the character of Don Draper, the other mad men on the show offer various portrayals of masculinity beleaguered by the vicissitudes of cultural instability and change. Like the female characters, all of the male characters on *Mad Men* have confronted personal and professional failures to varying degrees. But, as indicated by the series' representation of an historical feminist imperative, while characters like Peggy, Joan, Megan, and even Betty scramble for territorial purchase as they move slowly up the ladder of individuated social aspiration, Roger, Pete, Lane, Duck, and other male characters struggle, not valiantly, to maintain a foothold on what had seemed a guaranteed path of ascent if not bedrock stability. Their failures are frequently depicted as personal losses, in the dissolution of marriages and families, the diminution of their stature as patriarchs in the social realm. More important is the apparent loss, or threat of loss, of the imprimatur of white capitalist patriarchy, Freud's theory of castration as an *idea* of masculinity and its motivations. While the other male characters on *Mad Men* do not convey Don's larger-than-life dividedness, his dramatic hauntedness, they nevertheless exhibit a particular quality of desperation that speaks to time and place. There is a kind of isolation or isolated-ness to the men in *Mad Men* and a sense of thwarted purpose. This is especially true for most of the series with Pete Campbell, whose adolescent arrogance competes consistently with opportunities for growth, and Lane Pryce and Duck Phillips, whose characters bear the marks of being generationally and tragically out of step with the times. The imprint of generation marks younger and older male characters in consistently familial ways. Pete, the son, brash and impulsive in his behavior at home and in the office, frequently appears to be motivated both by a desire for the approval of parental figures and a determination to vanquish them. As the series develops, so does the character's sense of authority, however unfailingly mitigated by an immature impulsivity.[33] Alternatively, as indicative of patriarchal male decline, Duck's alcoholism and subsequent professional failure conveys the inevitability of constant drinking in the workplace, an activity tied to ritualistic male bonding (just as Peggy understands quickly that a drink signals camaraderie), but his story suggests from the outset that as an adman he is yesterday's news. Even more dramatically, Lane's suicide is shocking in its fatal response to professional and personal setbacks that convey masculine authority in failure and defeat. The narratives of these older male characters make clear the shifting tides in the mid-twentieth century of the economic and social playing fields for men who aren't adaptable to the new rules. Ironically, the character who perhaps most conveys this interaction of time and generation, despite his youth and promise, is Michael Ginsberg. Michael is, like Don, caught between past and future, and, though not a major character, his narrative offers a dramatic portrayal of melancholy becoming full psychosis. His family history marked by the horror of the Holocaust, Michael's anxieties about the future become focused on technological change in the workplace and what he perceives as the imminent erasure of his identity. His eventual breakdown and self-mutilation represent a grotesque expression of male crisis, at the very least a portrayal of identity out of step with its destiny.

To some extent, the narratives of these failed males reflect the exigencies of the characters' motivations, choices, and personal tragedies at odds with socially empowered identities. The fates of Lane, Duck and Michael falter despite their protected statuses as hegemonic males (Michael's Jewishness and youth offering somewhat less-secure footing) in the professional class. Importantly, however, the threat of failure and its eventuality is what connects these characters in their expressed masculinity. The instability of masculine identity, its future, and undermined coherence takes on particular significance through the stories of Sal Romano and Bob Benson. As gay men, the characters Sal and Bob represent particularly divided masculinities on *Mad Men*, and the narrative highlights their inability to align personal and professional identities despite generational shifts and cultural change. Sal, the suave and well-dressed art director with a young and needy wife, appears in seasons one and two as a well-integrated member of the boys' club at Sterling Cooper. Although it becomes clear by season three that Sal is himself performing a version of heteronormative drag, his ability to maintain the illusion allows him a pass, most significantly with Don. But when Sal's double identity is threatened with public exposure by his powerful client, the bullying and similarly closeted Lee Garner Jr., he loses his job in a scene that reinforces Don's sexual hypocrisy.[34]

Bob Benson, who appears in season six as a much younger executive on the way up, is more in the professional mode of Don Draper. Good looking, self-confident and ambitious, he capitalizes on relationships with the other executives, partners, and clients in a comfortable performance of male camaraderie. There is little appearance in Bob of the dividedness that haunts and eventually sabotages Sal, although his season seven proposal to Joan suggests the lengths to which the character is determined to go to in order to maintain the safe confines of the heternormative model.[35] In fact, Bob's relationship with Joan marks him in a distinctly contemporary version of maleness, on the one hand portraying him as an eager-to-please old-fashioned guy armed with flowers and candy, on the other an enlightened male who comfortably shares the cooking and childcare and looks good in an apron.

That Sal's queerness is tragic and Bob's normalized to some degree can of course be considered problematic in a show that has also been widely criticized for its lack of attention to the histories of marginalized communities during the sixties.[36] But both characterizations reflect the central problem with historical masculinity as a flawed and failing identity construct and they represent this breakdown from specifically historicized perspectives that convey cultural change. Sal's closeted, tormented existence, his personal and professional victimization, confirm our recognition of recent social history as inhospitable to difference, particularly sexual and gender difference, thus reaffirming our collective sense of cultural and political progress. In the same way that we see the conditions for women on the show as deplorable-but-improving from season to season (especially through the characters of Peggy and Joan), we can see the shift in focus from Sal's mistreatment to Bob's success (at least in the workplace) as a sign of progress that gestures to greater social tolerance or at least accommodation for a variety of masculinities. But the paradigm of hegemonic masculinity that allows Sal and Bob entry to the workplace in a way not afforded women inevitably fails these characters to varying degree and marks their difference in the trajectory of historical masculinity. Sal's meticulous masquerade of heternormativity in the workplace is unable to withstand the strain of its own apparatus, while Bob, whose performance of masculinity appears unconflicted and whose sexuality is to some degree accepted, is nevertheless compelled to attempt to manufacture an appropriate public persona of the "man on his way up," with beautiful wife, child, and picket fence as staged props.[37] While the viewer may be encouraged through the different narrative trajectories of these two gay characters to consider a progressive future for individuated and fully articulated expressions of masculinity, that possibility is not depicted here, at least not directly. Stonewall, like other politically defining events of the sixties, may be part of the historical memory the viewer brings to the narrative, but it has little transformative power for the characters. There is no burgeoning movement depicted, no groundswell of support. The male-identified and defining environment of the workplace, while creating at least a recognizable theater for gender performance and professional aspiration, offers no guarantee of success or even survival no matter who wears the pants.

By season seven, the workplace also offers a kind of staging ground or spectacle of salvation for Don Draper. Throughout the series, other male characters, at least the executives and partners at the agency, are represented in direct comparison to and competition with Don. He's the big dog in the office even when on probation, a "sensitive piece of horse flesh," as Pete refers to him in the episode *Waterloo* (7.7). Even through the loss of professional status subsequent to his confession in season six's *In Care Of* (6.13), Don's masculine dominance among peers conveys a recognizable and gendered authority. When Jim Cutler confronts him as "a bully and a drunk, a football player in a suit," he challenges and goads Don by mocking his hyper-masculinity. But here, as in the social realm, Don's male authority, an aspect of his glamour, mitigates his failure, even as that failure is premised on his very public drop of the mask. "The most eloquent I've ever heard you is when you were blubbering like a little girl about your impoverished childhood," says Jim in an assessment that ironically torpedos the most compelling story in the ad man's arsenal. "He's a pain in the ass," declares Bert, adding later to Roger that Don is "not a leader" (*Waterloo*, 7.7). These on-target critiques, however, do little to blunt the force of Don's masculine dominance in the workplace. In fact, his masculinity is thematically reinforced by his ejection from the firm in season six as that event calls attention to the crisis of identity at the heart of the narrative. This is the "fall of man" that *Mad Men* has been building to, the one the viewer has been waiting for. And it concretizes and makes explicit Don's relationship to the past; it performs his duality and duplicity, his woundedness, as spectacle for the other characters as well as the viewer. Explaining his firing, Don tells Sally "I told the truth about myself," telling the truth being perhaps the ad man's unpardonable sin. It is not clear whether it will set him free.

After Don's spectacular fall in the workplace, time and the character's relationship to it is reconfigured once again, as it has been throughout the series in relation to his personal failures, memories, and nostalgia. The reinvention of the self-made man sets the narrative agenda in "Time Zones" and "A Day's Work," the early episodes of season seven. This is not to suggest that Don's project of the self is transformed or redeemed, only that his past in becoming multi-directional as part of a before/after scenario is more clearly foregrounded for himself and the other characters. The past now operates as a public story about Don rather than as a narrative unconscious, one that has been available only to the viewer and a limited number of characters, and as such can be addressed directly. Early in season seven we see Don, banished from the office and alone in his messy apartment, in a self-conscious and ritual-istic performance of the identity he feels is integral to who he is: one who puts on a suit and gets to work.[38] As discussed above, the gray flannel suit, signaling a particular kind of masculinity, self-possession, and historical location to the viewer as it does to the character, is crucial to Don's relationship to work and, though it looks increasingly out of date on the street and in the boardroom, almost entirely outside of the fashion politics of the age, it gestures once again to a masculinized desire for coherence and self-actualization. It reinforces our understanding of Don as iconic, at once singular and representative of a certain kind of male identity in a particular place and time. "You have to work," Don says to Ted in the final scenes of *Waterloo* (7.7). "You don't want to see what happens when it's really gone."

The spectacle of male productivity offers, in a way, the illusion that mascu-linity itself rests on solid ground despite the prospect of turbulent social change and an anxious future. That spectacle is given dramatic historical play at the climactic midpoint of the final season, as many of the major characters gather to watch the Apollo moonwalk of 1969. On the verge of the 1970s, the decade that witnesses the growth of the women's and gay rights movements, racial and ethnic turmoil and momentum, Vietnam, the counterculture rejection of the status quo, an era of "deflated American masculinity,"[39] the collective experience of watching the performance of heroes in extraordinary circumstances, a vision of the future guaranteed by the triumphs of the past, reaffirms male identity and its *right stuff* as the engine, the machine of twentieth-century dominance and vitality. It restores, for a moment, the dream or fantasy of the Man.

Men, women, and the future

Ah, the future—it is perilous only if one denies feminist agency.[40]

The glamour and fantasy of male productivity and power, of masculinity, that imagines a vision of the future as it evokes nostalgia and a melancholic sense of loss begins to take on a different quality in seasons six and seven, in line with the viewer's recognition that *Mad Men*, and the 1960s, are coming to a close. The male characters have developed, or not, along sometimes surprising trajectories. Some have disappeared from the narrative altogether—even Bert, who spends his last moments watching the moon landing with his African-American housekeeper, utters his final dialogue in one emphatic word: "Bravo."[41] There is a semblance of resolution to workplace storylines and deceptively simple endings to complicated personal conflicts (Don and Megan's marriage, for example), all of which gesture to a future that is uncertain at best. The power of the past to assert its dominance remains key to our understanding of these developments, the characters' losses and failures, as well as our acute awareness of time passing and history happening before our eyes. A narrative focus in these final seasons that comes to embody the interactions of time, personal and social history, and the waning influence and stability of hegemonic masculinity can be found in relationships of fathers and daughters. We have seen a number of stories about fathers and daughters throughout the series. These narratives focus on the inheritance of frustration and lost opportunity in consistently Oedipalized scenarios: Betty's complex "daddy's girl" relationship with her father, Gene, which seems to be reintegrated into her marriage with the paternal and caretaking Henry;[42]

Roger's fraught relationship with his daughter Margaret, which shifts dramatically when she joins a cult, transforming the absent father into would-be rescuer who is inevitably forced to confront the full effect of his paternal failure;[43] Megan's supercilious, philandering communist father Emile, who presents a predictable springboard to another sexually unfaithful, emotionally unavailable older man, her husband Don. In these various characterizations, the themes of emotional disconnect and sexual competition between men and women are relayed through the past and future of generations, and similar Oedipalized failures occur in Don's performance as *paterfamilias*. But, as later seasons make clear, the father–daughter scenario comes to represent for Don his best hope for the future, some small measure of successful masculinity and ensured inheritance. This can be seen to some extent through the workplace relationship between Don and Peggy (in a way his professional progeny), but it is a dynamic that functions primarily through the interactions of Don and his daughter Sally.

Sally Draper represents a complex relationship to the successes and failures of Don's masculinity. Throughout the series, perhaps the most trenchant critique of hegemonic or historical masculinity comes through the eyes of Sally. From early episodes on, the character of Sally frequently acts as a psychological double for Don, or maybe a reverse image, in her capacity to trigger and mirror his interior analytical processes. His scenes with her consistently act as mirroring moments and there are frequent juxtapositions of her gaze activating his inward one, a dynamic that is staged dramatically in *Maidenform* (2.6), for example, when Sally, watching with adoration as her dad shaves, triggers a visual moment of introspection and self-loathing in Don, dramatically conveying his dividedness.

This sequencing is an effective cinematic device as the viewer comes to know Don's duplicitous and tortured self in part through his daughter's eyes. Her gaze in a sense strips him of his mask and the artifice of his performance of masculinity. But these scenes throughout the seasons of *Mad Men* also correspond to a developmental process of knowing and self-awareness in the character of Sally herself, staged in season six in a dramatic rehearsal of the Oedipal moment when Sally sees Don in the act of having sex with his neighbor Sylvia (*Favors*, episode 6.11). The image of Sally looking through

Figure 2   *Maidenform* (2.6)

the doorway of Sylvia's kitchen and upon her half-naked father and his companion, her own shock mirrored on Don's distraught face, has been replicated and analyzed throughout blogs and episode synopses over and over, the look exchanged between father and daughter a spectacle of betrayal and horror in that recognition. The image from the doorway is labeled in accompanying reviews as "Sally catches Don," but clearly Sally herself is caught as well, framed for the viewer at the threshold of what some critics might call the "loss of innocence," but what also may be considered as the coming of wisdom or truth, certainly a truth about Don. From *Mad Men*'s point of view, this scene and many others between Sally and Don convey a reciprocity between them that gestures at once to the truth of the characters' relationship inside and out of the "family romance," and to the viewer's engaged, dramatically visualized, recognition of Don's failures and seductions. This dynamic, particularly as it is staged as a highly sexualized spectacle of comprehension and self-awareness, allows us to identify with Sally while simultaneously observing her psychological development as "a woman." This not only informs our understanding of her as Don's daughter—it allows us to speculate on how she will use these experiences and realizations in her future, primarily through her own feminine agency.[44] But this dynamic or spectacle also engages once again our recognition of Don's masculinity and his sexualized and traumatic past as well as his ongoing project of controlling and contextualizing memory in pursuit of a coherent and unified self.

The final scene of *In Care Of*, the last episode of season six, conveys the power and primacy of this new exchange between father and daughter, character and viewer. The episode is bookended by vivid scenes from Don's childhood memories of the brothel and his return to that site with his own children. Both Bobby and Sally look back and forth from their father to the dilapidated structure in disbelief, a young African-American boy on the steps watching them. The exchange of looks between Don and Sally anchors the scene, offering a trajectory of new insight for the characters and visually registers for the viewer the connection between the past and future. This is the image that Matthew Weiner has said he had in his head at the beginning of season six, explaining:

> we start the whole season, usually I start it with an image in my head, and that was the image … What we wanted to do was show that Sally was both disgusted and illuminated and that she would—she, like the rest of the world, was going to see Don … I think Jon Hamm looked at her like take it or leave it, baby, this is what it is, I'm being honest with you. And she looked at it like that's gross, but oh my God, that's who you are. And the best thing is, to me, there are no words. This is where I grew up, no words, and that's the part that I find as a viewer sinks into me … And Jon had a depth and maybe carries, you know—even if it's fictional—a sense of a wound …[45]

Figure 3   *In Care Of* (6.13)

The impact of this scene and its implied exchange, as well as its power of identification for the viewer, is magnified through its silence and its evocation of history, of memory and loss. For Weiner, the actor's "wound" is conveyed through the character's story and deeply conflicted self but it is also visual, very much an aspect of his *look* and our interpretive gaze. This is melancholia embodied, for the viewer perhaps the most recognizable feature of Don Draper's masculinity, and here it is acknowledged fully by his daughter as it has been portrayed to us since the beginning of *Mad Men*. The exchange of information conveyed through the characters' mutual gaze frames Sally's new perception of Don, her fuller understanding of him, and reiterates and reaffirms what the viewer knows about him as it frames the doubling between the two characters and between characters and viewer. We see Don, in almost every shot of this scene, through Sally's eyes. And in this sequence, ending in a shot of father and daughter in profile, eyes directed toward the decaying "home," a place that exists spectacularly for Don and now somewhat definitively for Sally, we also see the past and future come together.

The mutuality achieved here between Don and Sally is not represented as a happy ending, nor is it meant to be a resolution to the Oedipal conflict or other psychical relationships depicted on the show. But Sally's comprehension of her father's history allows her a fuller understanding of her own subjectivity,

Figure 4   *In Care Of* (6.13)

giving her a story of her own. And in Sally, the viewer glimpses the possibilities of a future counteraction to hegemonic masculinity.[46] Who Sally is or will be has great potential for feminist analysis, especially from a generational perspective. After all, she is a child of the so-called second wave, one who will go to college with great numbers of women, who will enter the workforce under the auspices of Titles VII and IX, enjoy reproductive freedoms Betty, Joan, Peggy, or even Megan never knew. She will be shaped by the Civil Rights movement, Vietnam, queer nation and Act Up. In her potential for social and political change, Sally is the alternative to our memory of hegemonic masculinity, its historical primacy and its glamorous, melancholic thrall. If in the character of Sally we are once again invited to use our political imaginations in the service of fantasy or desire, it is a dynamic that offers the opportunity for new myths that may escape the interpretive pull of nostalgia. In the story of Sally, the daughter of Don, the depiction of possibilities characterized by futurity gives us an opening for an even better understanding of the feminist history that is yet to come. Perhaps *Mad Men* shows us not so much the end of men, certainly not the birth of women, but the promise of the imaginative engagement of historical memory to acknowledge cultural desire and create new stories about gender.[47]

Notes

1   Pierre Nora, "Reasons for the Upsurge in Memory," *Transit*, April 19, 2002, http://www.eurozine.com/articles/2002-04-19-nora-en.html (accessed August 23, 2014). Nora continues, "And increasingly rapid change, an accelerated precipitation of all things into an ever more swiftly retreating past. We must take the measure of this change for the way in which memory is organised. It is of crucial importance, for it has shattered the unity of historical time, that fine, straightforward linearity which traditionally bound the present and the future to the past."

2   "History was the sphere of the collective; memory that of the individual. History was one; memory, by definition, plural (since by nature individual). The idea that memory can be collective, emancipatory and sacred turns the meaning of the term inside out. Individuals had memories, collectivities had histories. The

idea that collectivities have a memory implies a far-reaching transformation of the status of individuals within society and of their relationship to the community at large. Therein lies the secret of that other mysterious shift which has occurred, and on which a little light needs to be thrown: the shift in our understanding of identity, without which it is impossible to understand this upsurge in memory." Ibid.

3   For a brilliantly detailed commentary on how image culture and fashion interact with the politics of *Mad Men*, see the blog Tom+Lorenzo: Fabulous & Opinionated, http://www.tomandlorenzo.com (accessed August 23, 2014).

4   Virginia Postrel, *The Power of Glamour: Longing and the Art of Visual Persuasion* (New York: Simon & Schuster, 2013), p. 41.

5   Ibid., p. 43.

6   Ibid., p. 178.

7   A. O. Scott describes *Mad Men*'s paradoxical perspective on historical gender in "The Post-Man," an analysis of the white male in pop culture: "From the start, 'Mad Men' has, in addition to cataloging bygone vices and fashion choices, traced the erosion, the gradual slide toward obsolescence, of a power structure built on and in service of the prerogatives of white men … Weren't those guys awful back then? But weren't they also kind of cool? We are invited to have our outrage and eat our nostalgia too, to applaud the show's right-thinking critique of what we love it for glamorizing." *New York Times* Magazine, September 14, 2014, p. 39.

8   Michael Ann Holly, *The Melancholy Art* (Princeton, NJ: Princeton University Press, 2013). Further, she quotes Henry James on the appearance of the uncanny in literary narrative as an "unsettling" of the past: "we are divided of course between liking to feel the past strange and liking to feel it familiar; the difficulty is … to catch it at the moment when the scales of the balance hang with the right evenness," p. 137.

9   Joan Wallach Scott, *The Fantasy of Feminist History* (Durham, NC: Duke University Press, 2011), p. 33.

10   Roland Barthes, "Myth Today," *Mythologies*, trans. Jonathan Cape Ltd. (New York: Hill and Wang, 1972), pp. 109–59. Barthes addresses the cultural power of myth to give us stories about ourselves, which substitute for historical interpretation: "What the world supplies to myth is an historical reality, defined, even if this goes back quite a while, by the way in which men have produced or use it; and what myth gives in return is a natural image of this reality. And just as bourgeois ideology is defined by the abandonment of the name 'bourgeois,'

myth is constituted by the loss of the historical quality of things: in it, things lose the memory that they once were made … Myth does not deny things, on the contrary, its function is to talk about them; simply, it purifies them, it makes them innocent, it gives them a natural and eternal justification, it gives them a clarity which is not that of an explanation but that of a statement of fact … What the world supplies to myth is an historical reality, defined, even if this goes back quite a while, by the way in which men have produced or use it; and what myth gives in return is a natural image of this reality," 142–3.

11   See Hanna Rosin's much-debated article in the *Atlantic Monthly* (July/August 2010) and her follow-up book, *The End of Men: And the Rise of Women* (New York: Viking, 2012).

12   See Amanda Lotz, *Cable Guys: Television and Masculinities in the 21st Century* (New York: New York University Press, 2014). See also her "Don Draper's Sad Manhood: What Makes 'Mad Men' Different from 'Breaking Bad,' 'Sopranos.'" http://www.salon.com/2014/04/11/don_drapers_sad_manhood_ what_makes_mad_men_different_from_breaking_bad_sopranos/ (accessed August 24, 2014). On the current fascination with television's "difficult men," see also Brett Martin's *Difficult Men: Behind the Scenes of a Creative Revolution: From the Sopranos and The Wire to Mad Men and Breaking Bad* (New York: Penguin, 2013).

13   Adam Sachs, "Jon Hamm: The Last Alpha Male." *Details*, October 1, 2010, http://www.details.com/celebrities-entertainment/cover-stars/201010/mad-men-actor-alpha-male-jon-hamm (accessed November 1, 2010).

14   Virginia Postrel calls this effortless male glamour a version of "sprezzuratura"; *The Power of Glamour*, p. 84. This quality of cool grace is seen in twentieth-century stars like Cary Grant, particularly as debonair action hero in films like *North by Northwest*.

15   See the *Mad Men* influence in a line of clothes for men at Banana Republic ("Mad About Style") or a *Rolling Stone* cover depicting Don Draper— grey-suited, Scotch in hand—as a high-rolling pimp with his stable of sexy female co-stars (September 16, 2010). In "From Boys to Men," a men's fashion review in the *New York Times*, writer Guy Trebay notes: "What the [designers] want is Jon Hamm. That Mr. Hamm's Don Draper so persuasively resembles an archetypal father on a time-travel visa from an era of postwar expansion and fixed gender roles can hardly be incidental to the success of Mad Men." *New York Times*, October 17, 2010, http://www.nytimes.com/2010/10/17/ fashion/17MANLY.html (accessed October 17, 2010).

16   See Anne Hollander's highly influential *Sex and Suits: The Evolution of Modern Dress* (New York: Knopf, 1994) for a full discussion of the power of the suit to convey the authority and primacy of the male body in modernity. Hollander notes that the endurance of the suit to connote masculinity is intrinsically related to cultural fantasies of the body: "this is the fantasy of the modern form as the proper material vessel of both beauty and power, of positive sexuality," p. 5. Furthermore, in not adhering to the dictates of ever-fluctuating women's fashions, the suit represents a kind of "truth" of masculinity and gender authority: "The suit remains the uniform of official power, not manifest force or physical labor—it suggests diplomacy, compromise, civility, and physical self-control, none of which are present in the fashionably ascendant … The suit reflects purposeful development … it has the modern look of carefully simplified dynamic abstraction …", p. 113.

17   Richard Yates' *Revolutionary Road* and Sloan Wilson's *The Man in the Gray Flannel Suit*, products of the transitional late fifties–early sixties, both depict male characters whose existential struggles with male identity are less than heroic, grappling with nostalgic memories of the role of masculine archetypes in their personal histories.

18   In a *Rolling Stone* article on the choice of Jon Hamm to play Don Draper, Weiner envisioned a particular pop cultural type of masculinity: "if Gregory Peck and James Garner had a baby, that guy …" Quoted in Erik Konigsberg, "A Fine Madness," *Rolling Stone*, September 16, 2010, p. 46.

19   Natasha Vargas-Cooper, *Mad Men Unbuttoned: A Romp Through 1960s America* (New York: HarperCollins, 2010), p. 60.

20   Quoted in ibid., p. 60.

21   Barbara Ehrenreich, *The Hearts of Men: American Dreams and the Flight from Commitment* (New York: Anchor, 1987), p. 106.

22   Weiner observes that Hamm "understood a kind of independence. And he had a wound." Quoted in Konigsberg, "A Fine Madness," p. 46. Art historian Holly connects Freud's idea of the open wound to "the cut between present and past—word and image," noting its "resistance to interpretation" (p. 116). These comments address the idea of absence or loss as a present and powerful visual characteristic of aesthetics.

23   In this genre, the man in gray flannel appears not as urbane Roger Thornhill, Cary Grant in *North by Northwest*, but more likely the tortured and emasculated Scotty Ferguson, Jimmy Stewart in *Vertigo*. Hitchcock's film, released on the cusp of the sixties, gives us the story of a man tormented by

anxiety, dread, and sexual obsession. Scotty may be seen as a version of the "hysterical male."

24 Freud's theory of the *"unheimliche"* or uncanny ("in reality nothing new or foreign, but something which is familiar and old-established in the mind that has been estranged only by the process of repression" [p. 148]) has particular resonance in *Mad Men*, primarily in the characterization of Don Draper, but to some extent in the viewer's relationship to the depiction of "history" itself in the narrative. The narrative identification with cultural notions of lost masculinity intentionally employs these kinds of associations which appear familiar though "past," as if they are memories rather than interpretations. See Sigmund Freud, "The Uncanny," in *On Creativity and the Unconscious*, ed. Benjamin Nelson (New York: Harper, 1958).

25 Weiner, quoted in Konigsberg, "A Fine Madness," p. 46.

26 Feminist film critic Molly Haskell addresses this interaction in a letter to the *New York Review of Books*: "As a card-carrying member of the *Mad Men* generation, I'm not only in thrall to the show but, having cut my professional teeth in advertising/PR, I'm unnerved at how closely it mirrors the workplace in which I came of age … But for me, with its deft blend of satire and sympathy, it has had the cathartic effect of well-imagined art in allowing me to both recognize and gain a forgiving distance from a sometimes embarrassing younger self." "In Response to 'The Mad Men Account,'" *New York Review of Books*, March 24, 2011, http://www.nybooks.com/articles/archives/2011/mar/24/mad-men-account/ (accessed August 23, 2014).

27 Sigmund Freud, "Mourning and Melancholia," *The Freud Reader*, ed. Peter Gay (New York: Norton, 1989), p. 586.

28 Ibid., p. 587.

29 Ibid.

30 Tammy Clewell, "Mourning Beyond Melancholia: Freud's Psychoanalysis of Loss," Journal of the American Psychoanalytic Association 52:1, p. 61, https://www.apsa.org/portals/1/docs/japa/521/clewell.pdf (accessed March 20, 2011).

31 Freud, "Mourning and Melancholia," p. 589. Melancholy becomes a repeating and regenerative aspect of the recognition of loss in the mourning process, and mourning itself—rather than satiated through the replacement of the lost loved one—becomes part of the consciousness of the mourner, part of his or her apprehension of the world. Clewell says, "working through depends on taking the lost other into the structure of one's own identity, a form of preserving the lost object as the self. In 'Mourning and Melancholia' Freud thought that

mourning came to a decisive end; however, in *The Ego and the Id*, he suggests that the grief work may well be an interminable labor" (p. 61).

32   It can be argued that this reading of twentieth-century anxiety about the shifting fates of hegemonic masculinity reflects another historical discourse about cultural identity as well—that of the American character as "the greatest nation" on the global stage. That this characterization is unquestionably masculinized—identified with male power and prowess—highlights the particularly gendered nature of the national crisis of postmodern politics for American identity, reinforcing the threat to "our way of life" in a new age of sweeping historical change and shifting cultural relevancies. It also explains to some extent the pervasive influences of nostalgia to resist or reify those changes even when they are recognized to be progressive. A detailed example of this kind of this social and political dynamic of reification can be found in Rick Perlstein's analysis of American political identity in the 1970s in *The Invisible Bridge: The Fall of Nixon and the Rise of Reagan* (New York: Simon & Schuster, 2014). Perlstein describes post-Vietnam, post-Watergate America reeling from a historical crisis of confidence, one familiarly gendered. He quotes a common lament: "For the first time, Americans have had at least a partial loss in the fundamental belief in ourselves. We've always believed we were the new men, the new people, the new society," p. xiv. Perlstein argues that the US's move to political conservatism in the late 1970s and 1980s, especially under the New Right's embrace of Ronald Reagan, is in part a nostalgic attempt to "re-capture" a more traditional and muscular national and global identity, one that is implicitly masculinized.

33   Other male characters reflect generational ideas about masculinity, with older characters often portraying specific and concrete relationships to war(s), traditional patriarchal family roles, and professional positions, while younger characters frequently exhibit a desire for the "new"—new ideas, interactions with male and female peers, and jobs—as they scramble for footing socially and professionally. Some examples of this can be found in characters like Stan Rizzo, who competes with Peggy to push the creative envelope, Abe Drexler, whose politics represent shifting cultural attitudes and youthful rejections of politics-as-usual, Paul Kinsey, whose experiments with eastern religious enlightenment suggest resistance to and rejections of dominant ways of seeing, and Harry Crane, whose relentless embrace of coming media trends meets with constant skepticism, even as it advances the creative successes of Sterling Cooper. While all of these characters convey to some degree new male identities, their aspirations nevertheless conform to a familiar paradigm of cultural masculinity

that emphasizes ambition, competition, and, to varying extent, sexual and social entitlement. They are not yet the sensitive new-age guys (or "snags") who come into being in the late 1970s as ideas about feminism assert themselves. And this same representation of entitlement is consistently satirized and shown to be foolish within the larger narrative (Paul's path to mysticism inspired by lust and leading to the Hare Krishna movement, for example) and through the eyes of other characters, suggesting an alternative critique of masculinity that is recognizably historicized but is unmarked by nostalgia or regret. It is tempting to see Ken Cosgrove's semi-blinding by hyper-masculine (and buffoonish) clients as an emasculating effect of the rituals and relationships of manhood, although that interpretation is off-set in his new appearance as a type of dashing "pirate" and double for the eye-patch version of the Arrow shirt man.

34   "Who do you think you're talking to?" Don asks Sal, ironically suggesting Don's own secret life. And he distances himself with a familiar epithet of the mainstream: "You people ..." Interestingly, although our last look at Sal confirms the continuation of his double life, calling wife Kitty from a phone booth in the park to say he is working late, the leather-clad male figures in the background suggest that at least, at last, Sal is seeking his own self-expression and satisfaction (*Wee Small Hours*, 3.9).

35   Critics speculated wildly on Bob Benson's mysterious background in his first episodes on the show, offering theories that the character is perhaps a gigolo, even a serial killer. Tom Fitzgerald and Lorenzo Marquez have a persuasive reading of Bob's closeted history and behavior as a gay man in the 1960s on their blog at www.tomandlorenzo.com.

36   See Ramy Zabarah, "Bob Benson and Mad Men's Disappearing Gay Characters," *Complex Pop Culture*, May 25, 2014, http://www.complex.com/pop-culture/2014/05/bob-benson-and-mad-mens-disappearing-gay-characters (accessed August 23, 2014).

37   See Tom and Lorenzo's insightful analysis of Bob Benson as a gay man in the 1960s: http://tomandlorenzo.com/2013/06/mad-style-favors; http://tomandlorenzo.com/2014/05/mad-men-the-strategy/ (accessed August 20, 2014).

38   See Tom and Lorenzo on Don's "crappy Bathrobe of Shame," http://tomandlorenzo.com/2014/04/mad-style-a-days-work/ (accessed August 20, 2014).

39   See Mark Asch, "Syllabus: Deflated American Masculinity in the 1970s," *The L Magazine*, September 22, 2010, http://www.thelmagazine.com/TheMeasure/archives/2010/09/22/syllabus-deflated-american-masculinity-in-the-1970s (accessed August 23, 2014).

40   Scott, *The Fantasy of Feminist History*, p. 43.

41   Bert Cooper's final appearance to the viewer pays tribute to the Broadway
     history of the actor who plays the character in his song and dance to "The Best
     Things in Life Are Free." Robert Morse is known for his role in *How to Succeed
     in Business Without Really Trying*, which, according to Matt Weiner, was another
     1960s influence for *Mad Men*. This scene engages cultural memory here in a
     specific way, although the reference is much more subtle and ironic than other
     direct allusions to popular culture on the show.

42   Some viewers speculated on the possibility of incest in the relationship between
     Betty and Gene, but that has never emerged as an aspect of the characterization
     or narrative. See for example Lisa Allender, in "Mad Men: Is Sexual Abuse/
     Incest About to be Revealed?" *Open Salon*, August 23, 2010, http://open.salon.
     com/blog/lisa_allender/2010/08/23/mad_men_is_sexual_abuseincest_about_
     to_be_revealed (accessed August 20, 2014).

43   In season seven's *The Monolith*, Roger's attempt to talk Margaret (newly
     Marigold) into returning to the young son she abandoned for the commune
     results in father and daughter groveling in the mud. "How could you just leave
     him?" Roger pleads. "He's your baby." "How did you feel when you went away
     to work, Daddy?" returns Marigold, her voice dripping with recrimination.
     "Your conscience must have been eating you alive. Calling your secretary from
     the hotel to pick out a birthday present for me? I'm sure you were sick. It's not
     that hard, Daddy. He'll be fine." This bitter and accusatory exchange between
     the two characters follows Roger's foolishly optimistic attempt to win back his
     daughter's heart with a nostalgic sleepover in the barn, a cozy familial reunion
     that Marigold abandons to join her lover.

44   Portrayed throughout the series as collateral damage of her parents' messy lives
     and bad parenting, Sally's fate has been second-guessed by many bloggers to
     include all the clichéd bad outcomes of 1960s excesses, especially as they relate
     to the burgeoning youth culture. Some of the prognostications for Sally include
     pothead or acid freak, runaway, commune inhabitant, cult follower, even serial
     killer. Interestingly, some of these same predictions have attached themselves to
     other young female characters like Megan or even made an appearance in the
     stories of Roger's daughter Margaret and Anna Draper's niece Stephanie, both
     of whom become members of communes or cults. These prognoses, especially
     in reference to Sally, depend to a large extent on the conventional narratives of
     pop psychology, the myths of the 1960s, and the mysteries and terrors of female
     sexuality. See for example Gwynne Watkins, "A Psychiatrist Analyzes *Mad Men*'s

Traumatized Sally Draper," *Vulture Magazine*, June 12, 2013, http://www.vulture. com/2013/06/psychiatrist-analyzes-mad-men-sally-draper.html (accessed October 30, 2013).

45   Matthew Weiner, interview with Terry Gross, "Fresh Air with Terry Gross," *NPR*, May 1, 2014: "I sometimes wake up in the middle of the night and I think, like, oh, my God. What if I didn't cast him? You know? Well, I wouldn't have a show." http://www.npr.org/2014/05/01/308608611/mad-men-creator-matthew-weiner-on-the-end-of-don-drapers-journey (accessed May 1, 2014).

46   "Feminists are not only political subjects but also desiring subjects and, as such, subjects who make history." Scott, *The Fantasy of Feminist History*, p. 43.

47   Thanks to Gloria-Jean Masciarotte and Astrid Henry for the discussions at the heart of this essay.

"You Can't Be a Man. So Don't Even Try": Femininity and Feminism in *Mad Men*

Natalie Fuehrer Taylor

"Are you Betty?" "Are you Joan?" The questions were posed in a mailing announcing Banana Republic's Fall 2011 clothing collection. The line was designed in collaboration with *Mad Men*'s costume designer and was "inspired by the razor-sharp tailoring and feminine silhouettes of 1960s style." The advertisement offered pieces for those who aspire to the classic beauty of *Mad Men*'s frustrated housewife Betty Draper Francis as well as those who aspire to the sex appeal of Sterling Cooper Draper Pryce's voluptuous office manager Joan Holloway Harris. Banana Republic's announcement did not ask "Are you Peggy?" Yet, many of *Mad Men*'s female viewers have more in common with the independent copywriter who, dissatisfied by the limited gender roles assumed by Betty and Joan, is successful in a profession once dominated by men. The series is popular among women who might be the daughters and the granddaughters of *Mad Men*'s female characters and who have enjoyed all the opportunity opened up to them by the women's movement of the late 1960s—a movement that critiqued the likes of Betty and Joan. They are affluent, well-educated professionals. Another print ad for the clothing collection featured a beautiful blonde (Betty?) in a suit (Joan?). Its caption encouraged viewers to "Get Mad in Stores or Online." Most obviously, the ad promised viewers the style and femininity of Betty Draper Francis and Joan Holloway Harris. It also indulged *Mad Men*'s viewers' righteous indignation about mid-century notions of femininity, which were limited to the kitchen and the bedroom and embodied by Betty and Joan. The sophisticated twenty-first-century audience knows that the women who gave us the "feminine silhouettes of 1960s style" had reason to be mad. Even as a later generation enjoys greater independence and opportunity won by the women's movement of the late 1960s, it seeks the femininity that the movement protested. *Mad Men*, like Banana Republic's advertising campaign, captures the challenge of reconciling femininity with the principles of second-wave feminism.

Second-wave feminism refers to women's political organizing, beginning in the mid-1960s and ending in the early 1980s with the defeat of the Equal Rights Amendment.[1] The second wave is characterized by a lively debate on the condition of women and the best avenue for ending sexual oppression. Betty Friedan's *The Feminine Mystique* is an early, and perhaps the most widely known, objection to femininity. "The feminine mystique says that the highest value and the only commitment for women is the fulfillment of their own femininity."[2] Although Friedan associates several attributes with the feminine mystique, such as sexual passivity and maternal love, her argument centers on that element of the feminine mystique that confines women to "domestic aspects of feminine existence—as it was lived by women whose lives were confined, by necessity, to cooking, cleaning, washing, bearing children—into a religion, a pattern by which all women must now live or deny their femininity."[3] Friedan founded the National Organization for Women (NOW) in 1966 to advocate for political and legal reforms, such reforms would allow women greater opportunities outside of the home and encourage equal partnership with men. By the late sixties, younger, more radical women broke with the sexist New Left in order to advance the cause of women's liberation.[4] They took with them the ideology and the tactics of the New Left. In contrast to the liberal or mainstream feminists (as they came to be called) affiliated with NOW, radical feminists argued that women could only affect their liberation by changing the society itself, since it was the sexism of the entire society that constrained all citizens, but most especially women. Power, including the power men exercised over women, is comprehensive and perpetuated by the private, as well as public, relations between men and women. "Everyday choices, like wearing stilettos or tying the knot, now had significant political consequences."[5]

In her history of the modern women's movement, Deborah Siegel examines the ambivalence of the next generation of American women toward second-wave feminism:

By 1992, a study of the most empowered female generation to date—women on college campuses—showed that most young women no longer wanted to be associated with feminism. According to a *Time*/CNN poll, while 77% of women thought the women's movement made life better, and 94% said it helped women become more independent, and 82% said it was still improving the lives of women, only 33% of women identified themselves as feminists.[6]

These young women would be the audience for *Mad* Men nearly twenty years later. Perhaps one of the reasons for their ambivalence is a perceived antagonism between feminism and femininity, especially as it has been associated with homemaking and with sex appeal.[7] Although not all the heirs to second-wave feminism have embraced the term feminist, some did. Third-wave feminists distinguish themselves from second-wave feminists by their willingness to accept, even celebrate, seemingly contradictory facets of women's lives, such as their feminist principles and femininity.[8] *Mad Men* does not merely condemn an earlier generation's sexism—it also reveals our contemporary ambivalence toward femininity as women continue to grapple with the meaning of "the personal is political."

Are you Betty?

It is not until the very end of the first episode that we meet *Mad Men*'s seemingly perfect suburban housewife, Betty Draper. Don returns to their Dutch colonial home, greets Betty warmly, and then goes into the room of their sleeping children. The beautiful, slim blonde in a pink satin nightgown watches from the bedroom door as her husband tucks their children into bed. With such a seemingly loving husband, peacefully sleeping children, and a comfortable home, Betty Draper would seem to fulfill a mid-century American feminine ideal. The closing music begins to play: "All at once I am several stories high, knowing that I am on the street where you live … Does enchantment pour out of every door. No it is just on the street where you live …"[9] Many viewers will recall that the song is from *My Fair Lady*, the story of two men's efforts to create an ideal woman. The play ran on Broadway from 1956–62. The allusion to it reminds us that to some extent the feminine ideal is a masculine construction. In this scene we are offered an idealized view of family life. Although we know that this suburban domestic scene is "staged" and much of the first episode belies its appearance, viewers may feel "a twinge in [our] heart[s]more powerful than memory alone" and a desire to go "[b]ack home again … to a place we know we were loved" (*The Wheel*, 1.13).

The ideal family vignette is threatened by Betty's anxiety as well as Don's chronic infidelity. There is no physical explanation for why Betty has sudden paralysis of her fingers in the early episodes of season one, so Don arranges for Betty to visit a psychologist to determine the reason for this condition. The source for Betty's anxiety is obvious to *Mad Men*'s audience. In 1963 (just three years after season one takes place and the year of season three) Betty Friedan published *The Feminine Mystique*, in which she diagnoses Betty (and millions of other housewives) with "the problem that has no name":

> The American housewife—freed by science and labor-saving appliances from the drudgery, the dangers of childbirth and the illnesses of her grandmother … was healthy, beautiful, educated, and concerned only about her husband, her children, her home. She found true feminine fulfillment.[10]

Despite her material comfort and security, the suburban housewife is unhappy but cannot articulate the source of her unhappiness. "The problem that has no name" is the guilty desire for "something more."[11] Friedan prescribes a cure for the problem that has no name, a "new life plan." The housewife must find meaningful employment outside the home in order to create an identity that is independent from her husband and her children.[12] Friedan's liberation narrative is linear. Women will find fulfillment by leaving the home and by rejecting femininity, which has been forced on them by popular culture. In their work *Sentenced to Everyday Life: Feminism and the Housewife*, Leslie Johnson and Justine Lloyd reconsider the relationship between domesticity and second-wave feminism. They argue that Friedan's liberation narrative for women is consistent with a modern political narrative, which privileges the autonomous individual. "But Friedan wanted women to do more than devise life plans for themselves. She advocated women undertaking a project of re-making themselves."[13] In a modern world that prizes the autonomy of the individual, the claims of the family seem to constrain the individual.

Furthermore, the autonomous individual is a masculine ideal. In her study of mid-century domesticity, *The Parlour and the Suburb*, Judy Giles observes:

> [I]nsofar as she [Friedan] wishes women to leave behind their "feminine" past and to enter fully into the experience of modernity, she challenges those accounts of modernity that relegated women to the margins of culture. The problem is that ... Friedan's image of the "full human identity" that should be their ideal is a masculine one.[14]

According to liberal feminist narratives, the solution to Betty Draper's sexist oppression is to become more like Don, who is quite literally a self-made man.

Betty Draper gets her shot in an episode entitled *Shoot*. As the episode begins Betty and her children watch as her neighbor releases pigeons from their cages and the birds fly from their suburban captivity. Later, a rival advertising executive, who is hoping to lure Don away from Sterling Cooper, invites Betty to model in a new ad for Coca Cola. Although Betty knows that the advertising executive is courting Don, she is undaunted and continuously reminds others (and herself?) that she once had a modeling career. And, of course, her beauty is undeniable. Modeling promises Betty a chance for at least temporary freedom from her suburban captivity. She tells her therapist, "My mother was always concerned about looks and weight ... She wanted me to be beautiful so that I could find a man. There's nothing wrong with that. But then what? You sit and smoke and then let it go until you're in a box" (*Shoot*, 1.9). Returning to her modeling career offers Betty "something more."

When Don refuses the executive's overtures (in part because he does not like the way that Betty is being used to entice him), Betty's modeling career comes to a quick and disappointing end. She puts on a brave face and tells Don that she doesn't want to work anyway because modeling leads her to neglect her responsibilities at home. Betty goes on to say that she doesn't like Manhattan on her own. It is "harsh." The home offers respite from the city, from modernity. Betty seems to appreciate that modernity, which prizes the autonomous individual, requires correction. Our attachment to those whom we love is also an important facet of the human condition. Don sounds typical of a later generation's efforts to reconcile Friedan's critique of "the happy housewife heroine" with the meaningful responsibility of raising children. He tells Betty that it is not important that she makes dinner for him or that she takes his shirts to the laundry. Betty's most important job is being a mother to their children. "You're mothering those two little people and you're better at it than anyone else in the world … I would have given anything to have had a mother like you. Beautiful and kind, filled with love, like an angel" (*Shoot*, 1.9). Even if Don has misrepresented Betty as an ideal mother, the importance of caring for children can be compelling to a generation of women (and men) who now struggle to find "work–life balance."[15]

The episode's closing scene takes place the following morning. Betty seems happy with her decision, but by 1.00 p.m. she is still not dressed. She goes outside wearing her feminine peignoir set, puts a cigarette in her mouth, pulls a bb gun to her shoulder, and begins to shoot her neighbor's pigeons. It is easy to understand this scene as Betty's rebellion against "the feminine mystique." She does seem to want to deny the birds the freedom from suburban captivity that has been denied to her. Yet, the scene is more complex and ambivalent than a simple protest against Betty's "comfortable concentration camp."[16] We should also interpret Betty's actions as a reaction—an overreaction, to be sure—to her neighbor's threats against her family, particularly her children. (Her neighbor did threaten to shoot their dog.) The scene combines Betty's femininity with the trappings of masculinity. The cigarette hangs from her mouth, rather than being poised between her fingers, and she rests the gun on her sheer nightgown. The juxtaposition of masculine and feminine elements reminds us how constructed and fragile the feminine mystique is. Yet, it also suggests the importance of women's differences from men. Resorting to anger and violence (as Don would have done had Betty allowed him to confront his neighbor when Sally woke up from a nightmare) undermines civil society. Femininity offers an antidote to that. Yet as Bobby Helms croons "You are my special angel … I'll have my special angel here to watch over me," Betty shoots the pigeons.[17]

As feminists and their daughters learned, Friedan's imperative to create "a new life plan," which entails leaving the private sphere for the public, remains challenging and riddled with compromise. While *Mad Men*'s viewers may have greater professional opportunities than Betty, they experience the same sense of love and responsibility for their children. Reconciling one's autonomy and professional aspirations with our desire to make a happy home for those we love remains difficult. Sometimes it seems as impossible as it did for Betty.

Betty's unhappiness is not solely due to her desire for "something more." (Her desire to create a life that is independent of Don and her children is the subject of only one episode. It is not until season seven that the possibility comes up again.) Betty's unhappiness is due to her inability to preserve her home. Her best efforts to live up to the ideal of post-war femininity are thwarted. Betty explains the reasons for her unhappiness to her therapist: "I can't help but to think I would be happy if my husband were faithful to me … He doesn't know what family is. He doesn't have one. It makes me sorry for him" (*Shoot*, 1.9). Perhaps the self-made man and his autonomy are wanting. Betty spends much of the second and third seasons asserting the importance of family and trying to preserve her own. Unable to preserve her own family with Don, Betty divorces Don and marries another man, Henry Francis.

Stephanie Coontz considers Betty's decision to remarry and viewers' reaction to it. "At the end of Season 3, when Betty exchanged one husband and provider for another, some critics complained that she did not experience any personal growth as a result; she didn't even demand a divorce settlement."[18] Coontz explains Betty's inability for "personal growth" by reminding her readers that "homemakers of the early 1960s had few options: Only eight states gave a wife a legal right to share the earnings her husband had accumulated during their marriage."[19] The implication is that "personal growth" is at odds with marriage (and not just a bad marriage); it entails autonomy and independence. Betty understands her decision to remarry differently. She does not divorce Don for the opportunity for independence that social conventions denied to her. Rather, she sees her divorce and her remarriage as a way to provide stability for her children. The sight of a dollhouse brings a rare smile to Betty's face, even as it suggests that a happy home is a product of children's imaginations (*The Chrysanthemum and the Sword*, 4.5). We would be obliged to admit that Henry is a better, more reliable husband than Don, and he seems sincere in his effort to provide a stable home for Betty and her children. Still, Betty's relationship to Sally becomes ever more fraught due to Sally's continued unhappiness over her parents' divorce. By season five Betty has moved her family into an old, dark, Victorian house. What we have come to refer to as the "traditional family"—a husband and wife living in a home with their children—seems old-fashioned.

Are you Peggy?

If Betty cannot—or does not want to—become Don, Peggy can and does. Peggy is hired at Sterling Cooper as a secretary, but it is not long before she begins to imagine a promotion. The time does seem right for women's success in advertising.[20] The era's affluence gives women more purchasing power, making it more important that men try to understand what women are likely to buy. Peggy's colleague, Paul Kinsley, tells Peggy that there are female copywriters, and that "you can always tell when a woman's writing copy, but sometimes she just might be the right man for the job" (*Ladies Room*, 1.2). Peggy seems to represent the promise of Betty Friedan's liberation narrative, but her story also represents the perils of it.

At a loss for what to do for a new advertising strategy for Belle Jolie lipstick, the all-male creative team decides to "throw it to the chickens." The secretaries are all gathered to try on lipstick while the creative team looks on from behind a two-way mirror, hoping to get a better understanding of the audience for their ad. "The chickens" delight in the break from the routine and the opportunity to try new lipstick. They behave in a silly, unself-conscious manner (and they are ridiculed for it). Peggy does not take part in the fun. She sits and watches. When asked why she did not try on any of the lipstick, she explains that someone else had already chosen the color and she does not want to be one of a hundred colors in a box. Freddie Rumsen appreciates Peggy's insight and she is asked to try her hand at writing copy. Peggy's reason for not trying on the lipstick becomes the strategy for Belle Jolie, and Peggy comes up with the tagline "Mark Your Man." Don uses logic that resonates with Friedan's liberation narrative in his pitch to Belle Jolie. "Every woman wants choice, but no woman wants to be one of a hundred. She's unique. She makes the choices and she's chosen him … He's her possession" (*The Hobo Code*, 1.8). The woman who wears Belle Jolie lipstick creates her own identity and is not dependent on a man for it. The client likes that the campaign signals a new understanding of femininity.

Joan observes the celebration and considers its import. "I'm not saying that Peggy doesn't have something upstairs. I'm just saying that at Sterling Cooper things are usually happening downstairs." Joan has not been the dupe of a sexist culture. She understands the reasons and the ways that women have been successful in the past and she has made the most of a sexist culture that she did not create, but she recognizes a shift in the way women will gain professional success. Hannah Farrell beautifully explains that the pen that Joan often wears around her neck announces the difference between her and Peggy. Farrell observes that the pen allows its wielder to shape reality with words. "Joan's potential to wield the power of the pen is rarely realized—rarely do we see Joan actually write with this particular pen—and it makes a good metaphor for the portrayal of her character."[21] Farrell elaborates, "Both Joan's body and the gold casing of her pen are merely decorative, and yet both define the value which they contain".[22] Peggy, unlike Joan, behaves like a man; she uses the pen to create a new life for herself. As the series progresses, Joan also creates a new life for herself, but instead of using the power of her pen, Joan uses the power of her body.

As Peggy enjoys success as a copywriter, she puts on some weight. Weiner explains the reason for Peggy's weight gain.

> Peggy succeeds because the men will take a good idea from anywhere … I wanted to do a story about a woman getting fat because she couldn't deal with being sexualized all the time, and that more important, she was never going to be taken seriously professionally until that happened. She becomes a guy, and they give her a big punch in her shoulder. She makes it.[23]

It seems to the junior executives and to Joan that Peggy has let that success go to her head and has neglected her femininity. Joan suggests that Peggy should devote more attention to her appearance if she would like to do well at Sterling Cooper. Peggy defends herself by reminding Joan that she is the first woman ("girl") to do any writing at the agency since the war. Still, Joan insists that Peggy should not hide a very attractive girl under "too much lunch." Peggy responds in a condescending tone: "I just realized something. You think you're being helpful" (*Shoot*, 1.9). Peggy seems to anticipate a feminist critique of feminine power associated with sex appeal: a woman's talent and intelligence are more important than her looks.

As the first season draws to a close, Peggy is promoted to junior copywriter. She seems to be on her way to realizing that modern, but masculine, ideal articulated by Betty Friedan. Peggy has defied the era's expectations for femininity and is creating a new life for herself. Yet, at the moment of her entrance into the ranks of a profession dominated by men, the writers of *Mad .Men* once again complicate the notion of feminine success. As Joan walks Peggy to her new office, she offers Peggy qualified congratulations that have a prescience of the limitations of Friedan's liberation narrative. "I said congratulations, didn't I? Although sometimes when people get what they want, they realize how limited their goals were" (*The Wheel*, 1.13). Just a few moments later, Peggy begins to experience terrible stomach pains. The doctor in the hospital informs Peggy that she is in labor.

Weiner explains that Peggy's pregnancy was a plot twist on the idea that Peggy would not be taken seriously as a copywriter as long as she was sexualized by her male colleagues. Although Weiner downplays Peggy's pregnancy as a twist, I would argue that it is one of the most interesting elements of the series. Peggy's weight gain was due to her pregnancy, not in defiance of conventional standards of feminine beauty and sexuality. Peggy "becomes a guy" by being a woman. When told by the doctor that she is going into labor, Peggy finds it impossible to believe. She has not recognized any of the changes that her body has undergone during the past nine months. After the baby is born, she silently refuses to hold or acknowledge him.

The second season begins several months later in the winter of 1962. Peggy is back at work. There is some speculation about her absence, but the viewer does not know what happened in the months following the birth of Peggy's baby. It is as if her pregnancy "never happened." What we learn about that time we learn from flashbacks. Immediately following the birth of her baby, Peggy remains in the hospital, but now in the psychiatric ward. When Don visits Peggy and he asks her what is wrong with her, she says that she does not know. He says firmly, "Yes you do. Do it. Do whatever they say." He advises her to do "whatever they say" in order to get released and then move forward with her life. "This never happened," he says. "It will shock you how much it never happened" (*The New Girl*, 2.5). Don speaks from his own experience. By assuming the name of a fallen soldier during the Korean

War, Don leaves behind the life that chance had given him and he creates a new life for himself.

In her essay "Not a 'Jackie,' Not a 'Marilyn'; *Mad Men* and the Threat of Peggy Olson," Mary Ruth Marotte argues that "Peggy is all too aware of the limitations of embracing the traditional female role of wife and mother."[24] Marotte sets up a dichotomy between the private and the public sphere and elevates the public while denigrating the private. "Peggy forces a stoic expression of determination to get out, to return to her workplace, to become not one who facilitates the work of others but the one who creates, the one who has a hand in defining what the world will be rather than stagnating in the world as it is."[25] Marotte emphasizes Don's advice to move forward with her life, but it is only one part of it. Don also tells Peggy that "It will shock you how much it never happened."

The implications of Peggy's determination to re-create a self beyond femininity as it had been defined by mere sexuality or maternity are indeed shocking. As season two comes to a close, the employees of Sterling Cooper and their families fear and prepare for a nuclear attack during the Cuban Missile Crisis. Peggy and Pete find themselves alone in Pete's office. Peggy rejects Pete's advances by confessing to him that she had their baby and gave it up. "I could have had you in my life forever if I wanted to ... I could have shamed you into being with me, but I didn't want to ... You got me pregnant. I had a baby and I gave it away. I had your baby and I gave it away ... I wanted other things" (*Meditations on an Emergency*, 2.13). Peggy explicitly rejects a certain kind of feminine sexual power that would have come from her affair with Pete and the birth of their child. The exercise of that power would have prescribed a different, more conventional life—a life similar to Betty Draper's—for Peggy. However difficult it was for Peggy, she was able to free herself, not only from tradition and authority, but also from biology, in order to create a self. Peggy describes her pregnancy and labor to Pete. "One day you're there and then all of a sudden there is less of you. And you wonder where that part went ... And you keep thinking maybe you'll get it back. And you realize that it's just gone." Stunned, Pete can only say, "Why would you tell me that?" Peggy is both haunted by her choice (throughout the series there are allusions to Peggy's child) and transcends it. Celebration of Peggy's liberation is tempered by the costs of it.

Don's mistress in season two, Bobbie Barrett, articulates the paradox of femininity—potentially a source of power, it might also be a means of repression in a sexist system. Bobbie tells Peggy that she is never going to get a corner office until she starts to treat Don like an equal. But Bobbie has further advice for Peggy: "And no one will tell you this, but you can't be a man. So, don't even try. Be a woman. Powerful business when done correctly" (*The New Girl*, 2.5). In becoming Don's equal, Peggy must be different from Don. How to reconcile an embodied, empowered sexuality and femininity with professional success and respect remain contemporary dilemmas, as viewers still try to unravel Bobbie Barrett's riddle.

Are you Joan?

Don is generally seen as Peggy's mentor. And to be sure, he does give her invaluable lessons about advertising. However, it is Joan who first takes Peggy under her wing and who mentors Peggy on gender politics in the workplace. When Peggy begins working at the firm, Joan makes her high professional standards clear, but also offers Peggy lessons in using her femininity for professional gain. If Betty Draper is a twenty-first-century television incarnation of Friedan's frustrated housewife, Joan Holloway Harris is a twenty-first-century incarnation of Helen Gurley Brown's vivacious, smart, sexy single girl. Published in 1962, a year before *The Feminine Mystique*, Gurley Brown's *Sex and the Single Girl* offers an alternative to "the feminine mystique." The single girl

> is engaging because she lives by her wits. She supports herself. She has had to sharpen her personality and mental resources to a glitter in order to survive in a competitive world and the sharpening looks good. Economically she is a dream. She is not a parasite, a dependent, a scrounger, a sponger or a bum. She is a giver, not a taker, a winner and not a loser.[26]

Gurley Brown encourages women to make the most of their resources, which, at the time she was writing, was quite often only themselves. "What you do have to do is work with the raw material you have, namely you, never let up. You must develop style. Every girl has one ... it is just a case of getting it out in the open."[27] Brown goes on to advise her readers that a girl's style need not conform to any particular attributes or uncommon intelligence in order to bring her professional and romantic success.

> Whatever it is that keeps you from saying anything unkind and keeps you asking bright questions even when you don't quite understand the answers will do nicely. A lively interest in people and things (even if you aren't *that* interested) is why bosses trust you with new assignments, why men talk to you at parties … and sometimes ask you out to dinner.[28]

Brown's advice goes even further. "Sex is a powerful weapon for a single woman in getting what she wants from life."[29] In *Mad Men*'s first few seasons, which take place during the early 1960s, Joan embodies the young, lively woman who lives by her wits and by her sex appeal.

As Peggy begins to achieve some success as a copywriter, Joan is there to ensure that Peggy makes the most of the sexist system, though she does not encourage Peggy to challenge it. Frustrated with the lack of respect that she receives from her male colleagues, Peggy approaches Joan in a confidential manner. "There's business going on and I am not invited." Joan whispers back, "What are you asking me?" Peggy is forced to acknowledge Joan's keen understanding of how the power in the workplace operates and to ask for Joan's advice. Joan tells her, "You're in their country. Learn to speak the language." Peggy points out that Joan doesn't speak their language. Joan responds that she doesn't need to. "You want to be taken seriously? Stop dressing like a little girl" (*Maidenform*, 2.6). Joan's advice is puzzling. On the one hand, she seems to be telling Peggy to behave more like the men in the office. On the other hand, Joan seems to be telling Peggy that she needs to behave more like a woman. Peggy will have to blend femininity with professionalism, which in mid-century is steeped in masculinity. After a presentation to clients Peggy overhears the junior executives making plans to meet the clients out on the town. The outing is to a strip club, but Peggy is undeterred. And she seems to have followed Joan's advice—all of it. Arriving at the strip club, Peggy participates in the ribaldry as if she is at home in "their country," but her evening clothes and sophisticated hairdo are sexually appealing.[30]

The shift that Joan noticed at Peggy's celebration continues and Joan's exploitation of her sex appeal becomes less and less effective in exerting power.[31] Season four of *Mad Men* takes place in 1965 and a new set of young men are employed at Sterling Cooper Draper Pryce. In contrast to the almost always inappropriate and usually offensive banter of Roger Sterling, the leers and innuendos directed toward Joan become more explicit and deliberate with the intention to belittle her (*The Summer Man*, 4.8). Farrell smartly observes the differences between the generations of men. "[M]en … faced in the mid-sixties a series of attacks on their privileged positions. The source of these 'attacks' included the nascent feminist and gay rights movements, changing roles in the workplace, and concern about America's involvement in Vietnam."[32] Men of the previous generation, like Roger, did not feel the "attacks" as acutely, in part because their masculinity had already been proven by war, fatherhood, and professional success.[33] The increasingly malicious insults directed towards Joan culminate when one of the young illustrators draws a sexually explicit picture of her with one of the partners. Peggy is angry and wants to see the man punished. They know that the drawing is disrespectful to all women, not just Joan. Although Peggy appeals to Don, Don understands that his involvement would not help Peggy. He tells Peggy, "You want some respect? Go out there and get it for yourself" (*The Summer Man*, 4.8). Peggy fires the man and, in doing so, demands respect for Joan and for all women. Marotte explains the significance of Peggy's action:

> As the creative force—the writer of copy—in the ad agency, she can reconstruct not only what women want but also reframe men's perceptions of female desire. In firing the illustrator for his pornographic depictions of Joan, she [Peggy] offers that his way of rendering women is passé. That the revolution is underway, and that she has joined the fight.[34]

But, before we become too satisfied, the writers of *Mad Men* challenge this simple solution. Joan is angry that Peggy interfered. She accuses Peggy of being motivated by her ambition more than by her concern. "No matter how powerful we get around here, they can always just draw another cartoon. So all you have done is proven to them that I'm just a meaningless secretary and you're a humorless bitch" (*The Summer Man*, 4.8). Marotte explains Joan's anger as typical of "plenty of women who will hold fast to old gender paradigms and resist revision."[35] Her implication is that some women, including Joan, are simply the dupes or victims of sexism. But this assumption is as belittling as the sexist assumption of the cartoonist. By interfering, Peggy may have garnered respect for herself, but rendered the sharp, lively woman who "lives by her wits" weak and a victim. Joan's anger is justified. Yet Joan's solution would have been to use her sexual power to get the man fired, and that too is unacceptable. Viewers are left to wonder what a satisfactory response could have possibly been. Joan's experience does not simply reveal the need for feminism. It also suggests a critique of feminism.

"The single girl" who honed her style and calibrated her intelligence in order to be pleasing to men would come under feminist scrutiny. As younger, more radical women came to the women's movement, the personal became political. In her defense of the "consciousness raising groups" that sprung up across the country, Carol Hanisch rejects their characterization as simply depoliticized "therapy." "Therapy assumes that someone is sick and that there is a cure, e.g., a personal solution … Women are messed over, not messed up! We need to change the objective conditions, not adjust to them. Therapy is adjusting to your bad alternative."[36] During a consciousness-raising session, members of the group respond to questions based on their own personal experience. The women identified the connections between the responses and generalized about women's shared oppression based on their particular answers. "One of the first things we discover in these groups is that personal problems are political problems. There are no personal solutions at this time. There is only collective action for a collective solution."[37] Political power operated through personal relations, including sexuality. Unconscious or unaware of how power operates, women—presumably women like Joan Holloway Harris—simply adjust to a bad alternative. "Women as oppressed people act out of necessity (act dumb in the presence of men), not out of choice. Women have developed great shuffling techniques for their own survival (look pretty and giggle to get or keep a job or man) which should be used when necessary until such time as the power of unity can take its place."[38] The implication of this radical critique of male power is that women are either fooled or victimized by this power, and that they would only be liberated when they came to recognize and reject it.

As the summer of 1968 comes to a close, members of New York Radical Women planned their protest of the Miss America pageant in Atlantic City. The protest would become a seminal moment in the Women's Liberation

Movement and the stuff of urban legend. The press release that announced the event identified ten points that would be protested. Among those points was an objection to Paul Kinsey's certainty that "women want to see themselves as men see them" (*Maidenform*, 2.6). They protested "the Degrading Mindless-Boob-Girlie Symbol. The Pageant contestant epitomizes the roles we are all forced to play as women … So are women in our society to compete for male approval, enslaved by ludicrous 'beauty' standards we ourselves are conditioned to take seriously." The New York Radical Women also opposed "The Consumer Con-Game. Miss America is a walking commercial for the Pageant's sponsors."[39] *Mad Men's* viewers have watched the con as mostly male advertising executives convince women to purchase beauty products in order to conform to beauty standards determined by men. They are promised empowerment from their sexuality even as they are degraded by it. The protest organizers suggested that protestors throw "articles of female torture," such as bras and girdles into "Freedom Trashcans." In its coverage of the event, *Time* magazine reported that there were "bra-burnings" in the "Freedom Trashcans" and brought to mind those who burned their draft cards in protest of the Vietnam war.[40] Feminists were dubbed "bra-burners" even though no bras were actually burned. In an unexpected twist to our "much-needed lesson on the devastating costs of a way of life," Joan Holloway Harris protests her own image as a "Mindless-Boob-Girlie Symbol" in her aggressive pursuit to become an "account man." It is a Fortune 500 company catering to what radical feminists argued are false and pernicious notions of female beauty, Avon, that allows Joan to liberate herself from her role as a "Mindless Boob-Girlie Symbol."

As Joan enjoys lunch with Avon's new marketing director, Andy Hays, it becomes clear that what she thinks is a date Andy thinks is a business lunch. When Joan tells Peggy that Avon is the potential client, Peggy's ambition is visible. She immediately knows that this would be a very important client and that she would be perfect for the advertising campaign. Joan is unsure what to do next; she doesn't "want to get kicked off the diving board" (*A Tale of Two Cities*, 6.10). Peggy imagines that Joan would be named "the account man" if she wanted, and suggests that they take the news to Ted. "He loves new business. He doesn't care where it comes from." But Ted immediately identifies

Pete as the account man and instructs Joan to set up a meeting between Avon's marketing director, Pete, and Peggy. When Joan and Peggy gently try to assert Joan's role, Pete—in his most condescending tone—explains the hierarchy and Joan's place in it. It is Joan's job to tell the new client how important Pete is within company hierarchy.

Joan should not be mistaken for a radical feminist, but there is an interesting, even if unexpected, comparison to be drawn between her and radical feminists. Joan has always understood how power operates and she is no longer willing to follow the rules that were established by and for the benefit of men. The next morning Joan arrives at the breakfast that she has arranged. Before the client arrives, Joan tells Peggy that Pete was not invited to the breakfast meeting. Peggy is stunned and asks Joan, "How the hell are we supposed to do this?" (*Tale of Two Cities*, 6.10). There are no rules or conventions to guide two women who are seeking to satisfy their professional ambitions in large measure because they are not supposed to have professional ambition. The client arrives and Joan tells him of Peggy's impressive experience writing copy for beauty products. The very products that are said to perpetuate women's subjugation have allowed for Peggy's professional success and they will allow for Joan's advancement.

It is only a matter of time before Pete finds out that he was excluded from the meeting and that the usual process for courting new business has been circumvented. Joan attempts to quiet Pete by saying that the important thing is that the client is happy. Angrily, Pete snaps at Joan, "I bet you are making him very happy," assuming that Joan is having sex with Andy Hays. Joan immediately retorts "It is better than being screwed by you"—a reference to Pete's part in prostituting Joan in order to secure the Jaguar account. For a woman who is only recognized as a "Mindless-Boob-Girlie Symbol," the language of the bedroom and the conference room are interchangeable. The power of sexual hierarchy is exercised on her in both places and in a similar manner. The only way for Joan to liberate herself from the sexual hierarchy is to break the rules that perpetuate it. Pete appeals to Ted. "What we have here is a breach of the fundamental rules of this business ... It's a "revolt" (*A Tale of Two Cities*, 6.10). Although Peggy has disagreed with Joan's tactics and, from Joan's perspective, has never respected Joan, at this moment "the sisterhood is powerful." She arranges for Joan to be told that Avon's marketing director is on the phone for her (he is not). Ted is eager to see the client happy and encourages Joan to take the call. This settles the matter: Joan will be on the account. Ted shrugs, "Possession is 9/10 of the law." Pete responds, "Only where there is no law!" (*A Tale of Two Cities*, 6.10).

Joan and Peggy are making their own rules rather than by following those that have been determined for them by others. Joan, however, does not see herself as vulnerable or as a victim, and she is certainly not duped. Joan's savvy resilience is an attractive quality to a later generation of women, who both felt empowered by the achievements of second-wave feminism and felt belittled by the idea that femininity made women victims of a sexist system. *Mad Men* captures this ambivalence toward femininity as smartly as it portrays the era's sexism.

Mad Men's writers depart from the feminist account of women's liberation that champions the "bra-burners" rather than the "Mindless-Boob-Girlie Symbol." It turns out that the "Mindless-Boob-Girlie Symbol" isn't mindless. Avon's business allows Joan to liberate herself from that role at Sterling Cooper & Partners and her professional expertise is recognized and rewarded in season seven. Peggy's work for companies such as Belle Jolie, Playtex, and now Avon has also positioned her for further advancement. As season six concludes, Don is forced to take a leave of absence. While the other employees of Sterling Cooper & Partners celebrate Thanksgiving, Peggy goes into Don's office to sort through the work he has left behind and that she will have to continue. Viewers are gratified to see Peggy look out on to the Manhattan skyline from Don's chair in his corner office. Intelligence, creativity, and hard work have won out over sexism. Yet, in narrative parallel to Don, who chose to be alone at Thanksgiving in season one, Peggy finds herself alone on Thanksgiving, highlighting both the costs and rewards of professional progress for women in the 1960s. Her polyester plaid pantsuit is a stark contrast to the "feminine silhouettes" from the series beginning in 1960, but also to those of Banana Republic's 2011 fall line. *Mad Men*'s viewers, who seek the clothes inspired by Betty and Joan rather than Peggy, remind us that there was never a simple or a singular way to reconcile femininity with second-wave feminism's critique of it.

"I Did it My Way"

As season seven opens, Betty, Peggy, and Joan are all experiencing the frustration of reconciling their femininity with their desire for "something more"—albeit in different ways and for different reasons. Yet, by the mid-season finale of season seven, these three characters seem to anticipate a life that includes personal attachments that have long been associated with the home or the private sphere as well as the autonomy associated with the public sphere.

Although Peggy has been able to create a new, independent life for herself in the public sphere, she has not been able to forge lasting romantic attachments in the private sphere that were compatible with her autonomy. In both her relationship with Abe and with Ted, Peggy was at the mercy of their choices. When Valentine's Day 1969 rolls around, Peggy arrogantly assumes that the red roses sitting on her secretary Shirley's desk are for her. She thinks that Ted has sent them to her and, angry at him for jilting her, she gives Shirley her own flowers. "I should have bought you flowers out of respect, not because of some holiday. Are these some symbol of how much we are loved? It's a joke" (*A Day's Work*, 7.2). Shirley confesses that the flowers were sent to her by her fiancé and the embarrassed Peggy takes her frustration out on Shirley. "Who cares about your stupid flowers? You have a ring on. We all know that you are engaged. You did not have to embarrass me. Grow up." Peggy childishly asks Joan to put another secretary on her desk. Peggy's frustration reveals the limits of her autonomy. She first takes a position of female solidarity and independence ("I should have bought you flowers out of respect" and rejection of Valentine tokens denoting women's worth to men). But when her mistaken assumption that Ted sent her the flowers is revealed, Peggy reacts with anger and humiliation. She is not free from either external or her own internal expectations of desirability, love, and connection. She would like the romantic attachments associated with femininity and the private sphere. We also watch as Peggy's maternal affection for her young neighbor grows. Although she has found the independence promised by Friedan, she still wants "something more."

Always ambitious, Joan was able to use her sex appeal to achieve a degree of power at work, but she had never won the professional respect that she deserved. At the start of season seven Joan schools a business professor in advertising, leaving no doubt that she knows the business better than anyone. The professor's interest in her mind, not her body, foreshadows Joan's coming professional success. Joan is exasperated by the many personnel requests she regularly fields when Jim Cutler stops in her office to ask her about Avon. Cutler notes to Joan: "I just realized that you have two jobs, don't you?" Perhaps fearful that Cutler will prevent Joan from continuing the account work, she tells him, "I'm not complaining." Cutler suggests that maybe Joan should complain. "Well, there's an office open upstairs. It's for an account man, not the head of personnel" (*A Day's Work*, 7.12). As the episode ends, Joan carries a box of her personal belongings upstairs to her new office. Her box holds a bouquet of yellow roses. She tells Roger that the roses are from her son, but she immediately thanks Roger for them. Joan seems to have finally settled into a relationship with Roger that is based on their affection for one another rather than sexual exploitation. Joan's yellow roses are not "the symbol of how much we are loved" but the symbol of how equal we are. The yellow rose is the flower worn by those who supported the Nineteenth Amendment, granting suffrage to women.[41]

Betty also begins to renegotiate the tension between the feminine mystique with Friedan's liberation narrative. Although Betty has not pursued (at least not seriously) work outside of the home, she now considers it. She meets her old friend and neighbor, Francine, for lunch. Francine takes pleasure and pride in her new job as a travel agent, and she tells Betty that she sees the job as a reward for her work in the home. Betty responds that "the children are the reward (*Field Trip*, 7.3). Despite Betty's efforts to be a good mother—attempts that often backfire or seem half-hearted to twenty-first-century viewers who still feel some anxiety about their relationships with their own children—Betty's connections with her children are tenuous and fleeting. As Gene sleeps sweetly on her breast, Betty feels that "it is only a matter of time" before her children will grow independent—maybe even resentful—of her. And being the wife of an elected official is not as satisfying as she once imagined. When Betty offers a political opinion at a party, Henry tells her to stick to hostessing: "Keep your conversation to how much you hate getting toast crumbs in the butter and leave the thinking to me" (*The Runaways*, 7.5).

Betty hasn't forgotten Henry's lack of respect the next day when he tells her that he does not want to join her and sit at the kitchen table "like the help." "The help? I'm going to assume that you're not referring to me … I am tired of everyone telling me to shut up. I'm not stupid. I speak Italian." Henry knows that Betty is referring to his comments at the party and apologizes for embarrassing her. Betty responds, "You're sorry you forgot to tell me what to think. Guess what; I think all by myself." Henry sarcastically suggests that Betty run for office. Without sarcasm or irony Betty tells him, "You know what, Henry, I don't know what I am going to do, but that's a good idea" (*The Runaways*, 7.5). Viewers, who have been waiting for Betty to "get mad" for six and a half years, have reason to anticipate that she will find her own way to reconcile the feminine mystique with a desire for "something more" in the public sphere. Despite the political efforts of both major parties to claim that they represent women, the diversity of political opinion among women resists easy categorization. Betty's political path, should she choose one, is likely to look more like those chosen by Phyllis Schlafly, Elizabeth Dole, or Sarah Palin than it is to resemble the paths of Nancy Pelosi, Geraldine Ferraro, or Hillary Rodham Clinton.

As a copywriter, a person who is paid to use words to create a desire for something new, Peggy articulates the changes to our notions of femininity that second-wave feminism (either as they are suggested early by Betty Friedan or later by more radical feminists, such as members of New York Radical Women) bring to Betty, Peggy, and Joan. Peggy is working on a new commercial for Burger Chef, which features a mother surrounded by her happy family at the dinner table at home. Although her colleagues like the ad, she is dissatisfied. Tired, drunk, and frustrated, Peggy asks Don, "Does this family exist anymore? Are there people who eat dinner and smile at each other instead of watching TV?" Don and Peggy are both self-made individuals. Yet both admit that they do not want to be alone. They reflect on their own personal choices. Peggy wonders, "What if there was a place where you could go where there was no TV and you could break bread. Anyone you were sitting with was family." The family, in other words, need not be bound together by the "happy housewife heroine." Peggy suggests that the ad take place not at a kitchen table in the home but at the Burger Chef restaurant.

By expanding the notion of family and bringing it into the public sphere, Peggy anticipates the variety of families that *Mad Men*'s viewers are familiar with nearly fifty years later. At that moment, Frank Sinatra's song "My Way" begins to play on the radio and Don and Peggy dance. Frank Sinatra is a singer Peggy explicitly identifies with an older generation of Americans. Yet these lyrics are somehow appropriate to the younger generation of Americans who defy convention. The song, both its singer and lyrics, capture Betty's, Peggy's, and Joan's effort to negotiate an older generation's notions of femininity even while taking advantage of the new opportunities made possible by second-wave feminism. It is a nostalgic choice for the heirs of second-wave feminism who have sought to reconcile the two.

Notes

1　First-wave feminism refers to the political efforts of women during the late nineteenth and early twentieth centuries to expand political and legal rights to women, most notably the right to vote. Third-wave feminism refers to efforts of a new generation of feminists to promote change, beginning in the 1990s. They sought to build a more racially and sexually diverse movement.

2　Betty Friedan, *The Feminine Mystique*. (New York: Bantam Doubleday Dell, 1983), p. 43.

3　Ibid.

4　Estelle B. Freedman, *No Turning Back: The History of Feminism and the Future of Women* (New York: Ballantine Books, 2002), p. 87.

5　Deborah Siegel, *Sisterhood Interrupted: From Radical Women to Grrls Gone Wild* (New York: Palgrave Macmillan, 2007), p. 2.

6　Ibid., p. 115.

7　See, for example, *What Our Mothers Didn't Tell Us* by Danielle Crittenden, *Sentenced to Everyday Life: Feminism and the Housewife* by Leslie Johnson and Justine Lloyd, and *To Hell with All That: Loving and Loathing Our Inner Housewife* by Caitlin Flanagan.

8　See, for example, "Motherhood" by Allison Abner or "'How Does a Supermodel Do Feminism?' An Interview with Veronica Webb" in *To Be Real: Telling the Truth and Changing the Face of Feminism*, Anchor Press, 1995, edited by Rebecca Walker.

9　Frederick Loewe and Alan Jay Lerner, "On the Street Where You Live," sung by Vic Damone, 1956, by Columbia Records 33014, used in closing credits of *Smoke Gets in Your Eyes* (1.1).

10	Friedan, *The Feminine Mystique*, p. 18.

11	Ibid., p. 33.

12	Ibid., p. 338.

13	Leslie Johnson and Justine Lloyd, *Sentenced to Everyday Life: Feminism and the Housewife* (New York: Berg, 2004), p. 12.

14	Judy Giles, *The Parlour and the Suburb: Domestic Identities, Class, Femininity and Modernity* (New York: Berg, 2004), p. 153.

15	Consider the recent essays by two women who have been highly successful in their professions and have also raised children. Anne-Marie Slaughter's article "Why Women Can't Have it All" appeared in *The Atlantic* in its July/August 2012 issue and Debra Spar's "Why Women Should Stop Trying to Be Perfect" appeared on *The Daily Beast* website in September 2012.

16	Friedan, *The Feminine Mystique*, p. 307.

17	Jimmy Duncan, "My Special Angel," sung by Bobby Helms, 1957, by Decca Records, used in *Shoot* (1.9).

18	Stephanie Coontz, "Why 'Mad Men' is TV's most feminist show," *Washington Post*, October 10, 2010. http://www.washingtonpost.com/wp-dyn/content/article/2010/10/08/AR2010100802662.html (accessed May 21, 2014).

19	Ibid.

20	See Kate Edenborg's chapter "Going Groovy or Nostalgic" for more on the changing advertising landscape and the integration of women and minorities into advertising during the 1960s.

21	Hannah Farrell, "Joey, Joan, and the Gold-Plated Necklace," in Heather Marcovitch and Linda E. Batty, eds, *Mad Men, Women, and Children: Essays on Gender and Generation* (Lanham, MD: Lexington, 2012), p. 50.

22	Ibid., p. 52.

23	Alex Witchel, "'Mad Men' Has Its Moment," *New York Times*, June 22, 2008. http://www.nytimes.com/2008/06/22/magazine/22madmen-t.html (accessed May 21, 2014).

24	Mary Ruth Marotte, "Not a 'Jackie,' Not a 'Marilyn': *Mad Men* and the Threat of Peggy Olson," in Marcovitch and Batty, (eds), *Mad Men, Women, and Children*, p. 36.

25	Ibid.

26	Helen Gurley Brown, *Sex and the Single Girl* (New York: Barricade Books, 2003), pp. 5–6.

27	Ibid., pp. 9–10.

28   Ibid., p. 10.

29   Ibid., p. 267.

30   Tom Fitzgerald and Lorenzo Marquez have astute commentary on all the characters' clothes at tomandlorenzo.com. More than any other female character, Peggy's clothes resemble her male counterparts'. Still, I would note that they are decidedly women's clothes, a further indication that Peggy seeks to redefine femininity.

31   In her essay "'So Much Woman': Female Objectification, Narrative Complexity, and Feminist Temporality in AMC's *Mad Men*," Fiona E. Cox demonstrates how Joan is complicit in the female objectification during the first four seasons as a way of "getting what she wants from life." Cox demonstrates that the power Joan exercises is diminished during the course of the first four seasons and that the series "gradually, but actively encourage[s]a feminist perspective in the viewer": *In Visible Culture*, Issue 17, May 2012. I would say that viewer's perspective is not linear, from an "unenlightened" nostalgia for Joan's sexual power to a feminist rejection of it. From the very beginning of the series, repulsion from Joan's exploitation of her sex appeal is mingled with attraction to her seductively swaying hips and knowing smile.

32   Marcovitch and Batty, (eds), *Mad Men, Women, and Children*, p. 46.

33   Ibid., p. 47.

34   Ibid., p. 41.

35   Ibid.

36   www.carolhanisch.org/CHwritings/PIP (accessed August 20, 2014).

37   Ibid.

38   Ibid.

39   www.redstockings.org

40   This proved to be an exaggeration of the protest. The organizers complied with police instructions not to endanger Atlantic City's historic wooden boardwalk and did not light fires (Seigel, *Sisterhood Interrupted*, p. 49).

41   In August of 1920, Tennessee was poised to be the thirty-sixth and the last state necessary to ratify the Nineteenth Amendment. The suffragists wore yellow roses and the anti-suffragists wore red. The vote came down to the youngest member of the assembly, Harry Burn, who wore a red rose. Although the political leaders of his district opposed ratification, Harry Burn's mother was for it. She had written to her son, "Hurrah! And vote for suffrage and don't keep them in doubt … Don't forget to be a good boy and help Mrs. Catt put the 'rat' in ratification." At the last moment, Harry Burn voted in favor of the amendment. Later, he explained that it always best to follow a mothers' advice. Mothering is a feminist act.

9

Invisible Men: The Politics and Presence of Racial and Ethnic "Others" in *Mad Men*

Linda Beail

As its seven seasons stretch across the 1960s, *Mad Men* reflects and interprets the social, political, and cultural changes happening in the United States during that pivotal and tumultuous decade. The narratives of Don Draper, his colleagues, and his family play out against the backdrop of the civil rights movement, second-wave feminism, the Vietnam war, and political assassinations. Changing roles and norms in American life—from dress to drug use to divorce—impact the look and the plotlines of the show. One of the things critics and fans noted from the beginning is *Mad Men*'s attention to detail; its creators and producers seem determined to capture a certain verisimilitude about the period. From the costumes to the lighting to the news stories flickering on the television set in the Draper living room, very few anachronisms appear. Indeed, watching an episode of *Mad Men* can be like experiencing time travel back to the 1960s. Just as Don Draper falls through space in the title sequence, viewers spin through time back into the world of post-war, pre-Watergate Madison Avenue.

Historians have noted ways in which film or television often use and portray the past, which is important to note as we discuss the ways in which *Mad Men* treats racial change and our own understandings of race. The show is not a documentary. It is not trying to present a historically factual or objective account of life in the 1960s in Manhattan's advertising world, though it borrows heavily from real events, styles, and trends. *Mad Men* is a imaginative account of life in that world, told with a particular aesthetic and perspective. The narrative choices made in the re-telling of this slice of American life, then, are important. One common way of dealing with a re-telling of historical events is to frame them with contemporary understandings. So a film about slavery will gesture to its audience that we *know* slavery is evil, and signal to us through its situations, characters, music, and visuals how to interpret the past in light of the present. We know who to despise, and who to root for, not in empathy with a complicated past, but via our own modern judgments and commitments. *Mad Men* presents little of this kind of overt editorializing or cue-giving in its treatment of racism, sexism, and anti-Semitism in our recent past. It offers a glimpse into office interactions that seem shockingly sexist and racist by today's standards, but are presented matter-of-factly and as utterly routine.

Some have argued that this type of presentation is even more powerful, since it shows how normalized and systemic things like sexual harassment and discrimination were in America's not-so-distant past. It is hard to dismiss such behavior as stemming from a few malicious or benighted bosses when it is so widespread and the secretaries themselves are accepting of it, even complicit in it, as simply "the way things are." One could assert that this realistic-yet-breathtaking depiction of sexism makes the show "feminist," as contemporary viewers are shocked into consciousness of the rampant objectification of women.[1] *Mad Men*'s audiences come to appreciate the necessity of feminism (in making changes so this treatment is, in fact, shocking and unfamiliar to us now). It might even link past to present, as some viewers recognize with new awareness vestiges of this objectification and devaluation that remain with us now, and make feminism still relevant. Yet there is also the possibility for confusion in interpretation. As audiences revel in the mid-century modern aesthetic of the show—searching for vintage Eames chairs, re-discovering cocktails like Don Draper's favorite Old Fashioned or Peggy Olson's Manhattan, and popularizing curve-hugging sheath dresses like the ones worn by Joan Holloway—one could also argue that the feminist critique implicit in the show's portrayal of 1960s limited roles and treatment of women has been lost. The enthusiastic embrace of the sexy "look" and glamorous appeal of those characters undermines the critical edge of the narrative, turning critique into commodification.

So, what are we to make of the politics of race in *Mad Men*? Certainly, one of the greatest shifts in American life during the 1960s happened with regard to race relations. The Civil Rights Movement, building momentum since World War II, began to come to fruition. Sit-ins, bus boycotts, Freedom Rides, passage of the Civil Rights Act of 1964 and the Voting Rights Act of 1965, as well as growing resistance to police brutality and economic inequality, race riots, and the murders of Malcolm X and Martin Luther King Jr.—all form the social and political landscape of the *Mad Men* era. Yet the show and its creator Matthew Weiner have been criticized for ignoring or downplaying racial issues in their portrayal of the 1960s. As the Civil Rights Movement and racial integration made major progress through the decade, many viewers and critics wondered why this show has not taken more advantage of the opportunity to depict these social changes and tell the stories of African Americans as fully developed characters. Daniel Mendelsohn complained in the *New York Review of Books* that *Mad Men*'s treatment of race was "little more than a lazy allusion."[2] In a high-traffic blog post at Slate.com, Latoya Peterson went further, accusing the show of being "truly written by cowards" for "ignoring race" and keeping black characters marginalized, "trapped in a romantic haze of noble, silent suffering" as ladies' room attendants, maids, elevator operators, janitors, and waiters.[3]

As each new season premiere neared, numerous media stories asked if this season would "Finally Bring Race into the Picture?" or assumed that, at long last, the show had progressed far enough into the 1960s that race must begin to play a more central role.[4] A headline at *The Atlantic* asked "Will *Mad Men* Ever Be as Good on Race as it is on Gender?" while its roundtable of editors bemoaned the fact that the topic had been addressed with mere "tentative scratches at race issues" and not "with anywhere near the complexity and nuance as ... gender."[5] The Root, a website for black news, opinion, politics and culture, began a "black people counter" for season four, simply listing the (paltry) number of times African-American characters appeared in each episode.[6] Actress Erika Alexander responded to her disappointment with the show's tokenism by writing her own 45-page *Mad Men* episode screenplay incorporating significant African-American characters seamlessly into the arc of the series' storylines. Entitled "Uptown Saturday Night," Alexander's original script has Don Draper headed to Harlem to collaborate with a black advertising executive in selling Seagram's whiskey, and, through their lively interaction, inventing the Seven and Seven cocktail. Alexander posted the screenplay on her website as a challenge to the show's prevailing whiteness and proof that black characters could be woven organically into the drama.[7]

While the criticisms are plausible, an argument can be made that *Mad Men* does not overlook or avoid the politics of race. Rather, the show is deliberate and sophisticated in critiquing racism by immersing viewers in the experience of "white privilege" typical of the time period, and still relevant to understanding race relations in the United States today. Putting blatantly racist statements into the mouths of its suave, attractive characters and refusing to "whitewash the white men" with the more egalitarian attitudes of the twenty-first century is what gives *Mad Men* its critical "edge."[8] As Tanner Colby explains, "Mad Men isn't cowardly for avoiding race. Quite the opposite. It's brave for being honest about Madison Avenue's cowardice."[9] By depicting the racial exclusion prevalent in 1960s corporate America, Matthew Weiner is "right on schedule, historically speaking."[10] But the show is not simply reflecting with accuracy its time period, or its swath of elite (and overwhelmingly white) men and women involved in advertising and commerce on the island of Manhattan. By so thoroughly and disturbingly demonstrating the ease and careless arrogance of white entitlement, with no imperative to consider or focus on the lives of those who are different, *Mad Men* is an "appropriate vehicle to highlight the stain of racism and the unconscious cruelty of white privilege" and offer a subversive critique of Roger Sterling et al.'s "adolescent ignorance."[11]

Creator Matthew Weiner has defended the whiteness of the show as an accurate representation of the advertising industry of the time, but also noted that he did not want to write a knee-jerk response to white guilt over racism or have the show become some kind of racial "wish fulfillment" in which whites are easily resuscitated or absolved from their own prejudice.[12] Critics have praised the show for not defaulting into tropes of either the exceptional negro or the white savior.[13] *Mad Men* is self-conscious about the politics of representation and the politics of nostalgia, knowing those with power are tempted to go back and rework history in their own image, fulfilling contemporary purposes and ideals. As Michael Berube points out, white people,

[l]ove stories about American history in which the drama of race is vividly front and center *and features some good white people.* Elsewhere I've called this the Huckleberry Finn Fantasy—"the seductive notion that if *we* were alive back then, even if we were poor backwoods kids whose only formal education included lessons about how abolitionism was immoral and lowdown, we would somehow, all by our lonesome, come to the conclusion that we should save Jim and go to Hell."[14]

That impulse to be "Good White People" produces pop culture representations of the 1960s like *Mississippi Burning* (1988) or *The Help* (2011), in which "sympathetic white people turn out to be the real heroes of the civil rights movement."[15] Berube concludes that *Mad Men* "does well to smack down that desire ASAP, by giving the structural role of the Good White Person to the cringe-inducing Paul Kinsey in season one."[16] The show does not allow its (white) characters to escape their culture or economic/political systems in a burst of solipsistic heroism, just as it does not allow its characters of other races to escape the social, economic, and political systems and norms that keep them powerfully at the margins—of the story, and of 1960s American society.

Mad Men consistently, from its first episode onward, presents African-American characters and raises questions about race and power. The very first scene of the pilot episode features Don Draper in a bar, trying to come up with ideas for a cigarette campaign, striking up a conversation with "Sam," an African-American man clearing tables. From the very beginning, it is clear how rigidly segregated this society is. A white waiter immediately asks Don if Sam is "bothering him" (though Don initiated the conversation, and Sam is too surprised and wary of the breaching of social norms to even answer him at first). *Mad Men* is not an all-white universe, oblivious to the existence of people of color. The first two characters we encounter are a black man and a white man. But *Mad Men* is a world of white privilege, made clear by their interaction. Throughout the show, African-American characters appear in silent and subordinate positions. They do real and necessary work (cleaning Sterling Cooper offices and caring for the Draper children), but we experience them only through the perspective of the white characters. We see Carla in the Draper kitchen, but we never get to follow her home or experience her multi-dimensional life (at one point, when Betty Draper is in anguish over her disintegrating marriage to Don, Carla offers an empathetic ear, noting that she has been married twenty years herself and hinting at a life beyond making the Draper existence possible). While some critics and viewers wonder what willful ignorance keeps the show from focusing on the rich interior lives of black characters as well as white, Ta-Nehisi Coates recognizes the political power of this representation:

> I actually think it's a beautiful, lovely, incredibly powerful omission. *Mad Men* is a show told from the perspective of a particular world. The people in that world barely see black people. They're there all the time—Hollis in the elevator, women working in the powder-room, the Drapers' maid, the janitors, the black guy hired at Leo Burnett—but they're never quite *seen*. I think this is an incredible statement on how privilege, at its most insidious, really works.[17]

The invisibility of racialized "others" is a key political strategy of the show. Just as Ralph Ellison used the invisibility of his protagonist in his 1952 novel to paradoxically shed light on twentieth-century racial politics, the invisibility of Jews and African Americans at the start of the series draws our attention and makes us notice their absence. The casual way in which Don Draper assures Roger Sterling that the agency has definitely not hired any Jews on his watch is startling to twenty-first-century viewers in its blatant anti-Semitism (*Smoke Gets In Your Eyes*, 1.1). The irony is that the absence of anyone Jewish is suddenly problematic, as they are preparing to pitch their services to Rachel Menken, a Jewish department store proprietor. What the firm has actively worked to not have to see, it now needs to show as a visible sign to this new client; Roger congratulates himself on finding a Jewish young man in the mailroom to sit in on the meeting with Miss Menken. Of course, Rachel Menken is unimpressed by this token sign or their pitch, which relies on the crudest ethnic stereotypes of Jewish parsimony. When she calls them out on their laziness (in assuming all she wants in the way of marketing is a coupon strategy, and in not even visiting her family's flagship store on Fifth Avenue), the ad men realize they have greatly underestimated the intelligence and the potential revenue stream of this client. Roger urges Don to rectify the situation and woo back her interest in employing the agency.

Mad Men does not choose to focus on anti-Semitism at the expense of racism. Rather, the show illustrates how very socially constructed the concept of race is as it contrasts the experiences of Jewish Americans with those of African Americans. While the show matter-of-factly depicts the blatant anti-Semitism of the early 1960s, it also illustrates the assimilation of Jews like Rachel Menken and copywriter Michael Ginsberg into the Madison Avenue realm of WASP culture and privilege via socioeconomic mobility, much as Karen Brodkin describes in her work *How Jews Became White Folks*.[18] While both Jewish people and African Americans begin the series as clearly "other," Jews are able to "pass" as white and actually join that world via their wealth and education; it is class that helps to determine the meaning of race, and skin color that tautologically blocks African Americans from being able to traverse those boundaries as well as being given meaning and definition by its very isolation. Blacks can't assimilate because of their race, and race is defined by being other/non-assimilated.

Post-war prosperity and government policies contributed to the burgeoning of the American middle class in the second half of the twentieth century. The GI Bill opened the doors to higher education for a far wider swath of the population than ever before, which allowed for greater professional ambitions and higher incomes, often at jobs made possible by the military–industrial complex and government investment in science, research, and technology. VA loans made home ownership possible for millions more, and proliferating suburbs were made more accessible by the development of federal interstate highways. Yet these policies were most beneficial to white veterans and often not fully available to returning black servicemen.[19] Jews and "white ethnics" were able to take advantage of these postwar economic opportunities in ways that African Americans were not (because of segregation in higher education and racially based redlining practices by home lenders, for example), and this intersection of class mobility with racial/ethnic identities led to the re-construction of meaning for those ethnic categories. Peggy Olson hails from a working-class, Irish immigrant family from Brooklyn; in the nineteenth century this heritage would have marked her as "non-white" (just as Italian and Eastern European immigrants were labeled as "other" races), but by the 1960s, she is able to cross into Manhattan (and out of the typing pool) as a person whose ethnicity no longer sets her apart as "other."[20] Even Roger Sterling, who exhibits such an anti-Semitic attitude at the start of the series, finds himself with a Jewish second wife, Jane, by the beginning of season three. (Jane, a beautiful twenty-year-old college graduate who came to work at Sterling Cooper as a secretary, is quick to note that she would like to change her Jewish surname, Siegel, to Sterling.)

In *Tea Leaves* (5.3), Peggy hires Michael Ginsberg to work in the creative department. He is young and brilliant; while his Jewish ethnicity is no secret, his neurotic, creative persona seems more along the lines of Sid Caesar or Lenny Bruce than the old-fashioned, non-assimilated image of his father, whom we see saying prayers in Hebrew and trying to arrange a match for his son with a "nice Jewish girl." While there are still moments in which lingering anti-Semitism exists, what we see in *Mad Men* over the course of the decade is the movement of Jews and "white ethnics" into the dominant racial culture of whiteness. When, in 1969, Joan's mother makes a disparaging comment about having fewer shopping options because "the Jews close everything on Saturday," a look of exasperated disbelief flashes across Joan's face and she quickly changes the subject (*The Strategy*, 7.6). The scene acknowledges that bigoted attitudes still exist, but clearly communicates that they are the vestiges of an outdated worldview, passing away with an older generation and not embraced by those (like Joan) who are seizing the future.

Mad Men also examines the notion that African Americans can be assimilated into the mainstream of American life as consumers, if not citizens. Account executive Pete Campbell notices an interesting fact in the market research for Admiral TV sets: sales are flat in most of the US, but growing in "Atlanta, Oakland, Detroit, Newark, DC, St. Louis and Kansas City" (*The Fog*, 3.5). When Paul Kinsey notes that these are also "great jazz cities," Pete wonders aloud if it is possible that Admiral sets are being bought largely by "negroes" and suggests an advertising campaign targeted at black consumers. Bert Cooper promptly shoots that idea down with a tart "Admiral Television has *no* interest in becoming a colored television company." (Interestingly, this notion that such a campaign would only harm the brand by being "tainted" by race is contested by the show when they have Lane Pryce, overseer of the firm's finances, presciently remark that "it *does* seem as though there is money to be made in the Negro market.")

Pete is optimistic that equality can be achieved through free markets and rational self-interest (a view that could be shared by contemporary viewers and political rhetoric). As he ponders the Admiral TV strategy, he strikes up a conversation with the black elevator operator Hollis about which brand of television he and his friends own. Hollis is uncomfortable with this conversation (maybe because Pete is asking him to risk violating the norm of black silence and invisibility usually observed in his service role, or maybe because he does not want to be co-opted for Pete's research and career advancement). He tells Pete that African Americans have "got bigger problems than this to worry about than TV, okay?" (*The Fog*, 3.5).

Pete responds "You're thinking about this in a very narrow way. The idea is that everyone is going to have a house, a car, a television—the American dream." Here we see the conflation of freedom and democracy with consumer choice, and the assumption that a rising tide of post-war prosperity can swamp racism by making the American (material) dream accessible to everyone. Blacks can buy televisions just like whites can: hence equal opportunity (to consume) as the end of racist exclusion, and social progress as a result of economic self-interest instead of political movement. Hollis seems skeptical of this view, as well he might considering how pervasive segregation and disenfranchisement remained and how little of the post-war American dream was accessible to African Americans. He looks at Pete with cold skepticism before starting the elevator car. When he continues to rebuff Pete's questions, demurring that he doesn't watch television, Pete exclaims, "You don't watch baseball? I don't believe you!" Hollis finally grins, admitting that much is true, as they share a mutual laugh. Note that the commonality Pete finds is in baseball—America's pastime, as patriotic as mom and apple pie. But we might well ask if shared fandom and purchasing power are enough to create true political equality.

In the following season, it is Peggy who makes an attempt to incorporate more racial diversity into an advertising campaign. When Fillmore Auto Parts comes to the agency for help because their stores are being boycotted in the South and they are losing business, Peggy suggests hiring popular

Caribbean–American singer and civil rights activist Harry Belafonte to help the company's image (*The Beautiful Girls*, 4.9). Peggy's co-workers scoff at this idea while Don, her boss, rejects it with this amoral rationale: "Our job is to make men like Fillmore Auto Parts, not to make Fillmore Auto Parts like negroes." Don espouses a position often heard, evading moral responsibility for taking action or taking a stand against injustice because "I'm just doing my job." In contrast to the earlier example with Admiral TVs, here racial justice will not be achieved through the invisible hand of the markets (though the economic lever of boycotts, it is suggested, can be a powerful tool when deliberately used for achieving social change). Instead, profit and pleasing the client are reasons for *not* addressing the moral and political issues at hand.

The solution to the Fillmore Auto Parts dilemma turns out to be shoring up white masculinity, which according to Dr. Faye Miller is under threat. She explains that men are losing the ability to be useful with their hands, to do tangible things, and that "they will pay a lot for that feeling." Thus the pitch incorporates the tagline "Fillmore Auto Parts. For the Mechanic in Every Man." The appeal to a rugged, self-sufficient masculinity, with connotations of working-class roots, asserts both masculine and white superiority, resisting whatever fears white men might have of becoming effeminate or racially contaminated.

Ironically, the reason Peggy becomes aware enough of the Fillmore boycotts to suggest Harry Belafonte for the ads is that she's been set up on a date with Abe Drexler, a journalist who tells her about how the auto parts company refuses to hire blacks. As Abe waxes on enthusiastically about the revolutionary moment they are living in and the importance of the civil rights struggle, Peggy tells him she agrees, but adds, "I have to say, most of the things negroes can't do, I can't do either. And nobody seems to care … Half of the meetings take place over golf, tennis, in a bunch of clubs where I'm not allowed to be a member, or even enter. The University Club said the only way I could eat dinner there was if I arrived in a cake." Here *Mad Men* shows Peggy's glimmering recognition of how systemic sexism can work in parallel ways to racism, and a slowly dawning consciousness that how she is treated might not be simply natural, but unjust. Abe's response is to scoff at how ludicrous this parallel seems. He laughs condescendingly, "All right, Peggy. We'll have a civil rights march for women." Offended and confused, she gets up from the bar and ends the date.

At the end of this same episode, Joyce reminds Peggy of how normalized—yet potentially unjust—gender relations are. "You gotta be their girl. It's the way they want it. Maybe it's biology." Joyce goes on to compare men to vegetable soup: "You can't put it on a plate or eat it off the counter. So women are the pot. They heat them up. They hold them. They contain them. But who wants to be a pot? Who the hell said we're not soup?" (*The Beautiful Girls*, 4.9). Peggy is silent, looking dumbfounded but intrigued by the idea that she could be "soup," the subject of her own life, and not merely a container or support for someone else's.

The women of *Mad Men* demonstrate how "the personal is political." Peggy, Joan, and Betty in particular have very different backgrounds, experiences, and reactions to the events of the 1960s. Yet the show questions and illustrates the limitations and changing possibilities of femininity in this decade. None of them becomes radicalized by a single incident or serves as a mouthpiece for a simple feminist ideology, yet all three embody a slowly dawning realization of sexist limits and some feminist consciousness. As the series opens, Joan aspires to marry a doctor and never work again. In season two, she goes beyond managing the office to help read TV scripts for Harry Crane, and discovers that she is quite good at it—so successful, in fact, that the firm decides to hire a man to do the job full-time (*A Night to Remember*, 2.8; *Six Month Leave*, 2.9). The look on Joan's face when she realizes her invisibility because she is a woman—that the ad men are oblivious to her talent and could not conceive of considering her for the job—speaks volumes, but she silently accepts that this is the way the world works. In fact, at the beginning of the series, she is the one who is constantly reminding Peggy of the "rules of the game" for women, advising her on how to use her feminine assets in the office, and also disapproving of Peggy's efforts to become "one of the guys" as a copywriter. However, by season seven, Joan has grown and changed. A divorced single mother who has survived being raped by her then-fiancé and endured the indignity of having to work to support her husband financially, she jumps at the chance to win an account of her own (*A Tale of Two Cities*, 6.10). Realizing the men in the agency still see her less as a partner to be trusted with her own client, and more as the sexually available female they prostituted in order to get a big car company account, Joan engages in a bit of well-planned deception in order to take the meeting with Avon herself. (And when Joan is caught, it is Peggy who comes to her aid and helps her keep the account: sisterhood is powerful.)

Mad Men has resisted the temptation to simply put a copy of *The Feminine Mystique* in the hands of unhappy housewife Betty Draper Francis. But by 1969, she is "tired of people telling [her] to shut up" (*The Runaways*, 7.5). Her husband Henry yells at her for expressing a differing political opinion at a party and embarrassing him, dismissively telling her to stick to discussions of how to keep toast crumbs out of the butter. Betty is still enraged the following day and lashes back, telling him that she resents his insinuation that she is "the help" and reminding him that she is educated, intelligent, and can think for herself: for goodness' sake, "I speak Italian!" Betty's personal experiences of gender roles and expectations may be starting to lead her to wider political awareness. When Henry utters the throwaway line "If you're so smart, why don't *you* run for office?" Betty responds coolly and ominously that she doesn't know what she's going to do, "but that's a good idea" (*The Runaways*, 7.5).

Again, many viewers and critics have wondered why racial consciousness has not been treated in the show with the same sophistication, depth, and complexity as this evolving awareness of sexism. We shouldn't excuse the show for ignorance or for simply being afraid to deal with race; but what if the dissimilar representations of sexism and racism actually tell us something true and important about how differently these two systematic modes of oppression operated?

Just as Peggy's consciousness perhaps started to be raised by Abe's ridicule of women's situation, the inclusion of sex discrimination in the Civil Rights Act of 1964 is often credited to a joke. Southern Congressmen hoping to block the bill viewed the notion of women's equality as ridiculous. How or why would women abandon their "feminine natures" and want the same treatment in the workplace or legal system as men? It seemed unthinkable, at least to Rep. Howard Smith of Virginia, who added the word "sex" to the list of prohibited discriminations in the bill in an effort to defeat it. Rep. Martha Griffiths of Michigan, and other feminist men and women, got the last laugh when the landmark bill was passed, with language outlawing discrimination on the basis of sex as well as race in place.[21]

In similar fashion, the breaking of Sterling Cooper's color barrier was not the result of intentional social change or anti-racist activism, but a reaction to a prank by a rival ad agency. In an incident inspired by a true story covered on the front page of the *New York Times* on May 28, 1966, the show depicts Sterling Cooper staffers' glee when executives at Young & Rubicam are embarrassed in the newspaper for throwing water bombs at protestors on the street below (in the actual story, a nine-year-old boy was one of the demonstrators hit).[22] Sterling Cooper runs a taunting ad in response, stating that their agency is "an equal-opportunity employer" whose "windows don't open" (*A Little Kiss*, 5.1). But the agency has only thought about how to give their rivals a hard time and not about the serious implications of their reaction. Sterling Cooper executives are surprised when dozens of African-American job applicants show up in the lobby in response. In an effort to cope with the fallout of this unplanned chain of events, Dawn Chambers, the first black secretary at the agency, is hired.

Through Peggy, viewers experience middle-class white ambivalence toward changes in race relations. When race riots in the city prevent Dawn from making it safely home to Harlem, Peggy generously invites Dawn to stay with her overnight (*Mystery Date*, 5.4). But the camera shot from Peggy's sight line of her cash-filled purse left by the couch, and Peggy's hesitation at leaving it within the black woman's reach overnight, signals her lingering racial fear and mistrust. Our emotional identification as viewers—whether repulsed by her reaction, or excusing it—is structured to be with Peggy's experience of the scene. Dawn remains inscrutable, her feelings and experience unsounded. By keeping this character at the margins, the show realistically presents the position of many people of color in the 1960s, and illustrates the political challenges of becoming visible and gaining power.

While both race and gender changes are huge and important, white privilege allowed Americans (and their understanding of their national identity) to remain separate and not transformed by their African-American fellow citizens' lives. Workplace and residential segregation, depicted in the show by the maids, elevator operators, and secretaries that commute from the black world of Harlem to the white world of Manhattan, allowed whites to remain oblivious, integrating very slowly, while conversely, women and their changing identities were intertwined directly with the lives of men (both black and white). As viewers, we experience how the personal becomes political change because the women are simply right there—in the offices, kitchens and bedrooms of the *Mad Men*. Yet at least until the late 1960s, the white privilege created by America's segregated customs and assumptions kept blacks literally and imaginatively separate and invisible.

This willingness and ability to literally "not see" black Americans' experience is demonstrated over and over again in the show. When Carla is watching a televised news report on the 1963 bombing of Birmingham's 16th Street Baptist Church, in which four young African-American girls were killed, Betty sweeps into the living room and switches the set off (*Wee Small Hours*, 3.9). Betty has the power simply to keep the Civil Rights Movement and the violence facing African Americans out of her consciousness and out of her home, where she does not have to deal with it at all.[23] When, at the end of season four, she feels implicitly judged and undermined by Carla's steady and reasonable care of the children (Carla disobeys an order that Betty, on a selfish and guilty whim, gives her to keep neighbor boy Glenn away from Sally), she fires Carla without any warning (*Tomorrowland*, 4.13). The loyal, long-suffering housekeeper disappears from the series without a trace, never to be seen again, because she has made Betty uncomfortable and Betty has the power to make her vanish.

Similarly, when Roger and Joan are mugged on an Upper West Side street by a black man, Roger (who seems to have been in this situation before) tells Joan to "look down" and assures the mugger that "we haven't seen anything" in an effort to escape the encounter by just being robbed of their valuables and not being physically harmed (*The Beautiful Girls*, 4.9). Even viewers only see the thief in shadow, portrayed stereotypically as large, imposing and dark, with naturally textured hair and a guttural voice: like Roger and Joan, we experience him only as a threatening caricature of a black man, not as a person we have to really see. In fact, it would be dangerous (to our worldview and privilege) to "see" him.

Well into season six we experience a notable first: two African-American characters having a conversation between themselves, with no white characters in sight. Perhaps this is the moment critics have been waiting for, when the fullness of black interiority can begin to come to light in a scene not structured by a white perspective. Dawn Chambers is sitting in a coffee shop, filled with other black diners, chatting with her friend Nikki about how strange it is to work at Sterling Cooper (*To Have and To Hold*, 6.4). But even here, the imperative of black silence and invisibility is referenced. She tells Nikki that she has seen a black man she knows in an unfamiliar context, walking toward her in a plaza in midtown Manhattan. While they made eye contact, they neither spoke nor acknowledged seeing one another. To survive in this white world, Dawn and her black acquaintance become invisible, not only to willfully ignorant whites, but to one another.

As the series moves toward the end of the 1960s, more black faces come to work at the ad agency. But they remain largely unknown and invisible. On Valentine's Day 1969, Dawn goes into the break room to find another black secretary, Shirley, drinking a cup of coffee. Dawn wryly greets her "Hello, Dawn," and Shirley answers, "Hello, Shirley" (*A Day's Work*, 7.2). Their in-joke of calling one another by each other's names immediately alerts viewers to how fungible they seem to the rest of the office. While the two women do not look alike, and are quite different in presentation (Dawn has straightened hair and is dressed conservatively in a dark-colored dress, while Shirley has an Afro and is wearing a brightly printed minidress), this scene communicates their realization that to their white bosses and co-workers, they are not seen as individuals. They are interchangeable black women, whose race determines their identities and renders every other detail about them forgettable or unremarkable.

In that same episode, both Lou Avery and Peggy find petty reasons to get angry at their respective secretaries (Dawn and Shirley) and demand that Joan reassign them.[24] Explicit racism, sanctioned by employment law, has been challenged enough by this point that neither Lou nor Peggy expect or demand that the women be fired outright. But they both make it clear that they do expect to not have to see or work with them again and tell Joan to "Fix it!" so they will not. Joan moves Dawn to the reception desk in the front lobby, to which senior partner Bert Cooper objects: "I'm all for the national advancement of colored people, but I do not believe they should advance all the way to the front of this office. People can *see* her from the elevator" (*A Day's Work*, 7.2). Bert expresses the insidious power of systemic racism. Of course, he is genial and not personally malicious or opposed to racial progress. He just objects to that progress when it might impact him personally or negate some of his own privilege (such as offending bigoted clients and costing the firm revenue). He is for black advancement, but not at his own expense, or when he will have to see and participate in it. Advancement can happen as long it remains out of sight and far away from real power. Joan presses Bert on his "suggestion" that she rearrange who sits at the front desk, trying to ascertain if this is a direct order that must be obeyed. Bert, with the confidence of one whose privilege and power are so established as to be unassailable, replies with a benevolent but firm smile that he is "requesting" the change. He walks away, ending the conversation and sure that his desire will be carried out. His white male privilege does not have to be enforced with brutality or anger. Racial power can wear a smiling face, as it closes its eyes to inequality it does not want to see.

One of the most incisive critiques of *Mad Men*'s strategies of racial representation comes from Kent Ono, who identifies the problem not simply as a lack of fully developed black characters, but a re-producing of the structural racist exclusion the show purports to condemn.[25] While immersion in white privilege may plunge viewers into the "shock of the banal"[26] and make us painfully aware of the absence of racial diversity and equality, Ono argues that it also makes it harder for audiences to grapple with continued racism in the present day. By portraying the "bad old days" of overt racism so compellingly, the show is complicit in creating a sense of "postracial beyondness" in the present.[27] By forcing us to see what we took for granted in the past—the silencing, the invisibility, the stereotyping—Ono wonders if *Mad Men* also lets us off the hook for racism in the present, allowing us to repress or forget continuing inequality by pushing notions of racism squarely onto the past. The show also does an inadequate job of pushing us beyond black–white notions of racial politics. It rarely includes characters or perspectives of other racial and ethnic groups; the scant attention given to Asian Americans trades wholly in stereotypes of Asians as primitive, comedic, or sexualized oriental figures.[28]

The show is self-conscious about race, but that does not absolve it from racism. For example, it is surely accurate to portray Carla's personal and interior life as invisible to her white employers in the 1960s. However, the absence onscreen of her life beyond the gaze of the Drapers has two effects: "First, it produces a historically realist representation of the irrelevance of her personal life to white people in the 1960s; second, it unnecessarily and objectionably produces the irrelevance of her personal life to television viewers now."[29] While defenders of the show's racial politics can point to its lack of sentimentality and the subversive critique implicit in its portrayal of unapologetic white privilege and superiority, Ono reminds us that this immersion in the white privilege of the past is also a reproduction of it in the present. While we might be dismayed that the Drapers neither knew nor cared about Carla's life, we in the twenty-first century are allowed to leave the show equally uninformed and unbothered, and with our stereotype of black women as "mammy" caring selflessly for white children undisturbed.

We viewers of *Mad Men* live in an era where residential and social segregation are no longer legally mandated, but are nevertheless increasing. Racial tensions may be overlooked until they spark, such as in the Trayvon Martin and Michael Brown shootings; then they become impossible to ignore, raising issues of inequality in policing, criminal justice, media representations, educational achievement, and economic opportunity. Despite acknowledgement of the power of black celebrities and the first African-American president, or discussion of entering a "post-racial" era, we have ongoing evidence that blacks and whites seems to live in two different worlds.[30] The starkly different reactions of whites and blacks to incidents in Ferguson, Missouri in the aftermath of Michael Brown's death in August 2014 demonstrates how little these groups see the world through the same lenses. While 76 percent of black Americans viewed the shooting as "part of a broader pattern in the way police treat black men," only about half that many whites agreed (40 percent).[31] And while an overwhelming majority of blacks agreed that Brown's death "raises important issues about race that need to be discussed" (80 percent), barely a third of white Americans would prioritize that conversation (37 percent).[32] One interesting cause of this division might be the very separate social worlds Americans inhabit. One study found that on average, whites' social networks are 91 percent white, and fully three-quarters of white Americans interact significantly with *no* people of other races and ethnicities.[33] The persistent homogeneity of white social worlds raises many questions, not only about political equality and policy outcomes, but importantly about politics of representation in popular culture as well. To take the racial politics of *Mad Men* seriously, we need to examine not only the messages within the text; we need to understand how the dissemination and reception of that text of popular culture are in themselves political acts, and how they challenge or perpetuate already-existing power relations.

Yet for all that the white characters and institutions of *Mad Men* might want to keep race and "others" at a safe remove, the challenges of racial identity and equality draw inexorably closer and cannot be ignored. By the time Martin Luther King Jr. is assassinated, in April 1968, we see all of the white characters impacted in some way and grappling to respond (*The Flood*, 6.5). Betty fears for Henry's safety when he joins New York Mayor Lindsay in the city, not knowing if there will be race riots. Pete yells at Harry for being more concerned with television ad revenue than this "shameful, shameful day," but then tries to exploit the tragedy for his own self-interest, attempting to use it as an excuse get back together with Trudy after she has kicked him out. Peggy tries to get a better deal on an apartment by capitalizing on the fact that the chaos and other people's racial fears might drive down property values. Joan gives Dawn an incredibly awkward hug, an unwelcome effort to comfort her over what is clearly not a shared grief.

Meanwhile, Don takes his son Bobby to the movies. The film they see, *Planet of the Apes*, is like *Mad Men* itself, an imaginative work that references and grapples with difference and race. Charlton Heston's keening rage and despair at the end of the film resonate and reflect the horror and confusion of the historical events in the episode, the assassination and riots. Afterward, a stunned and excited Bobby asks the African-American man cleaning the theater if he's seen the movie and muses that it must be cool to see movies for free. "Everybody likes to go to the movies when they're sad," Bobby tells the black man, in what is the episode's most authentic response of empathy by a white character. Of course, what Bobby's well-intentioned conversation overlooks is that it is quite different to go to a movie for escapism when something terrible is happening than it is to clean up after the people being entertained in order to survive economically. And given the intertextual reference to *Planet of the Apes*, we might do well to heed *Mad Men's* warning that popular culture is serious business, not mere distraction, and that there is no real escaping the past.

Three episodes later, the Draper children are startled by a stranger who has broken into Don and Megan's apartment in the middle of the night (*The Crash*, 6.8). Sally and Bobby have been left home alone, and a menacing, disheveled black woman comes in through the unlocked back door of the apartment.[34] She tells the terrified children that she is their "Grandma Ida," and proceeds to ransack the home for valuables while cooking them eggs and making chirpy conversation about their father, whom she claims to have raised after his parents died. Bobby is confused, asking his sister, "Are we negroes?" as he tries to process who this unknown grandmother could be. Sally is suspicious and tries to call the police, which is when we all know we are in real danger. Grandma Ida stops her with a blood-chilling stare and a lie to whomever is on the other end of the line. Eventually she departs, without harming Sally or Bobby, but with Don Draper's nice watch.

The sudden appearance of Grandma Ida is perplexing. Her character is an amalgam of some of the worst racial stereotypes, the mammy/matriarch and the menacing criminal (like the mugger in season four). Inserting her into the narrative seems like a risky move, one that might tap into the most blatant racist fantasies of viewers and reinforce their stereotypes. Sally is reading a horror novel in bed before Grandma Ida breaks in, and the subsequent inter-action clearly feels like the bizarre, destabilizing action of a horror story to Sally, who cannot quite get her bearings. She is not sure whether to trust her instincts about this stranger being dangerous, or to risk trusting Grandma Ida's incredible story. While Grandma Ida serves as an actual plot device to reference white middle-class fears of black crime and violence in 1968, she also serves as a metaphor for racial fears about vulnerability and identity, then and now. If all of *Mad Men* deals with themes of appearance and reality, truth and illusion, then the Grandma Ida incident taps directly into the ways these dilemmas are racialized. One of the great fears of American identity is miscegenation. Historically, there are grave consequences to not being racially pure, and to being someone different than you think you are (or that others believe you to be).[35] And this is not just an individual fear. Much of the United States was built, physically and economically, by slaves. The institution of slavery haunts our identity and undermines our democratic ideals. The stain of racism, from the brutal exploitation of slavery to the inhumanity of Jim Crow, continues to be a mark we would rather hide or deny. Bobby's inquiry—"Are we negroes?"—is one of the most terrifying we can imagine, for it might unearth guilt or undermine our sense of American identity. To be "American" was to share the perspective of English colonists resisting the Old World, to quote John Locke and pursue happiness with an assumption of Anglo legitimacy, not to identify with Native American "savages" driven off their land or enslaved peoples from the African continent. Acknowledging the complexity and moral ambiguity of that history could be a horrifying prospect.

Of course, Grandma Ida also stands as one of the many doppelgangers for Don Draper. A grifter, claiming a false identity, using deceit and charm to gain access to people or wealth in order to survive; she is the female, African-American version of Don, his mirror image in black and white, like the negative of a photograph. Grandma Ida's con is far less successful. She cannot "pass" to the Draper children, and is eventually caught with their stolen goods, waiting down at the police station for charges to be pressed. Without white, male privilege, her grift is a pathetic failed attempt in comparison with Don's sustained, suave illusion. Yet Don is also, at least symbolically, a negro like Grandma Ida. Dick Whitman is constantly "passing" as Don Draper. He is haunted and driven by his past, his fears of his true identity being revealed— and it is that hidden background which serves as his strength and his gift, as well his shame. As Ta-Nehisi Coates observes,

> Don Draper is, in the parlance of old black folks, passing. His origins are not proper and gentile—he is the child of a prostitute, who has reinvented himself for the Manhattan jet-set. He is Gatsby and Anatole Broyard, no? And yet the irony that animates *Mad Men* is the fact that, without that past, Draper would likely be the sort of pampered hack he despises. He'd be Pete Campbell. His double consciousness, makes him, indeed, doubly conscious, doubly aware. Don Draper sees more.[36]

Don Draper, the handsome creative genius admired for his many women, his vices, his wealth, his charisma—the epitome of post-war American success, holder of white male privilege, let into the room of elite power—also answers "yes" to the question, "Are we negroes?"

Mad Men employs the risky and creative strategy of allowing viewers to experience the suffocating insularity of 1960s white privilege and the "shock of the banal" at its blatant, unremitting racism and its marginalization of racial and ethnic "others." Even as the inequality of Jim Crow and racial subordination is being challenged by the historical events of the 1960s, *Mad Men* embodies the risks and reification of white privilege and illuminates why still, in the twenty-first century, we have not yet become a post-racial society.

Notes

1   Stephanie Coontz, "Why *Mad Men* is TV's Most Feminist Show," *Washington Post*, October 10, 2010, http://www.washingtonpost.com/wp-dyn/content/article/2010/10/08/AR2010100802662.html (accessed March 31, 2014).

2   Daniel Mendelsohn, "The *Mad Men* Account," *New York Review of Books*, February 24, 2011, http://www.nybooks.com/articles/archives/2011/feb/24/mad-men-account/ (accessed March 7, 2014).

3   Latoya Peterson, "Why *Mad Men* is Afraid of Race," *Slate Double X blog*, August 13, 2009, http://www.doublex.com/section/arts/why-mad-men-afraid-race (accessed April 19, 2010).

4   Gene Demby, "Will Mad Men's Sixth Season Finally Bring Race Into the Picture?," NPR's *Code Switch* blog, March 4, 2013, http://www.npr.org/blogs/codeswitch/2013/04/08/176531523/will-mad-mens-sixth-season-finally-bring-race-into-the-picture (accessed March 31, 2014); see also Alessandra Stanley, "Oblivious to the Battle Raging Outside, *Mad Men* Opens its Fifth Season on AMC," *New York Times*, March 22, 2012, http://www.nytimes.com/2012/03/23/arts/television/mad-men-opens-its-fifth-season-on-amc.html (accessed March 7, 2014).

5   Eleanor Barkhorn, Ashley Fetters, and Amy Sullivan, "Will *Mad Men* Ever Be as Good on Race as it is on Gender?," *The Atlantic*, April 22, 2013, http://www.theatlantic.com/entertainment/archive/2013/04/will-i-mad-men-i-ever-be-as-good-on-race-as-it-is-on-gender/275149/ (accessed March 7, 2014).

6   Tanner Colby, "*Mad Men* and Black America," *Slate*, March 14, 2012,
     http://www.slate.com/articles/arts/culturebox/features/2012/mad_men_
     and_race_the_series_handling_of_race_has_been_painfully_accurate_/
     mad_men_and_race_why_season_5_may_finally_put_the_civil_rights_
     movement_front_and_center_.html (accessed March 7, 2014).

7   Aisha Harris, "If *Mad Men* Really Addressed Race," *Brow Beat: Slate Culture
     Blog*, April 10, 2013, http://www.slate.com/blogs/browbeat/2013/04/10/mad_
     men_with_black_characters_erika_alexander_s_screenplay_uptown_saturday.
     html (accessed March 31, 2014).

8   Stanley, "Oblivious to the Battle."

9   Colby, "*Mad Men* and Black America."

10   Ibid.

11   Otis Moss, "*Mad Men* Highlights Invisible Black People and Stain of Racism,"
     Daily Beast, March 27, 2012, http://www.thedailybeast.com/articles/2012/03/27/
     mad-men-highlights-invisible-black-people-and-stain-of-racism.html
     (accessed March 7, 2014).

12   Demby, "Bring Race into the Picture?"

13   Ibid.

14   Michael Berube, "A Change is Gonna Come, Same As it Ever Was," in Lauren M. E.
     Goodlad, Lilya Kaganovsky, and Robert Rushing (eds), *Mad Men, Mad World: Sex,
     Politics, Style and the 1960s* (Durham, NC: Duke University Press, 2013), p. 351.

15   Ibid.

16   Ibid. In later seasons, the obnoxious Pete Campbell is sometimes the person at
     the agency who unexpectedly calls out racism (such as after Martin Luther King
     Jr.'s assassination in *The Flood*, 6.5), which makes this point as well.

17   Ta-Nehisi Coates, "Race and *Mad Men*," *Atlantic* (blog post), August 17,
     2009, http://www.theatlantic.com/entertainment/archive/2009/08/race-and-
     mad-men/23372 (accessed July 22, 2014).

18   Karen Brodkin, *How Jews Became White Folks and What that Says About Race in
     America* (New Brunswick, NJ: Rutgers University Press, 1998).

19   Glenn C. Altschuler and Stuart M. Blumin, *The GI Bill: A New Deal for Veterans*
     (New York: Oxford University Press, 2009); see also Brodkin, *How Jews Became
     White*.

20   Though class is still a significant barrier that divides her from someone like Pete
     Campbell, an elite WASP from one of the oldest families in New York. Pete is
     willing to have a drunken one-night stand with Peggy after his bachelor party,
     but does not see her as a suitable partner for a relationship; instead he marries

the equally WASP-ish Trudy. Peggy's working-class roots are not just portrayed as a liability, however. They also seem to be in large part the motivation for her drive, determination, and creativity, which propels her forward professionally and helps her take advantage of opportunities opening up for women in the workplace. Her energy and ambition (much like Don's, which also springs from a non-privileged background) is what makes her successful and part of the striving American future, not identified with suffocating tradition or a stagnating past.

21   Gail Collins, *When Everything Changed: the Journey of American Women from 1960 to the Present* (New York: Little, Brown & Co., 2009), pp. 75–7, 81.

22   John Kifner, "Poverty Pickets Get Paper-Bag Dousing on Madison Avenue," *New York Times,* May 28, 1966, A1, http://www.documentcloud.org/documents/328527-new-york-times-may-28-1966.html (accessed March 11, 2014).

23   In an interesting side note, Betty has a Demerol-induced dream while in labor with her third child that features Medgar Evers' bloodied, murdered body. In the dream, her mother tells Betty to be quiet: "You see what happens to people who speak up?" Leslie Reagan elaborates on this in her essay "After the Sex, What? A Feminist Reading of Reproductive History in *Mad Men*," in Goodlad et al., (eds), *Mad Men, Mad World* pp. 92–110. Reagan makes the point that the show is using a black body to send a message to its white female characters about the dangers of deviating from norms of silence and subordination. If that is true, then it is also another example of how the show can enact, not just reflect, white privilege and structural racism in appropriating black experience as a vehicle to instruct or benefit white characters, rather than treating it as significant in its own right.

24   Lou tries to blame Dawn for his own oafishness, and Dawn refuses to take the blame. In a perfect articulation of his racial privilege and inability to take any responsibility for it, he storms, "Do you understand it's not my problem? None of this has to do with me. I'm sorry if I said the wrong thing." Peggy, meanwhile, is embarrassed that she thought Shirley's Valentine roses were actually meant for her. When she realizes her own arrogant mistake, she lashes out at Shirley. Instead of feeling solidarity with a female subordinate, Peggy uses her position of power to strike back, stemming from her own insecure feelings regarding her attractiveness and failed relationship with Ted Chaough.

25   Kent Ono, "*Mad Men's* Postracial Figuration of a Racial Past," in Goodlad et al. (eds), *Mad Men, Mad World*, pp. 300–19.

26   Caroline Levine, "The Shock of the Banal: *Mad Men's* Progressive Realism," in
     ibid., pp. 133–44.

27   Ono, "Postracial Figuration," p. 315.

28   For example, Pete returns from his honeymoon to find what appears to be a
     family of Asian villagers has taken up residence in his office, complete with a live
     chicken on his desk, as a prank by his colleagues. Don Draper has an encounter
     with an Asian waitress in a restaurant which draws on geisha stereotypes of
     Asian women as eroticized and sexually available. Erotic overtones are also
     present in Bert Cooper's love of Asian art and culture, particularly the painting
     in his office. See Ono, "Postracial Figuration," p. 311, for more.

29   Ibid., pp. 305–6.

30   Robert P. Jones, "Self-Segregation: Why it's So Hard For Whites to Understand
     Ferguson," *Atlantic*, August 21, 2014, http://www.theatlantic.com/politics/
     archive/2014/08/self-segregation-why-its-hard-for-whites-to-understand-
     ferguson/378928/ (accessed August 26, 2014).

31   Ibid.

32   Ibid.

33   Ibid. People of other races and ethnicities are not quite as insulated from
     those of different identities; social network racial homogeneity among black
     Americans averages 65 percent, while for Hispanic Americans it is typically
     46 percent.

34   It seems significant that it is the Draper children who interact with Grandma
     Ida, since they represent the future, in whom the experiences and socio-
     political changes of the 1960s are going to come to fruition, and that the show
     increasingly seems to be watching the actions of the adult characters through
     their eyes. Thus it is more interesting to see what reactions and racial fears
     Grandma Ida taps from Bobby and Sally than from, say, Bert Cooper, Roger
     Sterling, or even Betty Draper, for whom a different set of racial categories and
     relations are already firmly in place.

35   See, for example, Kate Chopin's powerful 1893 short story "Desiree's Baby,"
     which dramatizes the dire consequences of racial difference being revealed.
     A Louisiana orphan girl, raised by an elite white family, marries into another
     elite white family. When the beloved newlyweds welcome a baby, rumors swirl
     about the baby's mulatto skin, and eventually even the besotted husband admits
     his wife's unknown parentage must include negro blood, which causes him to
     reject her. Desiree despairingly wanders with her child out into the bayou, to
     their deaths; her dishonored husband burns all material traces of her and the

baby. The cruel twist at the end of the story is the revelation that it is actually Armand, the husband, whose maternal parentage contains negro blood, and whose racial features were passed on to his innocent child.

36 Ta-Nehisi Coates, "The Negro Don Draper," *Atlantic*, October 27, 2008, http://www.theatlantic.com/entertainment/archive/2008/10/the-negro-donald-draper/6129/ (accessed July 22, 2014).

Part Four

Conclusion

10

Tomorrowland: Contemporary Visions, Past Indiscretions

Rebecca Colton Josephson

So we beat on, boats against the current, borne back ceaselessly into the past.

F. Scott Fitzgerald, *The Great Gatsby*

Watching *Mad Men*

Let's face it, watching *Mad Men* can be hard. Every episode has those moments when we find ourselves cringing or looking sideways at the screen, thinking: *No! Don't do it! Don't head down that road!* Yet we don't look away or head for the fridge for a drink, or turn off the screen. In fact, we keep watching, and afterward, we rehash the pain of that episode with friends and colleagues, partly gossiping about shocking decisions but also sensing that this dark vision of the storied sixties is saying something important to us. The show is ironic and beautiful, sad, but somehow hopeful. Characters seem trapped in a corrupt, constraining society; what goodness is to be found here? We feel both revulsion (*How could they live this way?*) and recognition (*Some things are still a lot like this*). We watch seven seasons because in *Mad Men* we recognize not only unresolved social and political issues of today, but also the fundamental tension for individuals in an aging democracy. We are struggling to balance our love of originality with our need for foundations, diversity with equality, expanding gender roles, and changing sexual values. More than ever before, we are connected to society through media images and digital culture; the idea of a private life or personal time is rapidly shifting, and with it the concept of individualism and self-reliance. Our economy is changing too, and we must adjust to increased economic insecurity and shifting distribution of wealth. Racial division and inequality of opportunity persist. The fear of a military–industrial complex continues as America is accused of using military force to create and protect an amorphous empire. To top it all, during *Mad Men*'s run we have passed through a presidency that began with a popular mandate but is closing with executive orders and a Congress immobilized by partisan politics, effectively gridlocked. We keep returning to *Mad Men* because it addresses these issues as well as a central conundrum for a free society: our individual identities and liberty, even in America, are partially constrained and constructed by our society and our understanding of our past.

In *Mad Men*, we recognize that though liberty and justice may increase, we can never be entirely free and virtuous because our past and our current society haunt our creative efforts, and our virtue includes our relations to others. As Fitzgerald notes at the end of *Gatsby*, even as we hope for the future, all we can do is keep rowing against an unseen current. Thus *Mad Men* is really about us at the beginning of America's third century. It reminds us of our daily stresses and our specific concerns for society, our desire for the ideals of democracy, and our inability to achieve those goals fully. Meanwhile, as we face more choices about who we are and how we should act, we feel increased anxiety and isolation, an increased need to connect to one another. We watch *Mad Men* because it reminds us that Americans have survived transitions before. We recognize ourselves in a mythic time of transition, an era which might evoke nostalgia for childhood. However, the show pushes us to move beyond nostalgia to an understanding of current challenges. *Mad Men* confronts the fundamental and recurrent problem in our liberal democracy: we are urged to be free individuals, but we exist in a social context, so we must negotiate our identities between who we want to be and who the community allows us to be. This idea, our own identity combined with who or what the community expects or allows, may sketch out part of what it means to be a citizen, to negotiate between social or political expectations and individual aspirations. *Mad Men* reminds us that we are not entirely free, but neither are we entirely shaped by our culture; the construction of our identities is analogous to the ad man's creation of an original message that connects to current consumer culture. Watching *Mad Men*, we hope for a just resolution for these characters in a mythic yet remembered era, for their lives speak directly and existentially to the tensions of contemporary society. We watch because we want to know who we were, who we are, and who we wish to be.

Yesterday and *Tomorrowland*

As Americans we are well practiced at aiming for progress while craning over our shoulders, looking at the past. We love innovation and originality; we believe in social progress. At the same time, the political and economic uncertainty of our contemporary lives and ambitions for the future don't sustain us. Americans often turn to a romanticized image of the past as a source of comfort. We find ourselves looking backwards with a combination of affection and revulsion. Many of the chapters in this volume pay attention to how *Mad Men*'s use of material culture in props, set design, and costumes works to connect the audience with the historical sixties. We delight in seeing lost artifacts of an earlier time—the electric typewriter, the slide carousel, short bangs and wide skirts—but *Mad Men* simultaneously subverts nostalgia with its unblinking portrayal of the unhappy, harmful elements of the past. *Mad Men* gives us the sixties, but the era is not as glorious or as free either as we remember or as we would like to believe.

Whatever one's opinion of the 1960s, the decade is synonymous with pivotal change. In the popular mind, the Civil Rights Movement, the second wave of feminism, the rise of youth culture, and the anti-war movement reach a climax in the 1960s. Interwoven into our memory of social change is a sense of increasing personal liberty, including free love, the introduction of the Pill, and experimentation with hallucinogens to access a different reality. Whether or not we think of these changes as progress, and though they certainly did not perfect the democratic culture, these social movements promised to steer America away from Jim Crow, the objectification of women, unfettered militarism, and a social Darwinism that would deny basic needs and services to the poor. Optimistically speaking, the sixties changed the country and gave us a fresh start.

This optimism is a part of our national character. We have long maintained the belief that we can freely choose to start anew. As Goren points out, our literature embraces the motif of the self-made man, and he (and occasionally she) reappears with some consistency from Ben Franklin to Jay Gatsby. The self-made man can leave behind his past limitations and vices, leave behind the identity that society has given him; he can remake himself into a more virtuous, happier individual through will, wit, work, and luck (although improvement does not seem to captivate us so much as renewal). Both as individuals and as a society, Americans love the idea of leaving the past behind, heading out to the perpetually new frontier. We celebrate a break with the past as a new beginning; thus we have mythologized the sixties as a decade when America started over. Part of what happened in the 1960s was a rebirth, but just like Dick Whitman's recreation as himself as Don Draper, it is impossible to completely leave behind the vestiges of the past, no matter how much it may seem like the past never happened.

As Beail and Goren remind us at the outset, founding narratives are important for any republic; documents and stories quite literally "constitute" the political community, and the rhetoric of founding narratives defines the values and identity of the polis. Yet the *enthusiasm* for refounding is particular to the United States for historical and geographical reasons. First, we lack some common ancestry for our national identity. As a population of mostly slaves and immigrants, we do not share a primordial mythic past contributing to an American identity and connecting us to the land. We do not claim Native American heroes, and we share no Lear or Charlemagne, no Romulus and Remus whom we claim as our own foundational characters. So in starting over, we seek to choose our cultural character and leave our earlier identities behind. Second, because our past as a nation is so brief (1776 is not so long ago, an event of historical record only partially shrouded in myth), and because we are an invented nation with an identifiable founding, we see no reason why we cannot start over again, and again, and again. If our democracy has stalled, either in its innovation, its virtue, or as a land of the free and the brave, what must we do? Refound the republic, overthrow or abolish old ways, and create something fresh and new.[1] Third, as the global political settings shift, Americans seek a national identity that defines and reflects America's role. In the post-World War II period the US was, in many ways, "refounded" as a superpower with a modern political identity. Today contemporary political rhetoric makes claims of a "homeland" that requires securing, which contradicts our historical beginnings. Now we may need to decide which identity we will claim: did we come from elsewhere or from this "homeland"? Are we a Christian nation, or an ecumenical melting pot? Are we one people or many? The tensions in our identities may stem from our habit of clinging to nostalgic visions of America that see our nation as both good and righteous, but these tensions are also heightened by contemporary concerns. *Mad Men*'s focus on the 1960s draws our attention to America's particular enthusiasm for new beginnings and to how social movements and individual choices contribute to the gradual reimagining of American identity, creating myths of a more egalitarian and inclusive revolution that eventually steer the polis in a new direction. *Mad Men* asks us to reflect on the consequences and possibilities of a refigured America in the 1960s and today.

As Heyman, Goldman, and Naranch all point out, *Mad Men* subverts our romantic notion of a fresh start in the sixties. Though we imagine that the popular social movements sparked epiphanies and inspired renewed virtue, In *Mad Men* these revolutionary moments merely play in the background on the television or radio. Individuals most often cannot recognize their own impotence in an economic and geo-political world governed by a "power-elite." Rather than representing the sixties as a new beginning, a cleansing wave of change, teeming with new insights, *Mad Men* shows the sixties as comprising quotidian responses to social pressures that create incremental change, a gradual shifting in values that erodes and rebuilds the social and political identity over time. Only when circumstances force characters to contend with social change (and often because they believe it will affect their economic success) do they deviate from the old ways. Though the assassination of the Kennedys and Martin Luther King cause some characters to pause, perhaps even to wonder about whether their lives will change, these individuals carry on, the plots of their lives, their daily machinations, barely altered. These individuals are firmly rooted in the social expectation of their times. They struggle with isolation, and, as Naranch posits, their lives lack meaningful intimacy, co-operation, trust, and kindness. In *Mad*

Men, those historical events that we have come to think of as the epicenters of change provide context but not motivation for individuals. Though we are occasionally delighted by moments of dawning social awareness in these characters, we are more often frustrated by their frequent inability to respond to the injustices in their own economic and social systems. Change here is gradual, and it appears in fits and starts, yet this, too, is strangely familiar to us. This draws us, the contemporary audience, into the narrative itself, paying attention to the shifting responses, the dramatic tension of these fits and starts of change. These characters, perhaps like us, are too busy living in the society to challenge it significantly.

But if the show corrects our image of the 1960s as our latest "cultural revolution," and in so doing frees us from nostalgic longing, then we may watch *Mad Men* because it inspires in us a kind of cautious hope for our future. As we compare the sixties with today, we recognize that society has changed in terms of greater equality of opportunity, security, and tolerance among a diverse population, and even though change seems frustratingly slow, we can hope for better times ahead. In his fifth State of the Union Address, President Barack Obama referred to the slow pace of change when he commented "It's time to do away with [discriminatory] workplace policies that belong in a *Mad Men* episode,"[2] recognizing that, to move forward, we need to leave behind our nostalgia for the past. Because of social and political differences between then and now, *Mad Men* inspires us with a cautious optimism for our contemporary culture. Just as President Obama campaigned in 2008 with the themes of "Hope" and "Change," to capture the zeitgeist of the electorate, we remain hopeful, as individuals and a nation; we want to feel that we can make a difference. In *Mad Men*, we see characters shaped by their times, and we celebrate with them when they occasionally manage to overcome the expectations of what we recognize, retrospectively, as a corrupt culture. We know that we too are, to some degree, products of our society, but we need to believe that as individuals we have freedom to act, and in fact, that this is our identity and role as citizens in a liberal democracy.

In the twenty-first century, where the pace of technological change is breathtaking, we live with a growing sense of personal alienation, fear, a sense of stagnation, and a lack of national purpose. Watching *Mad Men*, we recognize our parents, our grandparents, and ourselves, our not-so-distant past illuminating our current society. Over seven seasons, we see characters shaped by their times; we watch *Mad Men* and compare: *How are we still like that? How can I avoid being so determined by my society?* We are forced to evaluate our current politics and values and examine whether we have the individual freedom to confront and change injustices. But these characters surprise themselves and us with their occasional deviance, their occasional yet significant freedom, which helps us to believe that we too, though shaped by powerful social forces, have freedom to choose who we are and what we do. In the first episodes, we felt this shock of dual recognition: the continual smoking and drinking, the objectification of women, the marginalization of minorities, and the shallow *bonhomie* of the workplace all seemed both distinctly alien and alarmingly familiar. We may no longer smoke or gulp whiskey in the office, but we have our own status-marking habits with which we negotiate the professional world: expensive coffees, hooking up, long commutes with endless work hours, and digital umbilical cords eroding any sense of solitude or individual identity. *Mad Men*'s world is not so distant from our own, and we can see our own politically constrained identities in the choices characters make.

Memory, Nostalgia, and Freedom

Though *Mad Men* masks itself as a show about memory and nostalgia, it actually addresses the fundamental issue that a freely constructed identity is always realized in the context of memory and society. *Mad Men* examines this conundrum in its portrayal of gender roles, the uneasy daily balance of personal and professional identities, and tensions of class and race. Watching *Mad Men* is harder than watching other examinations of the past (*Friday Night Lights* or *Downton Abbey*); *Mad Men* asks us to integrate today's issues with the world of the 1960s. Here again, the dual recognition mediates our understanding: some elements of life have changed, but certain questions around freedom and identity are essentially the same.

As Fuehrer Taylor and Witzig both argue, *Mad Men* begs a comparison with contemporary tensions surrounding female and male identity and the extent to which characters can respond freely to society's gender constructions. The men and women of the show have little freedom from social norms in both professional and domestic spheres. Men and women are defined and valued according to their conformity to circumscribed gender definitions and expectations. We often find it painful to watch men and women trapped in a culture of domination, objectification, and subservience, especially as cultural constraints limit freedom. But our concern reflects back on current society as well: what does it mean in the twenty-first century to be a man or woman in America? Gender identity is complex; the social and political structure of society is often grounded in a communal understanding of gender norms and expectations. *Mad Men* suggests that during the 1960s both women and men develop politically through elements of their private lives and personal identities. The self-knowledge of women and men in *Mad Men* reflects complexities of identity in our time. We value sexual freedom and psychological self-awareness; contemporary media images sexualize both men and women, celebrating sexual pleasure, and implying that power is implicit in sexual agency and emotional detachment. *Mad Men* treats these elements differently for men and women, but for both, empowerment results from self-knowledge and from intimate connection and communication. From the first season of *Mad Men*, female identity, ambition, and the construction of femininity are obvious themes, and we may compare these to masculinity, as Witzig does in her analysis of Don Draper's growth and a modern cultural crisis of manhood.

The arrival of an outsider, Peggy Olson, into the culture of the ad agency makes clear the cultural expectations and limitations for young professional women. Paradoxically, women's submissiveness and perceived femininity grant them greater (though limited) freedom. Individuality is constrained by social identity which includes sexuality, but women can create elements of their identities as well, as Peggy Olson does, and in *Mad Men* this self-construction gives women greater control, freedom, and power. In contrast, for Don Draper, individual agency increases as he remembers his past and becomes more self-aware. In juxtaposing Don's childhood memories and his frequent trysts (as well as bouts of drinking and fleeing office or family responsibilities), *Mad Men*'s viewers understand before the character does the complex connection between his childhood and his sexuality. As he integrates his childhood with his current life, and as he shares that life with others, Don seems to gain agency in the world of appearances in which he operates.

Mad Men suggests that for both women and men, growing awareness of the private elements of their lives, often taboo in the public sphere (sexuality, emotional vulnerability) grants agency in the life of the polis. Women must learn to navigate the social taboos of sexual identity, and men must learn to feel emotion even under the social expectation of male invulnerability. Fuehrer Taylor and Witzig note that these tensions are ongoing for women and men today. The contemporary dialogue around sexuality often pits the argument in favor of the liberty to choose how to express one's sexuality against the societal expectations that often tie female expressions of sexuality and sexual agency to moral, religious, and cultural norms. Discussion of masculinity and male identity and psychological awareness also suggests that social expectations are slowly changing, but still media images imply that real men must be physically powerful and relatively unreflective. Furthermore, *Mad Men* suggests that the question of sexual and emotional agency is not as simple as conforming and rebelling, but that even the most personal decisions reflect and recreate identity and agency. The personal is, in this way, political, and these private understandings, as incremental learning, are integral to the public, political person's wisdom.

A slow politicization of the individual through his or her personal decisions occurs in *Mad Men*, and we see that development continuing today. *Mad Men* suggests that the feminist "revolution" of the 1960s is a continual development rather than a sudden reversal of values. In the examination of individual characters engaged in particular, private choices, we see the roots of new directions for women and men, and in contemporary society we see the continued shifting of individual identity and agency within the context of the society.

The tension between the private and the public selves is likewise related to *Mad Men*'s attention to the tension between appearance and reality. Edenborg's and Goldman's commentaries on the tension between the private and the public in *Mad Men* tie this tension to a basic problem in the republic, living as a free individual in a republic. While appearances can protect the individual from social pressure, the show suggests that this dichotomy can constrict agency. The personal and public selves are conjoined, and separating them limits personal liberty and happiness. *Mad Men* comments on identities fragmented between work and home, professional (or public) responsibilities, and personal (private) needs. Characters seek to keep their private identities distinct from their professional personae, but more and more, as the seasons continue, the two worlds connect. Increasingly, characters find themselves dealing with children and parents while juggling professional duties. In his brief connection with Conrad Hilton in season three, Don Draper finds himself taking work calls in the middle of the night, at home, in bed with Betty. The personal is public and the public is personal.

In this mixing of the professional and private spheres, we can recognize contemporary difficulties of working people negotiating their shifting identities as workers, adult children, and mothers and fathers. Many contemporary families have all parents working away from home, and we are required to prioritize multiple vital roles. Which is more important: excellence at work or commitment and presence at home? Either compromise is fraught with danger. With digital technology, the two worlds are further integrated; parents and children stay connected when parents are working, and the office reaches into our homes in the evening and weekends when we might have once dedicated ourselves to family. Though this integration may seem to ease the tension for working parents by unifying the public and private selves, the change nevertheless causes anxiety as we mediate these shifting identities at work and at home.

The Bifurcated Self

Tensions in the bifurcated self are echoed in the economic and social divisions of the nation. *Mad Men*'s sixties shows an America that is more oligarchic than democratic and more prejudiced than equal. Economic power and security are limited to an enviable few, whom Goldman identifies as examples of C. Wright Mills' "power elite" that undermines the agency of the rest of society. While Edenborg elaborates on the growing consumer culture of the time, many of the ambitious employees of Sterling Cooper are also insecure; both executives and staff are concerned that they are in danger of losing their jobs. The firm itself seems to perpetually struggle against much larger, older advertising firms. The presence of a ruling power elite implies that class aspirations are based on a false sense of economic opportunity. The power of a few extremely wealthy individuals (such as Conrad Hilton) constrains the majority's agency and further segments the society.

Similarly, *Mad Men*'s America is cruelly prejudiced, as Beail demonstrates in her discussion of *Mad Men*'s portrayal of racial and ethnic minorities. African-American characters are present in each episode, but always on the edges of the narrative, a focus that critiques white privilege and power in the professional world of the show. Though this tension between the haves and have-nots was a focus of the social and political awareness of the sixties, reflected in the Johnson administration's 1964 "War on Poverty" and the 1965 Voting Rights Act, in spite of governmental interventions (Social Security, Food Stamps, Head Start, elementary and secondary school funding), the country continued to be divided by inequality along race, class, and geographical lines. Interestingly, *Mad Men* walks a fine line here in allowing the viewer to embody positions of privilege without justifying or normalizing this privilege. Through this narrow perspective, we reflect on the injustice of the society from the perspective of the elite, and we can recognize that inequality persisted even in this mythic era of democracy and continues to exist today, even after the implementation of multiple programs to alleviate injustice.

Watching *Mad Men*, we can't help but recognize our own frustrated ambition and insecurity as well as contemporary America's economic and social inequities. *Mad Men* debuted in July 2007, only two months before the revelation of the subprime mortgage crisis in September and the market collapse one year later, both leading to persistent economic insecurity. In our time, 75 percent of the total wealth in the United States is held by 5 percent of the population, and, to little avail, the Occupy Wall Street movement of 2011 protested this concentration of wealth and power. The concentration of wealth intensifies, poverty increases, and the middle class dwindles. The political marginalization of minorities also has intensified in the last decade. As Michelle Alexander's 2010 *New Jim Crow* points out, American society is still deeply divided along racial lines, and America cannot claim to have eradicated racism and racial inequality. Today, as we congratulate ourselves for electing a black president, an extraordinary percentage of the African American community has been imprisoned (a result of the federal "War on Drugs" initiative), denied civil and human rights, and gunned down by police without legal recourse.

Contemporary frustrations with constraints on individual liberty may also be echoed nationally and internationally as America senses limitations to its economic and political power. Just as *Mad Me*n suggests that the myth of the self-invented or remade man is not sufficient for individual agency and liberty, the show also implies, by analogy, that the nation as a whole cannot move forward through a naive hope in re-founding. Rather, a republic demands a more incremental understanding of change and progress. In the half century since the 1960s, America has found itself in increasingly complex international situations, scenarios wherein an American empire not only cannot be fulfilled, but seems to be part of the problem. The national identity that claims America is selfless in its intervention in foreign conflicts now seems naive, and we must create a new national identity that comprehends the tension between self-interest and serving others.

Watching *Mad Men*, we learn that national politics are neither as pure nor as powerful as the myth of the sixties suggests; legislation does not quickly change desires and habits. Here, Edenborg's point about innovation in the market place seems particularly significant: *Mad Men*'s characterization of the reflexive, conservative nature of advertising, even in the hip sixties, shows that media creativity is only marginally innovative; the economy of risk ties all creative ventures safely back to images of past acceptable, and sometimes beloved, aesthetics. Today, as the US claims to be an economy of innovation (particularly in technology, medicine, and education),[3] *Mad Men* reminds us that the market often constrains true experimentation of wholly innovative ideas and approaches. We must temper our national self-image to recognize that free creativity in business is ultimately controlled by the drive for profit and market share, and then move forward with that understanding.

Politically as well as economically, we recognize in *Mad Men* the limits of our power. Goldman's subtle conclusion about the optimism implied in *Mad Men* seems particularly important as America faces limitations to its international economic and political influence. Goldman's and Heyman's chapters each highlight the common impotence resulting from a lack of self-knowledge, from being fooled into believing in apparent, but empty power. *Mad Men* shows both the lack of freedom and the lack of power for individuals who cannot recognize the social forces underlying their own decisions. By analogy, America needs to be clear in the underlying economic and political forces which drive foreign policy. To ignore these influential forces, whether they be environmental, economic, or social, reduces the nation's power around the globe. Likewise, the show implies that American goals in global settings may need to be more co-operative and incremental to be both authentic and effective. As it explores the myth of the autonomous self, *Mad Men* suggests that in America's third century we need to refine our patriotism and national identity for a post-empirial age, but here, too, nostalgia alone will not lead us forward.

Specific elements of *Mad Men*'s 1960s bring to mind our current political struggle. We consider the sixties as an era of political change, but the assassination of national leaders and the rise of the Nixon administration suggest a national electorate seeking security in the face of innovation. We analogize to our own times: the federal government seems to be gridlocked in partisan politics while the issues call for action; the imbalance of wealth implies economic insecurity connected to corporate power and global markets; our environmental prognosis suggests insurmountable disaster. Similarly, the fear and threat of terrorism since 9/11, to which the United States has responded with a never-ending "War on Terror," demands an effective and wise government that can create new solutions. Perhaps much like the Korean and Vietnam conflicts did in their eras, today's military engagement may redefine our understanding of war and our place as a nation in the world. As a nation, our motives are suspect; our allies are not trustworthy, terrorism continues to punch holes in our ideas of indomitability, and so we wonder if we are any longer the shining beacon of democracy to the rest of the world. As we watch *Mad Men*, we may long for the post-war economic growth of the

1950s and for a new enlightenment in America that will grant greater opportunity for more people, but *Mad Men* does not allow us to rest in nostalgia for
a more secure era. Our insecurity today is connected to our current struggle
to understand what America is ethnically, racially, culturally, economically,
and politically. That the sixties were not a better time means our nostalgia is
misplaced.

In the third American century, we are coming to a new understanding of
our democratic challenges and failings. We have not widened the diversity
of citizens included in the economics of possibility, and wealth and status
are held by only a few, limiting the liberty of the rest. *Mad Men*'s critique of
inequality and prejudice addresses the fundamental tension between liberty
and equality for individuals, the society, and the nation. The show is not an
explicit call to action, but as we compare current social division with the
injustices of the 1960s, we recognize our own frustration with economic and
racial inequalities. Implied in this critique is the notion that we must look
forward with creative vision to solve these damaging inequities. Nostalgia and
hubris will not accomplish the important work of creating an America that
overcomes the haunting injustices of the past.

The Examined Life

By framing current societal tensions in the setting of the storied 1960s,
Mad Men does much more than entertain us. It teaches us something about
ourselves and America. We watch *Mad Men* because the show affirms our
experience of gender roles, divided selves, and injustice, and it implies that
we will not resolve these problems through either the heroic individualism of
prophets and reformers, or the collective action of social movements and legislation. Instead, *Mad Men* suggests a more complex cause for hope; the show
affirms the necessity of individual agency perpetually constrained by society.
Progress will not come through romantic self-reliance, but through self-
knowledge and courageous creativity within the society. To solve America's
problems, we must do the work of knowing our past, but not mythologizing
or being trapped by it. In a liberal democracy, thinking and acting freely are

both important and difficult. The roles and values taught by society create a powerful conservative force, and not surprisingly, we often cannot resist it. At some point, each of *Mad Men*'s characters is guilty of perpetuating the objectifying culture, of not resisting injustice or inequality, of passivity in the face of corruption. Blinded by nostalgia and cultural expectations, he or she often cannot see an alternative, a way forward. Even if these characters consider acting differently, social and economic insecurity often limit their individual agency. When they occasionally choose to reject society's norms, separation and alienation, even from a corrupt culture, grants neither liberty nor happiness.

We don't watch *Mad Men* because it leaves us feeling cynical, however; this show does not leave us hopeless. It reveals a slow, challenging path to individual virtue and social progress in America. Looking back at the 1960s, an era we remember for its liberating individuality, *Mad Men* reminds us that, even then, it was a struggle to be both free and good. Social conformity may lead to immediate gains in status or wealth, but not long-term happiness—just ask Don Draper. *Mad Men* thus pushes us toward a limited individualism that allows for both freedom and connection, suggesting that this limited individualism can help society to progress. The show draws us in with a promise of entertaining nostalgia, a drama set in a more hopeful time, but what we find in *Mad Men* is a commentary on contemporary society. It suggests that, if we could be hopeful then, when society was clearly more corrupt, when we were clearly struggling with tensions of individual liberty, justice, and equality, then we can also be hopeful now.

Mad Men moves us because it implies that, essentially, being American means grappling with living freely in association with others. Our continued struggle to mediate our own liberty and the needs of others implies optimism for the future rather than failure. It reminds us of Aristotle's primary definition that a citizen is one who has a share in ruling.[4] The citizen needs practical wisdom and self-knowledge to know justice. *Mad Men* demonstrates that lack of self-knowledge limits individual agency, and imbalanced liberty or constraint risks cruelty and disaffection. Similarly, we must allow neither unmediated nostalgia nor ambition to overwhelm our understanding of the current moment. America is still maturing, and the present moment requires our attention; we must resist longing for some past golden era, which, according to Weiner's production, was not nearly as golden as contemporary citizens imagine. When nostalgia goes unchecked, it keeps us from freely responding to society and circumstance. When ambition requires forgetfulness, the past can control us, and again we cannot clearly see the current situation. Simply put, we can never be rid of nostalgia and ambition, but our struggle to balance them is not failure, but part and parcel with living in a liberal democracy.[5] We are constantly drawn forward by a love of progress and held back by a connection to our origins. *Mad Men* demonstrates that progress is more gradual than the popular myth of the 1960s would have us believe, but our democracy is changing (we no longer live in the world of *Mad Men*), and our progress stems as much from individual knowledge and creativity as from social and political action. As we balance liberty with society, we gradually, optimistically learn who we are and what it means to be America, slowly moving forward in the slim lane between nostalgia for the past and ambition for the future.

Notes

1   In his book *Lincoln at Gettysburg* (New York: Simon & Schuster, 2006), and in a 1992 article in *The Atlantic*, Garry Wills makes this argument about Lincoln's Gettysburg Address—that it rewrote the Constitution and gave America a fresh start: "The crowd departed with a new thing in its ideological luggage, the new Constitution Lincoln had substituted for the one they had brought there with them. They walked off from those curving graves on the hillside, under a changed sky, into a different America. Lincoln had revolutionized the Revolution, giving people a new past to live with that would change their future indefinitely …" www.theatlantic.com/magazine/archive/2012/02/the-words-that-remade-america/308801/ (accessed September 18, 2014).

2   White House, President Obama's State of the Union Address, January 28, 2014, http://www.whitehouse.gov/the-press-office/2014/01/28/president-barack-obamas-state-union-address (accessed September 19, 2014).

3   President Barack Obama, in his 2011 State of the Union Address, argued for new American innovation: "We need to out-innovate, out-educate, and

out-build the rest of the world." http://www.whitehouse.gov/the-press-office/2011/01/25/remarks-president-state-union-address (accessed September 19, 2014).

4   Aristotle, *Politics*, Ernest Barker, trans. (Oxford: Oxford University Press, 1995), p. 85. *Politics*, III.i 1275a19, "The citizen in this strict sense is best defined by the one criterion that he shares in the administration of justice and in the holding of office."

5   FX's *The Americans*, about two KGB agents posing as Americans in suburban Washington, DC, during the 1980s, also examines the balance between nostalgia and ambition in a liberal democracy concerned with Cold War anxiety.

Appendix I: Products of *Mad Men*

The following are lists of new advertisements and products mentioned in the AMC recaps of each episode.

Season 1 = 15 products
Lucky Strike
Mencken Department Store
Right Guard
Nixon Election
Bethlehem Steel
Liberty Capitol Savings Bank
Maytag
Rio de Janeiro
Israeli Tourism Board
Belle Jolie Lipstick
Secor Laxatives
Dr. Scholl's
Electrosizer
Kodak
Clearasil

Season 2 = 8 products
Mohawk
Utz
Playtex
Martinson Coffee
Heineken
Samsonite
Aerospace
Popsicle

Season 3 = 12 products
London Fog
Penn Station
Madison Square Garden
Patio Cola
Pampers
Bacardi
Jai alia
Admiral
John Deere
Hilton Hotels
Western Union
Caldecott Farms

Season 4 = 12 products
Jantzen
Sugarberry Ham
Glo-Coat
Topaz
American Cancer Society
Pond's Cold Cream
Vicks Chemical
Honda
Life Cereal
Filmore Auto Parts
Heinz
Philip Morris

Season 5 = 6 products

Butler Footwear

Jaguar

Cool Whip

Manischewitz

SnoBall

Chevalier Blanc

Season 6 = 7 products

Koss Headphones

Chevrolet

Avon Cosmetics

Carnation

Sunkist

Ocean Spray

St. Joseph's

Season 7 = 6 products

Accutron Watches

H. Salt and Fish Chips

Chevalier Noir

Burger Chef

Lease Tech

Commander Cigarettes

Appendix II: *Mad Men* Episode Listings

1.1, *Smoke Gets in Your Eyes*
Written by Matthew Weiner
Directed by Alan Taylor
July 19, 2007

1.2, *Ladies Room*
Written by Matthew Weiner
Directed by Alan Taylor
July 26, 2007

1.3, *Marriage of Figaro*
Written by Tom Palmer
Directed by Ed Bianchi
August 2, 2007

1.4, *New Amsterdam*
Written by Lisa Albert
Directed by Tim Hunter
August 9, 2007

1.5, *5G*
Written by Matthew Weiner
Directed by Lesli Linka Glatter
August 16, 2007

1.6, *Babylon*
Written by Andre Jacquemetton and Maria Jacquemetton
Directed by Andrew Bernstein
August 23, 2007

1.7, *Red in the Face*
Written by Bridget Bedard
Directed by Tim Hunter
August 30, 2007

1.8, *The Hobo Code*
Written by Chris Provenzano
Directed by Phil Abraham
September 6, 2007

1.9, *Shoot*
Written by Chris Provenzano and Matthew Weiner
Directed by Paul Feig
September 13, 2007

1.10, *Long Weekend*
Written by Bridget Bedard, Andre Jacquemetton, Maria Jacquemetton, and Matthew Weiner
Directed by Tim Hunter
September 27, 2007

1.11, *Indian Summer*
Written by Tom Palmer and Matthew Weiner
Directed by Tim Hunter
October 4, 2007

1.12, *Nixon vs. Kennedy*
Written by Lisa Albert, Andre Jacquemetton, and Maria Jacquemetton
Directed by Alan Taylor
October 11, 2007

1.13, *The Wheel*
Written by Robin Veith and Matthew Weiner
Directed by Matthew Weiner
October 18, 2007

2.1, *For Those Who Think Young*
Written by Matthew Weiner
Directed by Tim Hunter
July 27, 2008

2.2, *Flight 1*
Written by Lisa Albert and Matthew Weiner
Directed by Andrew Bernstein
August 3, 2008

2.3, *The Benefactor*
Written by Matthew Weiner and Rick Cleveland
Directed by Lesli Linka Glatter
August 10, 2008

2.4, *Three Sundays*
Written by Andre Jacquemetton and Maria Jacquemetton
Directed by Tim Hunter
August 17, 2008

2.5, *The New Girl*
Written by Robin Veith
Directed by Jennifer Getzinger
August 24, 2008

2.6, *Maidenform*
Written by Matthew Weiner
Directed by Phil Abraham
August 31, 2008

2.7, *The Gold Violin*
Written by Jane Anderson, Andre Jacquemetton, Maria Jacquemetton, and Matthew Weiner
Directed by Andrew Bernstein
September 7, 2008

2.8, *A Night to Remember*
Written by Robin Veith and Matthew Weiner
Directed by Lesli Linka Glatter
September 14, 2008

2.9, *Six Month Leave*
Written by Andre Jacquemetton, Maria Jacquemetton, and Matthew Weiner
Directed by Michael Uppendahl
September 28, 2008

2.10, *The Inheritance*
Written by Lisa Albert, Marti Noxon, and Matthew Weiner
Directed by Andrew Bernstein
October 5, 2008

2.11, *The Jet Set*
Written by Matthew Weiner
Directed by Phil Abraham
October 12, 2008

2.12, *The Mountain King*
Written by Robin Veith and Matthew Weiner
Directed by Alan Taylor
October 19, 2008

2.13, *Meditations in an Emergency*
Written by Kater Gordon and Matthew Weiner
Directed by Matthew Weiner
October 26, 2008

3.1, *Out of Town*
Written by Matthew Weiner
Directed by Phil Abraham
August 16, 2009

3.2, *Love Among the Ruins*
Written by Cathryn Humphris and Matthew Weiner
Directed by Lesli Linka Glatter
August 23, 2009

3.3, *My Old Kentucky Home*
Written by Dahvi Waller and Matthew Weiner
Directed by Jennifer Getzinger
August 30, 2009

3.4, *The Arrangements*
Written by Andrew Colville and Matthew Weiner
Directed by Michael Uppendahl
September 6, 2009

3.5, *The Fog*
Written by Kater Gordon
Directed by Phil Abraham
September 13, 2009

3.6, *Guy Walks into an Advertising Agency*
Written by Robin Veith and Matthew Weiner
Directed by Lesli Linka Glatter
September 20, 2009

3.7, *Seven Twenty Three*
Written by Andre Jacquemetton, Maria Jacquemetton, and Matthew Weiner
Directed by Daisy von Scherler Mayer
September 27, 2009

3.8, *Souvenir*
Written by Lisa Albert and Matthew Weiner
Directed by Phil Abraham
October 4, 2009

3.9, *Wee Small Hours*
Written by Dahvi Waller and Matthew Weiner
Directed by Scott Hombacher
October 11, 2009

3.10, *The Color Blue*
Written by Kater Gordon and Matthew Weiner
Directed by Michael Uppendahl
October 18, 2009

3.11, *The Gypsy and the Hobo*
Written by Marti Noxon, Cathryn Humphris, and Matthew Weiner
Directed by Jennifer Getzinger
October 25, 2009

3.12, *The Grown-Ups*
Written by Brett Johnson and Matthew Weiner
Directed by Barbet Schroeder
November 1, 2009

3.13, *Shut the Door. Have a Seat*
Written by Erin Levy and Matthew Weiner
Directed by Matthew Weiner
November 8, 2009

4.1, *Public Relations*
Written by Matthew Weiner
Directed by Phil Abraham
July 25, 2010

4.2, *Christmas Comes But Once a Year*
Written by Tracy McMillan and Matthew Weiner
Directed by Michael Uppendahl
August 1, 2010

4.3, *The Good News*
Jonathon Abrahams and Matthew Weiner
Directed by Jennifer Getzinger
August 8, 2010

4.4, *The Rejected*
Written by Keith Huff and Matthew Weiner
Directed by John Slattery
August 15, 2010

4.5, *The Chrysanthemum and the Sword*
Written by Erin Levy
Directed by Lesli Linka Glatter
August 22, 2010

4.6, *Waldorf Stories*
Written by Brett Johnson and Matthew Weiner
Directed by Scott Hombacher
August 29, 2010

4.7, *The Suitcase*
Written by Matthew Weiner
Directed by Jennifer Getzinger
September 5, 2010

4.8, *The Summer Man*
Written by Lisa Albert, Janet Leahy, and Matthew Weiner
Directed by Phil Abraham
September 12, 2010

4.9, *The Beautiful Girls*
Written by Dahvi Waller and Matthew Weiner
Directed by Michael Uppendahl
September 19, 2010

4.10, *Hands and Knees*
Written by Jonathon Abrahams and Matthew Weiner
Directed by Lynn Shelton
September 26, 2010

4.11, *Chinese Wall*
Written by Erin Levy
Directed by Phil Abraham
October 3, 2010

4.12, *Blowing Smoke*
Written by Andre Jacquemetton and Maria Jacquemetton
Directed by John Slattery
October 10, 2010

4.13, *Tomorrowland*
Written by Jonathon Igla and Matthew Weiner
Directed by Matthew Wiener
October 17, 2010

5.1–2, *A Little Kiss*
Written by Erin Levy and Matthew Weiner
Directed by Jennifer Getzinger
March 25, 2012

5.3, *Tea Leaves*
Written by Erin Levy and Matthew Weiner
Directed by Jon Hamm
April 1, 2012

5.4, *Mystery Date*
Written by Victor Levin and Matthew Weiner
Directed by Matt Shakman
April 8, 2012

5.5, *Signal 30*
Written by Frank Pierson and Matthew Weiner
Directed by John Slattery
April 15, 2012

5.6, *Far Away Places*
Written by Semi Chellas and Matthew Weiner
Directed by Scott Hombacher
April 22, 2012

5.7, *At the Codfish Ball*
Written by Jonathon Igla
Directed by Michael Uppendahl
April 29, 2012

5.8, *Lady Lazarus*
Written by Matthew Weiner
Directed by Phil Abraham
May 6, 2012

5.9, *Dark Shadows*
Written by Erin Levy
Directed by Scott Hombacher
May 13, 2012

5.10, *Christmas Waltz*
Written by Victor Levin and Matthew Weiner
Directed by Michael Uppendahl
May 20, 2012

5.11, *The Other Woman*
Written by Semi Chellas and Matthew Weiner
Directed by Phil Abraham
May 27, 2012

5.12, *Commissions and Fees*
Written by Andre Jacquemetton and Maria Jacquemetton
Directed by Christopher Manley
June 3, 2012

5.13, *The Phantom*
Written by Jonathon Igla and Matthew Weiner
Directed by Matthew Weiner
June 10, 2012

6.1–2, *The Doorway*
Written by Matthew Weiner
Directed by Scott Hombacher
April 7, 2013

6.3, *Collaborators*
Written by Jonathon Igla and Matthew Weiner
Directed by Jon Hamm
April 14, 2013

6.4, *To Have and to Hold*
Written by Erin Levy
Directed by Michael Uppendahl
April 21, 2013

6.5, *The Flood*
Written by Tom Smuts and Matthew Weiner
Directed by Christopher Manley
April 28, 2013

6.6, *For Immediate Release*
Written by Matthew Weiner
Directed by Jennifer Getzinger
May 5, 2013

6.7, *Man With a Plan*
Written by Semi Chellas and Matthew Weiner
Directed by John Slattery
May 12, 2013

6.8, *The Crash*
Written by Jason Grote and Matthew Weiner
Directed by Michael Uppendahl
May 19, 2013

6.9, *The Better Half*
Written by Erin Levy and Matthew Weiner
Directed by Phil Abraham
May 26, 2013

6.10, *A Tale of Two Cities*
Written by Janet Leahy and Matthew Weiner
Directed by John Slattery
June 2, 2013

6.11, *Favors*
Written by Semi Chellas and Matthew Weiner
Directed by Jennifer Getzinger
June 9, 2013

6.12, *The Quality of Mercy*
Written by Andre Jacquemetton and Maria Jacquemetton
Directed by Phil Abraham
June 16, 2013

6.13, *In Care Of*
Written by Matthew Weiner and Carly Wray
Directed by Matthew Weiner
June 23, 2013

7.1, *Time Zones*
Written by Matthew Weiner
Directed by Scott Hombacher
April 13, 2014

7.2, *A Day's Work*
Written by Jonathon Igla and Matthew Weiner
Directed by Michael Uppendahl
April 20, 2014

7.3, *Field Trip*
Written by Heather Jeng Bladt and Matthew Weiner
Directed by Christopher Manley
April 27, 2014

7.4, *The Monolith*
Written by Erin Levy
Directed by Scott Hombacher
May 4, 2014

7.5, *The Runaways*
Written by David Iserson and Matthew Weiner
Directed by Christopher Manley
May 11, 2014

7.6, *The Strategy*
Written by Semi Chellas
Directed by Phil Abraham
May 18, 2014

7.7, *Waterloo*
Written by Matthew Weiner and Carly Wray
Directed by Matthew Weiner
May 25, 2014

Bibliography

Aceyalone [Edwin Hayes, Jr.]. *Magnificent City*, prod. by RJD2, © 2006 by Decon Records, DCN 34, CD.

Adorno, Theodor W., *Minima Moralia*, trans. Edmund Jephcott (London: Verso, 2005).

Adorno, Theodor W. and Max Horkheimer, *Dialectic of Enlightenment*, trans. E. Jephcott (Stanford: Stanford University Press, 2000).

Agger, Ben, *The Sixties at 40: Leaders and Activists Remember and Look Forward* (Boulder, CO: Paradigm Publishers, 2009).

Ahmed, Sara, *The Promise of Happiness* (Durham, NC: Duke University Press, 2010).

Allender, Lisa, "Mad Men: Is Sexual Abuse/Incest About to be Revealed?" Open Salon (2010), http://open.salon.com/blog/lisa_allender/2010/08/2 mad_men_is_sexual_abuseincest_about_to_be_revealed (accessed July 7, 2013).

Altschuler, Glenn C. and Stuart M. Blumin, *The GI Bill: A New Deal for Veterans* (New York: Oxford University Press, 2009).

Anderson, Terry, *The Sixties* (Boston: Pearson, 1998).

Arendt, Hannah, *The Human Condition* (Chicago: University of Chicago Press, 1958).

Aristotle, *Politics*, trans. Ernest Barker (Oxford: Oxford University Press, 1995).

Aronowitz, Stanley, *Taking it Big: C. Wright Mills and the Making of Political Intellectuals* (New York: Columbia University Press, 2012).

Asch, Mark, "Syllabus: Deflated American Masculinity in the 1970s," *The L Magazine* (2010), http://www.thelmagazine.com/TheMeasure/archives/2010/09/22/syllabus-deflated-american-masculinity-in-the-1970s (accessed July 7, 2014).

Barkhorn, Eleanor, Ashley Fetters, and Amy Sullivan, "Will *Mad Men* Ever Be as Good on Race as it is On Gender?" *The Atlantic*, April 22, 2013.

Barthes, Roland, "Myth Today," in *Mythologies*, trans. Jonathan Cape Ltd. (New York: Hill and Wang, 1972).

Batty, Nancy E., "*Mad Men*'s Epoch Eclipse: Marking Time with Sally Draper," in Heather Marcovitch and Nancy E. Battys (eds), *Mad Men, Women, and Children: Essays on Gender and Generation* (Lanham, MD: Lexington, 2012), pp. 191–206.

Benjamin, Walter, "The Work of Art in an Age of Mechanical Reproduction," in Hannah Arendt, ed., *Illuminations*, trans. Harry Zohn (New York: Shocken, 1968), pp. 217–52.

Berebitsky, Julie, *Sex and the Office: A History of Gender, Power and Desire* (New Haven, CT: Yale University Press, 2012).

Berube, Michael, "A Change is Gonna Come, Same As it Ever Was," in Lauren M. E. Goodlad, Lilya Kaganovsky, and Robert Rushing (eds), *Mad Men, Mad World: Sex, Politics, Style, and the 1960s* (Durham, NC: Duke University Press, 2013), pp. 345–60.

Bevan, Alex, "Nostalgia for pre-digital media in mad men," *Television and New Media*, 14:6 (November 2013), pp. 546–59.

Brodkin, Karen, *How Jews Became White Folks and What that Says About Race in America* (New Brunswick, NJ: Rutgers University Press, 1998).

Brown, Helen Gurley, *Sex and the Single Girl* (New York: Barricade Books, 2003).

Butler, Judith, *Bodies That Matter: On the Discursive Limits of Sex* (New York: Routledge, 1993).

Caputo, Philip, *A Rumor of War* (New York: Holt, 1996).

Chandler, Alfred and James Cortada (eds), *A Nation Transformed by Information: How Information has Shaped the United States from Colonial Times to the Present* (Oxford: Oxford University Press, 2000).

Chevallier, Gabriel, *Fear* (London: Serpent's Tail, 2011).

Chomsky, Noam, *Year 501: The Conquest Continues* (Boston: South End Press, 1993).

Chow, Lisa, "'Mad Men' Haven't Changed Much Since the 1960s," *NPR*, January 14, 2010, http://www.npr.org/templates/story/story.php?storyId=122545036 (accessed July 22, 2014).

Ciasullo, Ann M., "Not a Spaceship, but a Time Machine: Mad Men and the Narratives of Nostalgia," in Danielle M. Stern, Jimmie Manning, and Jennifer C. Dunn (eds), with assistance from Igor Rustic, *Lucky Strikes and a Three Martini Lunch: Thinking about Television's Mad Men* (Newcastle upon Tyne: Cambridge Scholars Publishing, 2012), pp. 14–26.

—"What Do a Meaningless Secretary and a Humorless Bitch Have in Common? Everything: Or Joan, Peggy, and the Convergence of *Mad Men*'s Career Girls," in Heather Marcovitch and Nancy E. Battys, eds, *Mad Men, Women, and Children: Essays on Gender and Generation* (Lanham, MD: Lexington, 2012), pp. 19–31.

Clewell, Tammy, "Mourning beyond melancholia: Freud's psychoanalysis of loss," *Journal of the American Psychoanalytic Association* 52:1 (2004), pp. 43–67.

Coates, Ta-Nehisi, "Race and *Mad Men*," *Atlantic* (blog post), August 17, 2009, http://www.theatlantic.com/entertainment/archive/2009/08/race-and-mad-men/23372/ (accessed July 22, 2014).

—"The Negro Don Draper," *Atlantic*, October 27, 2008, http://www.theatlantic.com/

entertainment/archive/2008/10/the-negro-donald-draper/6129/ (accessed July 22, 2014).

Colby, Tanner, "*Mad Men* and Black America," Slate.com, March 14, 2012, http://www.slate.com/articles/arts/culturebox/features/2012/mad_men_ and_race_the_series_handling_of_race_has_been_painfully_accurate_/ mad_men_and_race_why_season_5_may_finally_put_the_civil_rights_ movement_front_and_center_.html (accessed March 7, 2014).

Collins, Gail, *When Everything Changed: The Amazing Journey of American Women from 1960 to the Present* (New York: Little Brown & Co., 2009).

Coontz, Stephanie, "Why *Mad Men* is TV's Most Feminist Show," *Washington Post*, October 10, 2010, http://www.washingtonpost.com/wp-dyn/content/ article/2010/10/08/AR2010100802662.html (accessed March 31, 2014).

Courrier, Kevin, *Randy Newman's American Dreams* (Toronto: ECW Press, 2005).

Cracknell, Andrew, *The Real Mad Men* (Philadelphia: Running Press, 2011).

Dahl, Robert, *Who Governs?* (New Haven, CT: Yale University Press, 1961).

Del Vecchio, John, *The 13ᵗʰ Valley* (New York: St. Martin's Griffin, 1999).

Demby, Gene, "Will Mad Men's Sixth Season Finally Bring Race into the Picture?," NPR's Code Switch blog, March 4, 2013, http://www.npr.org/blogs/ codeswitch/2013/04/08/176531523/will-mad-mens-sixth-season-finally-bring-race-into-the-picture (accessed March 31, 2014).

Dobrow, Larry, *When Advertising Tried Harder. The Sixties: The Golden Age of American Advertising* (New York: Friendly Press, 1984).

Duncan, Jimmy, "My Special Angel," sung by Bobby Helms, 1957, by Decca Records.

Dunn, George A., "'People Want to be Told What to Do So Badly That They'll Listen to Anyone': Mimetic Madness at Sterling Cooper," in James B. South, Rod Carveth and William Irwins (eds), *Mad Men and Philosophy: Nothing is As it Seems* (Hoboken, NJ: Wiley-Blackwell, 2014), pp. 20–33.

Dyson, Freeman J., *Disturbing the Universe* (New York: Harper & Row, 1979).

Edgerton, Gary R., "Introduction: When Our Parents Became Us," in Gary R. Edergerton, ed., *Mad Men: Dream Come True TV* (London: I. B. Tauris, 2011), pp. xxi–xxxvi.

Ehrenreich, Barbara, *The Hearts of Men: American Dreams and the Flight from Commitment* (New York: Anchor, 1987).

Ellison, Ralph, *Invisible Man* (New York: Vintage Books, 1972).

Farrell, Hannah, "Joey, Joan, and the Gold-Plated Necklace," in Heather Marcovitch and Nancy E. Battys (eds), *Mad Men, Women, and Children: Essays on Gender and Generation* (Lanham, MD: Lexington, 2012), pp. 45–55.

Fitzgerald, F. Scott, *The Great Gatsby* (New York: Scribner, 1925).

—*The Great Gatsby* (New York: Charles Scribner's Sons, 1953).

Fitzgerald, Tom and Lorenzo Marquez, Tom + Lorenzo: Fabulous & Opinionated, http://www.tomandlorenzo.com/ (accessed August 20, 2014).

Frank, Thomas, *The Conquest of Cool: Business Culture, Counterculture, and the Rise of Hip Consumerism* (Chicago: University of Chicago Press, 1997).

Frank, Thomas and Matt Weiland (eds), *Commodify Your Dissent: Salvos from the Baffler* (New York: Norton, 1997).

Freedman, Estelle B., *No Turning Back: The History of Feminism and the Future of Women* (New York: Ballentine, 2002).

Freud, Sigmund, "The Uncanny," *On Creativity and the Unconscious*, Benjamin Nelson, ed. (New York: Harper, 1958).

—"Mourning and Melancholia," in Peter Gay, ed., *The Freud Reader* (New York: Norton, 1989), pp. 584–9.

Frick, Daniel, *Reinventing Richard Nixon: A Cultural History of an American Obsession* (Lawrence, KS: University Press of Kansas, 2008).

Friedan, Betty, *The Feminine Mystique* (New York: Dell Publishing, 1983).

Geary, Daniel, *Radical Ambition: C. Wright Mills, the Left, and American Social Thought* (Berkeley, CA: University of California Press, 2009).

Gilens, Martin and Benjamin Page, "Testing theories of American politics: elites, interest groups, and average citizens," *Perspectives on Politics*, 12:3 (2014), pp. 564–81.

Giles, Judy, *The Parlour and the Suburbs: Domestic Identities, Class, Femininity and Modernity* (New York: Berg, 2004).

Gitlin, Todd, *The Sixties: Years of Hope, Days of Rage* (Toronto: Bantam Books, 1997).

—*The Whole World is Watching: Mass Media in the Making and Unmaking of the New Left* (Berkeley, CA: University of California Press, 1980).

Goffman, Erving, *The Presentation of Self in Everyday Life* (New York: Anchor, 1959).

Goldman, Loren, "In defense of blinders: On Kant, political hope, and the need for practical belief," *Political Theory*, 40:4 (2012), pp. 497–523.

Goodlad, Lauren M. E., "The *Mad Men* in the Attic: Seriality and Identity in Modern Babylon," in Lauren M. E. Goodlad, Lilya Kaganovsky, and Robert A. Rushing (eds), *Mad Men, Mad World: Sex, Politics, Style, and the 1960s* (Durham, NC: Duke University Press, 2013), pp. 257–78.

Goodlad, Lauren M. E., Lilya Kaganovsky, and Robert A. Rushing, "Introduction" in *Mad Men, Mad World: Sex, Politics, Style, and the 1960s* (Durham, NC: Duke University Press, 2013), pp. 1–33.

—*Mad Men, Mad World: Sex, Politics, Style and the 1960s* (Durham, NC: Duke University Press).

Gopnik, Adam, "The Forty Year Itch," *The New Yorker*, April 23, 2012, http://www.newyorker.com/magazine/2012/04/23/the-forty-year-itch (accessed May 9, 2014).

Goren, Lilly, ed., *You've Come a Long Way, Baby: Women, Politics, and Popular Culture* (Lexington, KY: University Press of Kentucky, 2009).

Graeber, David, *The Democracy Project* (New York: Spiegel & Grau, 2013).

Greenwald, Andy, "Men in Crisis: *Mad Men*'s Curious, Frustrating, and Ultimately Disappointing Sixth Season', Grantland.com, June 19, 2013, http://www.grantland.com/story/_/id/9402724/mad-men-disappointing-sixth-season (accessed July 15, 2013).

Habermas, Jürgen, "The Concept of the Lifeworld and the Hermeneutic Idealism of Interpretive Sociology," in S. Seidman, ed., *Jürgen Habermas on Society and Politics* (Boston: Beacon, 1989), pp. 165–87.

Harris, Aisha, "If *Mad Men* Really Addressed Race," *Brow Beat: Slate Culture Blog*, April 10, 2013, http://www.slate.com/blogs/browbeat/2013/04/10/mad_men_with_black_characters_erika_alexander_s_screenplay_uptown_saturday.html (accessed March 31, 2014).

Haskell, Molly, "In Response to 'The Mad Men Account,'" *New York Review of Books*, March 24, 2011, http://www.nybooks.com/articles/archives/2011/mar/24/mad-men-account/ (accessed July 7, 2014).

Hayden, Tom, *Radical Nomad: C. Wright Mills and His Times* (Boulder, CO: Paradigm, 2006).

Heidegger, Martin, *Die Selbstbehauptung der Deutschen Universität* (Frankfurt: V. Klostermann, 1990).

Hollander, Anne, *Sex and Suits: The Evolution of Modern Dress* (New York: Knopf, 1994).

Holly, Michael Ann, *The Melancholy Art* (Princeton, NJ: Princeton University Press, 2013).

Jaarsma, Ada, "An Existential Look at *Mad Men*: Don Draper, Advertising, and the Promise of Happiness," in James B. South, Rod Carveth and William Irwins (eds), *Mad Men and Philosophy: Nothing is As it Seems* (Hoboken, NJ: Wiley-Blackwell, 2014), pp. 95–111.

Jaspers, Karl, *The Atom Bomb and the Future of Mankind*, trans. E. B. Ashton (Chicago: University of Chicago Press, 1963).

Johnson, Leslie and Justine Lloyd, *Sentenced to Everyday Life: Feminism and the Housewife* (New York: Berg, 2004).

Jones, Adrian, "All About Betty: Selling the Suburban Housewife in *Mad Men*,'" in Danielle M. Stern, Jimmie Manning, and Jennifer C. Drums (eds), *Lucky Strikes and a Three Martini Lunch: Thinking about Television's Mad Men* (Newcastle upon Tyne: Cambridge Scholars Publishing, 2012), pp. 144–58.

Jones, Robert P., "Self-Segregation: Why it's So Hard for Whites to Understand Ferguson," *Atlantic*, August 21, 2014, http://www.theatlantic.com/politics/archive/2014/08/self-segregation-why-its-hard-for-whites-to-understand-ferguson/378928/ (accessed August 26, 2014).

Jünger, Ernst, *Storm of Steel* (New York: Penguin Classics, 2004).

Kant, Immanuel, *Critique of Practical Reason*, trans. M. Gregor, in Immanuel Kant, *Practical Philosophy* (Cambridge: Cambridge University Press, 1999).

Keefe, Patrick Radden, Slate.com, "Mad Men Season 5," June 5, 2012, http://www.slate.com/articles/arts/tv_club/features/2012/mad_men_season_5/ week_11/mad_men_review_betty_and_sally_still_need_each_other_.html (accessed March 11, 2014).

Kessler-Harris, Alice, *In Pursuit of Equity: Women, Men and the Quest for Economic Citizenship in 20th-Century America* (Oxford: Oxford University Press, 2001).

Kidd, Dustin, "Harry Potter and the functions of popular culture," *Journal of Popular Culture*, 40:1 (2007), pp. 69–89.

Kifner, John, "Poverty Pickets Get Paper-Bag Dousing on Madison Avenue," *New York Times*, May 28, 1966, A1, http://www.documentcloud.org/documents/328527-new-york-times-may-28-1966.html (accessed March 11, 2014).

Knight, Michael Muhammad, *The Five Percenters: Islam, Hip Hop and the Gods of New York* (London: Oneworld, 2007).

Konigsberg, Erik, "A Fine Madness", *Rolling Stone*, September 16, 2010, pp. 43–9.

Laqueur, Thomas, "The rise of sex in the eighteenth century: historical context and historiographical implications," *Signs*, 37:4, *Sex: A Thematic Issue* (Summer 2012), pp. 802–13.

Lawrence, Jerome and Robert Edwin Lee, *Inherit the Wind*, 12th edn, vol. 8 (New York: Random House, 1955), Act II, Scene 2, p. 83.

Lehman, Katherine, "More Than Just a 'Marilyn': Peggy, Joan and the Single Working Woman of the 1960s," in Danielle M. Stern, Jimmie Manning, and Jennifer C. Dunn (eds), with assistance from Igor Rustic, *Lucky Strikes and a Three Martini Lunch: Thinking about Television's Mad Men* (Newcastle upon Tyne: Cambridge Scholars Publishing, 2012), pp. 159–76.

Light, Enoch and his Orchestra, "Autumn Leaves," music by Johnny Mercer. On *Melody of Love*, © 1958 by Waldorf Record Corp., MHK 33-1232, LP.

Loewe, Frederick and Alan Jay Lerner, "On the Street Where You Live," sung by Vic Damone, 1956, by Columbia Records 33014.

Lotz, Amanda, "Don Draper's Sad Manhood: What Makes 'Mad Men' Different from 'Breaking Bad,' 'Sopranos,'" *Salon*, April 11, 2014, http://www.salon.com/2014/04/11/don_drapers_sad_manhood_what_makes_mad_men_different_from_breaking_bad_sopranos/ (accessed July 7, 2014).

Maas, Jane, *Mad Women: The Other Side of Life on Madison Avenue in the 60s and Beyond* (New York: Thomas Dunne, 2012).

Mad Men (2007–14), TV program, Seasons 1–7. Matthew Weiner, Creator. AMC.

Mailer, Norman, *The Naked and the Dead* (London: Picador, 2000).

Marotte, Mary Ruth, "Not a 'Jackie,' Not a 'Marilyn': Mad Men and the Threat of Peggy Olson," in Heather Marcovitch and Nancy E. Battys (eds), *Mad Men, Women, and Children: Essays on Gender and Generation* (Lanham, MD: Lexington, 2012), pp. 33–44.

Martin, Brett, *Difficult Men: Behind the Scenes of a Creative Revolution: From the Sopranos and The Wire to Mad Men and Breaking Bad* (New York: Penguin, 2013).

Martin, Geoff and Erin Steuter, *Pop Culture Goes to War: Enlisting and Resisting Militarism in the War on Terror* (Lanham, MD: Lexington, 2010).

McQuaid, Kim, *Uneasy Partners: Big Business in American Politics 1945–1990* (Baltimore and London: Johns Hopkins University Press, 1994).

Melville, Herman, *The Confidence Man: His Masquerade*, Hershel Parker and Mark Niemeyer (eds), Norton Critical Edition, 2nd edn (New York: Norton, 2006).

Mendelsohn, Daniel, "The *Mad Men* Account," *New York Review of Books*, February 24, 2011, http://www.nybooks.com/articles/2011/feb/24/mad-men-account/ (accessed March 7, 2014).

Mills, C. Wright, *The Power Elite* (New York: Oxford University Press, 1956).

—*The Sociological Imagination* (New York: Oxford University Press, 1959).

Moss, Otis, "*Mad Men* Highlights Invisible Black People and Stain of Racism," *Daily Beast*, March 27, 2012, http://www.thedailybeast.com/articles/2012/03/27/mad-men-highlights-invisible-black-people-and-stain-of-racism.html (accessed March 7, 2014).

Nora, Pierre, "Reasons for the Upsurge in Memory," *Transit*, http://www.eurozine.com/articles/2002-04-19-nora-en.html (accessed July 7, 2014).

North by Northwest (1959), [Film] Dir. Alfred Hitchcock. Burbank, CA: Warner Home Video, 2010. DVD.

Nussbaum, Emily, "Working the Street," August 14, 2010, http://nymag.com/arts/tv/reviews/67491/ (accessed September 17, 2014).

Obama, Barack, State of Union Address, January 25, 2011, http://www.whitehouse.gov/the-press-office/2011/01/25/remarks-president-state-union-address (accessed September 19, 2014).

—State of the Union Address, January 28, 2014, http://www.whitehouse.gov/the-press-office/2014/01/28/president-barack-obamas-state-union-address (accessed September 19, 2014).

Ono, Kent, "*Mad Men's* Postracial Figuration of a Racial Past," in Lauren M. E. Goodlad, Lilya Kaganovsky, and Robert A. Rushing (eds), *Mad Men, Mad World: Sex, Politics, Style, and the 1960s* (Durham, NC: Duke University Press), pp. 300–19.

Owen, Joseph, *Colder than Hell: A Marine Rifle Company at Chosin Reservoir* (New York: Ballantine, 1996).

Perlstein, Rick, *The Invisible Bridge: The Fall of Nixon and the Rise of Reagan* (New York: Simon & Schuster, 2014).

Peterson, Latoya, "Why *Mad Men* is Afraid of Race," Slate.com, Double X blog, August 13, 2009, http://www.doublex.com/section/arts/why-madmen-afraid-race (accessed April 19, 2010).

Pickering, Michael and Emily Keightley, "The modalities of nostalgia," *Current Sociology*, 54:6, pp. 91–4.

Poe, Edgar Allen, *Saturday Courier* (Philadelphia), October 14, 1843, Vol. XIII, No. 655, 1843.

Postrel, Virginia, *The Power of Glamour: Longing and the Art of Visual Persuasion* (New York: Simon & Schuster, 2013).

Rasmussen, Angela and Andrea Reid, "Tearing Out the Kitchen" in Heather Marcovitch and Nancy E. Battys (eds), *Mad Men, Women, and Children: Essays on Gender and Generation* (Lanham, MD: Lexington, 2012), pp. 159–72.

Reagan, Leslie J., "After Sex What?: A Feminist Reading of Reproductive History in *Mad Men*," in Lauren M. E. Goodlad, Lilya Kaganovsky, and Robert Rushing, eds, *Mad Men, Mad World: Sex, Politics, Style, and the 1960s* (Durham, NC: Duke University Press, 2013), pp. 92–110.

Remarque, Erich Maria, *All Quiet on the Western Front* (New York: Ballantine, 1987).

Ricoeur, Paul, *Time and Narrative*, vol. 1 (Chicago: University of Chicago Press, 1984).

RJD2 [Ramble John Krohn], "A Beautiful Mine," on *Magnificent City Instrumentals*, © 2006 by Decon Records, DCN 38, 2LP.

Rosin, Hanna, "The End of Men," *The Atlantic*, June 8, 2010, http://www.theatlantic.com/magazine/archive/2010/07/the-end-of-men/308135/ (accessed January 12, 2015).

Rosin, Hannah, *The End of Men: And the Rise of Women* (New York: Viking, 2012).

Rousseau, Jean-Jacques, "Discourse on Inequality," in *The Discourses and Other Early Political Writings*, Victor Gourevitch, ed. and trans. (Cambridge: Cambridge University Press, 1997).

Sachs, Adam, "Jon Hamm: The Last Alpha Male," *Details*, October 1, 2010, http://www.details.com/celebrities-entertainment/cover-stars/201010/mad-men-actor-alpha-male-jon-hamm (accessed October 15, 2010).

Schattschneider, E. E., *The Semisovereign People* (New York: Holt, Rinehart and Winston, 1960).

Schlosser, Eric, *Command and Control: Nuclear Weapons, the Damascus Accident, and the Illusion of Safety* (New York: Penguin, 2013).

Scott, A. O., "The Post-Man," *New York Times*, September 14, 2014, pp. 39–41.

Scott, James, *Domination and the Arts of Resistance* (New Haven, CT: Yale University Press, 1991).

Siegel, Deborah, *Sisterhood Interrupted: From Radical Women to Grrls Gone Wild* (New York: Palgrave Macmillan, 2007).

Silverstein, Michael, "The 'message' in the (political) battle," *Language and Communication*, 31:3, pp. 203–16.

Simons, Natasha, "*Mad Men* and the Paradox of the Past," *National Review*, July 19, 2010, http://www.nationalreview.com/articles/243490/i-mad-men-i-and-paradox-past-natasha-simons (accessed August 2, 2014).

Sinatra, Nancy, "You Only Live Twice," music by John Barry, © 1967 by Unart Music Corp. BMI, Reprise Records 0595, 45RPM.

Sivulka, Juliann, *Soap, Sex and Cigarettes: A Cultural History of American Advertising* (Belmont, CA: Wadsworth, 2012).

Slaughter, Anne-Marie, "Why Women Still Can't Have It All," *The Atlantic*, June 13, 2012, http://www.theatlantic.com/magazine/archive/2012/07/why-women-still-cant-have-it-all/309020/ (accessed January 12, 2015).

South, James B., Rod Carveth, and William Irwin (eds), *Mad Men and Philosophy: Nothing is As it Seems* (Hoboken, NJ: Wiley-Blackwell, 2010).

Spar, Debora, "Why Women Should Stop Trying to Be Perfect, *Newsweek*, September 24, 2012, http://www.newsweek.com/why-women-should-stop-trying-be-perfect-64709 (accessed January 12, 2015).

Stanley, Alessandra, "Oblivious to the Battle Raging Outside, *Mad Men* Opens its Fifth Season on AMC," *New York Times*, March 22, 2012, http://www.nytimes.com/2012/03/23/arts/television/mad-men-opens-its-fifth-season-on-amc.html (accessed March 7, 2014).

Stern, Barbara B., "Historical and Personal Nostalgia in Advertising Text: The Fin de siècle Effect," *Journal of Advertising*, 31:4, pp. 11–22.

Sweet, Lynn, "Bill Clinton Pitches Health Care; Muses on 'Mad Men,'" *Chicago Sun-Times*, November 11, 2009, http://blogs.suntimes.com/sweet/2009/11/bill_clinton_in_chicago_pitche.html (accessed August 2, 2014).

Teschner, George and Gabrielle Teschner, "Creating the Need For the New: 'It's Not the Wheel. It's the Carousel'" in James B. South, Rod Carveth and William Irwin (eds), *Mad Men and Philosophy: Nothing is As it Seems* (Hoboken, NJ: Wiley-Blackwell, 2010), pp. 126–40.

Tocqueville, Alexis de, *Democracy in America*, Harvey C. Mansfield and Delba Winthrops, eds and trans. (Chicago: The University of Chicago Press, 2002).

Tom + Lorenzo, "Review of Mad Men: The Other Woman," May 28, 2012, http://www.tomandlorenzo.com/2012/05/mad-men-the-other-woman.html (accessed June 4, 2012).

Trebay, Guy, "From Boys to Men," *New York Times*, October 17, 2010, http://www.nytimes.com/2010/10/17/fashion/17MANLY.html (accessed October 17, 2010).

Tyree, J. M., "No Fun: Debunking the 1960s in *Mad Men* and *A Serious Man*," *Film Quarterly*, 63:4 (2010), pp. 33–9.

Vargas-Cooper, Natasha, *Mad Men Unbuttoned: A Romp Through 1960s America* (New York: HarperCollins, 2010).

Varon, Jeremy, "History Gets in Your Eyes: *Mad Men*, Misrecognition, and the Masculine Mystique," in Lauren M. E. Goodlad, Lilya Kaganovsky, and Robert A. Rushing (eds), *Mad Men, Mad World: Sex, Politics, Style, and the 1960s* (Durham, NC: Duke University Press, 2013), pp. 257–78.

Vaughn, Justin S. and Lilly J. Goren, *Women and the White House: Gender, Popular Culture, and Presidential Politics* (Lexington, KY: University Press of Kentucky, 2012).

Wallach Scott, Joan, *The Fantasy of Feminist History* (Durham, NC: Duke University Press, 2011).

Watkins, Gwynne, "A Psychiatrist Analyzes *Mad Men*'s Traumatized Sally Draper," *Vulture*, June 12, 2013, http://www.vulture.com/2013/06/psychiatrist-analyzes-mad-men-sally-draper.html (accessed September 1, 2013).

Weiner, Matthew, Radio interview with Terry Gross, "Fresh Air with Terry Gross,"

NPR, May 1, 2014, http://www.npr.org/2014/05/01/308608611/mad-men-creator-matthew-weiner-on-the-end-of-don-drapers-journey (accessed May 2, 2014).

Weisberg, Joe, *The Americans*, FX Network (2013, 2014).

Wills, Garry, *Lincoln at Gettysburg: The Words that Remade America* (New York: Simon & Schuster, 1992).

—"The Words that Remade America," *The Atlantic*, November 23, 2011, http://www.theatlantic.com/magazine/archive/2012/02/the-words-that-remade-america/308801/ (accessed September 18, 2014).

Wilson, Julia C. and Joseph H. Lane Jr., "Is *This* the Traditional American Family We've Been Hearing So Much About?: Marriage, Children, and Family Values in *Mad Men*," in Heather Marcovitch and Nancy E. Battys (eds), *Mad Men, Women, and Children: Essays on Gender and Generation* (Lanham, MD: Lexington, 2012), pp. 77–90.

Wilson, Sloan, *The Man in the Gray Flannel Suit* (Cambridge, MA: Da Capo, 2002).

Witchel, Alex, "'Mad Men' Has Its Moment," *New York Times*, June 22, 2008, http://www.nytimes.com/2008/06/22/magazine/22madmen-t.html (accessed May 21, 2014).

Yates, Richard, *Revolutionary Road* (New York: Vintage, 2000).

Zabarah, Ramy, "Bob Benson and *Mad Men*'s Disappearing Gay Characters," *Complex Pop Culture*, May 25, 2014, http://www.complex.com/pop-culture/2014/05/bob-benson-and-mad-mens-disappearing-gay-characters (accessed July 7, 2014).

Index